# BIODIVINITY AND BIODIVERSITY

This book is concerned with the argument that religious traditions are inherently environmentally friendly. Yet in a developing country such as India, the majority of people cannot afford to put the 'Earth first' regardless of the extent to which this idea can be supported by their religious traditions. Does this mean that the linking of religion and environmental concerns is a strategy more suited to contexts where people have a level of material security that enables them to think and act like environmentalists?

This question is approached through a series of case studies from Britain and India. The book concludes that there is a tension between the 'romantic' ecological discourse common among many western activists and scholars, and a more pragmatic approach, which is often found in India. The adoption of environmental causes by the Hindu Right in India makes it difficult to distinguish genuine concern for the environment from the broader politics surrounding the idea of a Hindu *rashtra* (nation). This raises a further level of analysis, which has not been provided in other studies.

D1807576

# Biodivinity and Biodiversity

## The Limits to Religious Environmentalism

EMMA TOMALIN
*University of Leeds, UK*

Routledge
Taylor & Francis Group

LONDON AND NEW YORK

First published 2009 by Ashgate Publishing

2 Park Square, Milton Park, Abingdon, Oxon OX14 4RN
711 Third Avenue, New York, NY 10017, USA

*Routledge is an imprint of the Taylor & Francis Group, an informa business*

First issued in paperback 2016

**British Library Cataloguing in Publication Data**
Tomalin, Emma
  Biodivinity and biodiversity: the limits to religious
  environmentalism
  1. Environmentalism – India 2. Environmentalism – Religious
  aspects – Hinduism
  I. Title
  294.5'177

**Library of Congress Cataloging-in-Publication Data**
Tomalin, Emma.
  Biodivinity and biodiversity: the limits of religious environmentalism / Emma Tomalin.
    p. cm.
  Includes bibliographical references and index.
  ISBN 978-0-7546-5588-6 (hardback : alk. paper) 1. Nature—Religious aspects.
  2. Environmentalism—Religious aspects. I. Title.
  BL65.N35T66 2008
  201'.77–dc22

                                                                            008041390


ISBN 978-0-7546-5588-6 (hbk)
ISBN 978-1-138-26515-8 (pbk)

# Contents

# Foreword

A century and a half ago, spurred by the invention of the internal combustion engine and fuelled by easily accessible petroleum, humanity's power to rapidly transform and degrade the habitats upon which it depends intensified. A few great thinkers took note and expressed alarm. Perhaps most notably among them was Henry David Thoreau, the American naturalist who was deeply influenced by the Transcendentalist worldview of his friend Ralph Waldo Emerson. Thoreau avidly read not only Emerson but the land, human societies, and the Hindu Vedas, trying to fuse scientific ecology and religious perceptions and ethics. In this he was both reflecting and participating in a longstanding encounter between the religious cultures of the western world and those originating in Asia – an encounter that has been increasingly embroiled in contentious claims about which traditions tend to promote environmental decline and social inequality, and whether any of them might help arrest, ameliorate, or reverse such trends.

In *Biodivinity and Biodiversity*, Dr Emma Tomalin focuses on this encounter in general and on 'religious environmentalism' in particular, namely, on forms of religious perception and practice where nature is considered sacred and in need of protection. Tomalin proves to be an able guide into this deeply contested terrain. Some assert, for example, that certain kinds of religious ideas are valuable if not essential underpinnings for environmentally sustainable societies. In part of her study, Tomalin analyses the views of those who assert that indigenous traditions or religions originating in Asia are more naturally friendly to the environment than cultures grounded in other religious orientations. She also analyses those who vehemently disagree with such views, and who find little reason or evidence to believe that any religious beliefs promote environmental responsibility.

Tomalin takes a more judicious approach than most of the contending parties. She fair-mindedly reviews the main perspectives articulated by those engaged by and supportive of 'religious environmentalism' as well as of those skeptical or critical of it. As importantly, more so than many of the critics whose views she discusses, by bringing her fieldwork into her analysis, which explores individuals and groups that in different ways consider nature to be sacred, and supplementing this information with other ethnographic studies, she avoids the oversimplified analysis that too often characterises the work of those with little or no on-the-ground experience with the individuals and movements they discuss. Demonstrating that when it comes to understanding social phenomena there is no substitute for fieldwork, Tomalin brings to light evidence that is supportive and qualifying to virtually all the contending perspectives. The result is a more nuanced discussion that neither exaggerates the potential or salutary role of religion-related environmentalism nor denies that for many, and not only for those who already have food security and a modicum of creature comforts, such spirituality can be a powerful motivation for environmental action.

Much of the ferment in environmental ethics during the past century and a half has been based on the premise that to create environmentally sustainable and equitable societies, misperceptions and bad ideas must be identified and corrected – and many of these are religious ideas. Thoreau himself, as well as the Scotland born John Muir, who immigrated as a child to America, eventually founding and becoming the first President of the Sierra Club in 1892, and the ecologist and forester Aldo Leopold, whose *A Sand County Almanac*, published posthumously in 1849, has become a sacred text to many environmentalists, and Rachel Carson, whose early writings expressed a deep spiritual connection to nature in general and the sea in particular, and whose 1962 book *Silent Spring* helped launch the modern environmental movement, all critiqued the instrumental view toward nature that they found in the Christianity prevalent during their times. They would all have agreed with the Historian Lynn White, who in 1967 published a now-famous article that blamed Christianity, and its anti-pagan and anti-animistic worldview, for fostering environmental destruction by disenchanting nature. In their own ways, these authors, and a growing chorus of others, have offered what they consider to be environmentally friendly religious alternatives to the prevailing western Christianity. Typically the prescription has been to turn to the East, or to indigenous traditions, or to home-grown nature mysticism.

To evaluate the most typical diagnoses and prescriptions that have been articulated since Darwin published *On the Origin of the Species* 150 years ago, more is needed than a good hunch or an interesting theory about the pernicious role of ideas in precipitating environmental decline. Careful and sustained critical inquiry into what are the relationships between the Earth's diverse environments and human beliefs and practices is needed. *Biodivinity and Biodiversity* is a substantial step in the right direction. It is also a reflection of the maturing of the 'religion and nature' field wherein scholars are beginning to test proffered hypotheses with on-the-ground analysis. Those who wish to move beyond wishful thinking in the guise of scholarship, and transcend the kind of skepticism that all too often represents a scholarly fashion rather than careful analysis, will find much to appreciate in this book.

Bron Taylor
Author, *Dark Green Religion: Nature Spirituality
and the Planetary Future* (2009)
Editor, *The Encyclopedia of Religion and Nature* (2005)
Gainesville, Florida, December 2008

# Acknowledgements

This book began life as a PhD thesis and I am most grateful for the advice and discussion provided by my supervisors Graham Chapman, Geoffrey Samuel and Bronislaw Szerszynski, as well as to the British Academy and the Leverhulme Trust for funding this work. I updated and supplemented the doctoral research, during my time working for Independent Broadcasting Associates as a researcher for a series of radio documentaries about the River Ganges in India, and would like to thank the producer, Julian Crandall Hollick, for enabling me to extend this research.

I am also indebted to all the people who gave me their time in allowing me to interview them, in both India and the UK. In India I lived at the Institute for Social and Economic Change, in Bangalore, and, in its own way, it became my home-from-home: both staff and students welcomed me to their institution and allowed me to come and go as I pleased. All the groups, gatherings and protest sites that I visited and stayed at during this research were always friendly and open to me as both a participant and an academic researcher.

Finally, I would also like to acknowledge those who have read and commented upon various drafts, in particular, Bron Taylor, Thomas Jones and James Tomalin. The book is dedicated to my boys: Andy, Reuben and Toby.

# Chapter 1
# Introduction

## Religion and the Environmental Crisis

> In the ancient spiritual traditions, man [*sic*] was looked upon as a part of nature, linked by indissoluble spiritual and psychological bonds with the elements around him. This is very much marked in the Hindu tradition, probably the oldest living religious tradition in the world...[T]he natural environment also received the close attention of the ancient Hindu scriptures. Forests and groves were considered as sacred, and flowering trees received special reverence...The Hindu tradition of reverence for nature and all forms of life, vegetable or animal, represents a powerful tradition which needs to be re-nurtured and re-applied in our contemporary context (WWF, 1986, pp. 17–19).

> We know that God pervades the whole universe...It is due to this knowledge alone that we never have thought of nature as inanimate and never did we make the mistake of over exploiting it for our own benefit...That is why an average Indian has always had an inclination to worship everything in nature...This knowledge of the divinity of nature which has been with us as part of our nature and tradition ought to be protected. In our country before setting foot on the ground after waking up in the morning, people address it as mother and ask mother earth's forgiveness for stepping on it. We regard rivers as *tirtha-s* (places of pilgrimage) and worship gods whose abode is in lakes and mountains from which rivers originate (Banwari, 1992, pp. 7–8).

It has become increasingly common for religious traditions to be drawn into discussions about environmental sustainability. The first quotation is part of the Hindu contribution to the 1986 Assisi Declarations, when representatives of five of the world's major religions (Christianity, Buddhism, Islam, Hinduism and Judaism) met in Assisi, Italy, to make statements concerning the environmental nature of their religious traditions.[1] The Assisi Declarations comprised the first significant attempt by religious traditions to come together to discuss the relationship between their teachings and practices and the environment. Within this debate it is frequently argued that humanity has 'forgotten' the sacredness of

---

[1]   This meeting was jointly organised by WWF (the World Wide Fund for Nature) and the International Consultancy on Religion, Education and Culture (ICOREC), an organisation based in Manchester, UK. As the patron of WWF, Prince Philip, the Duke of Edinburgh, attended this event.

nature and that this needs to be rediscovered in order to address the environmental crisis. Thus, religious teachings have been reinterpreted, extended or synthesised in order to express concern for the environment, old rituals have been given new content and new rituals have been devised to reinforce the idea that there is a need for a re-evaluation of humanity's relationship to the natural world (Gottlieb, 1996). While this 'religious environmentalist' discourse can be applied to *all* religious traditions, non-Abrahamic traditions tend to be depicted as having more resonance with environmentalist thinking. For instance, eastern religions or Native American traditions are often seen as intrinsically oriented towards environmental protection. This is clearly expressed in the second quotation, where the 'average Indian' (here considered to be a Hindu) is depicted as respecting nature due to the influence of certain religious beliefs and practices.

This book reflects upon these discourses about religion and nature and assesses their place within, and relevance for, contemporary forms of environmentalism. There is unlikely to be much disagreement with the suggestion that in developing countries religiocultural traditions have some impact upon people's relationship to the natural world, thereby influencing (albeit in a complex fashion) their access to and use of natural resources, as well as the ways in which they might protect themselves from the consequences of ecological change. However, academic disciplines that are interested in environmental sustainability, such as environmental and development studies, have tended to ignore or downplay the role that religious traditions play in shaping human-nature relations or in providing a basis for ecological action and movements. Such disciplines have tended to take a more technocratic and positivistic approach to the issue of environmental sustainability, but it is also the case that they are grounded in the modernist assumption that religion will disappear once societies 'develop' and become more like the West. Nevertheless, in recent years – particularly since the terrorist outrages of 2001 – religion has been firmly placed on the public agenda. On the one hand, the limitations of theories about secularisation are acknowledged, and these theories have been abandoned or modified. On the other hand, secular policy makers, as well as erstwhile modernist academic disciplines, are increasingly concerned to know about and understand the impact of religious identities upon both private identities and public engagement. Considering this 'resurgence of religion', coupled with a renewed concern for environmental issues that has gripped people's attention across the globe (from high level policy makers to average citizens concerned to map and curtail their carbon footprint), a fresh analysis and interrogation of *religious environmentalism* is particularly timely.

A discussion of religious environmentalism may have a renewed significance in the 2000s, but is not, however, a contemporary debate. In the seminal 1967 article *The Historical Roots of our Ecological Crisis*, Lynn White Jr. argued that religion was the cause of, as well as the potential solution to, environmental problems. He wrote that 'Christianity bears a huge burden of guilt' for the environmental crisis facing humanity (1967, p. 1206) and considered that the displacement of Paganism by Christianity had led to the desacralisation of nature. The Christian God was seen as transcendent to creation and humanity was granted dominion over the natural world. This, he argued, opened the way for humans to begin the domestication and transformation of nature. On the one hand, the growth of science was predicated upon the desire to understand God's 'mind' and, on the other hand, the development of technologies to manipulate the natural world were an 'Occidental, voluntarist realization of the Christian dogma of man's [*sic*] transcendence of, and rightful mastery over, nature' (1967, p. 1206). In tracing the roots of the contemporary environmental crisis to the union of science and technology in the nineteenth century, which created the conditions for the industrial revolution, he concludes that 'more science and more technology are not going to get us out of the present ecological crisis until we find a new religion, or rethink our old one' (1967, p. 1206). He suggests that religious traditions such as Zen Buddhism hold an environmentally friendly view of the humanity-nature relationship: such eastern traditions are represented as emphasising the interconnectedness of humanity and nature rather than their separation (Callicot and Aimes, 1991). Or that a stewardship model, which draws upon the example of St Francis of Assisi, subverts and challenges the dominant attitudes towards nature, which are 'deeply grounded in Christian dogma' (1967, p. 1207).

This conceptualisation of the environmental crisis as a religious problem, both in terms of its cause and its remedy, has become an element of contemporary environmentalist discourse. Although this book will focus upon expressions of religious environmentalism in Britain and India, the recourse to religious ideas, values and practices has become a feature of environmentalism across the globe.[2] In the British context, this book will be concerned with expressions of 'spirituality' in the radical environmental direct action (EDA) movement, which has engaged in various styles of direct action against perceived environmental threats, such as road building, quarrying and nuclear power. Despite the anarchistic backdrop to this style of ecopolitics, many activists describe themselves as 'spiritual', consider the Earth to be sacred and, echoing Lynn White's narrative, criticise Christianity for supporting a worldview that has generated an ecological crisis. They also articulate an anarchic 'neo-primitivism', which looks back to (assumed) ecological affinities of preindustrial communities and forwards in terms of attempting to model contemporary ecolifestyles on the past (Smith, 2002). These contemporary styles of ecospirituality typically draw upon or borrow from eastern (including Hindu) and Native American beliefs and practices. However, we also find that some environmental movements in the developing world articulate their concerns in religious language. In India, for instance, the idea that the Hindu tradition is environmentally friendly (as the two opening quotations suggest) is frequently expressed in both grey literature and scholarly publications concerned

---

[2] See, for instance, the website of the Yale University Forum on Religion and Ecology. This includes ample reading lists that clearly indicate the appeal of religious environmentalism across different traditions and within different regions, http://fore.research.yale.edu/ (last accessed 04/03/08).

with ecological problems (Banwari, 1992; Dwivedi, 1993a; 1993b; 1996; 1999; Dwivedi and Tiwari, 1987; Sen, 1992). This might not seem particularly surprising in a country where religion, rather than secular ethics or scientific explanations, continues to provide the ultimate source of meaning in the lives of most people.

However, in tandem with literature that provides environmental interpretations of religious and cultural traditions, there have emerged critiques of such exegeses. Some critics argue that religiocultural traditions can also be interpreted to contradict contemporary environmentalist thinking (Harris, 1991; Nelson, 1998b). For instance, Nelson is concerned that the frequent disregard for the material world in Hinduism, as an impediment to spiritual progress, is problematic for claims that the tradition is environmentally friendly. He questions the sentiments towards nature that a passage such as the following might suggest:

> Pure non-attachment is disregard for all objects – from the god Brahma down to plants and minerals – like the indifference one has toward the excrement of a crow (cited in Nelson, 1998, p. 81).[3]

Would this inspire the devotee to revere nature as part of a spiritual life, or 'would it rather teach…the irrelevance of nature to spiritual life?' (1998, p. 81). Other critics of this position have argued that environmentalist interpretations of religion are anachronistic, that they are reading contemporary concerns into religious or cultural traditions (Freeman, 1994; Pederson, 1995). They argue that the contention that religious traditions are environmentally friendly is an *interpretation of tradition* rather than a *traditional interpretation*. Thus, although the idea of the sacredness of nature (*biodivinity*) is found within many of the world's religiocultural traditions, the claim that their adherents will necessarily think and behave like modern environmentalists is flawed. In India, for example, we find many examples of the worship of elements of the natural world that do not result in behaviour that is directed towards environmental conservation. For instance, while people in India worship the dangerously polluted River Ganges as the goddess *Ganga Ma*, there is little evidence that this religious practice motivates devotees to engage in initiatives to prevent any further pollution of the river (Alley, 1998; 2000; 2002). Similarly, there is a strong tradition of sacred grove preservation in India, yet it can be suggested that people worship these forests because they are the abode of the deity rather than to conserve biodiversity (Freeman 2004). Thus, the idea of the *intrinsic value* of nature is not necessarily implied by these examples of nature worship. Elements of the natural world may be considered as sacred without any explicit consciousness about the relevance of this to environmental protection.

In this book I will use the term 'religious environmentalism' to describe the conscious and reflexive process of applying religious ideas to the issue of the

---

[3]    From the Aparokshanubhuti, a text associated with the eighth century Indian philosopher Shankara.

destruction of the environment. This is to distinguish a fundamentally modern phenomenon, which arose alongside the emergence of the environmental movement since the 1960s, from the very ancient religious practice of worshipping features of the natural world – 'nature religion', which exists across many cultures. Within religious environmentalism we find the selective appropriation of beliefs and practices that support the idea of nature as sacred (*biodivinity*), taken from within religious traditions across the globe. Moreover, the existence of nature religion is typically taken as proof that certain communities were/are environmentally friendly. The reason why religious environmentalists tend to confuse nature religion with conscious environmental protection is an unquestioning acceptance of 'the myth of primitive ecological wisdom'.

## The Myth of Primitive Ecological Wisdom and the Two Religious Environmentalist Assumptions

The anthropologist Kay Milton has called the tendency to essentialise the values and lifestyles of non-industrial communities as environmentally friendly, the 'myth of primitive ecological wisdom' (1996). She does not use the word 'myth' to suggest that non-industrial peoples never live in harmony with their environment, but instead she argues that the idea of primitive ecological wisdom is taken as a dogma which is 'in no need of proof and not easily amenable to refutation' (1996, p. 31). She suggests that this view, while questionable, is nonetheless integral to much environmentalism that relies upon this 'myth' in support of the argument that industrialisation is the cause of environmental destruction. Drawing upon anthropological studies, she questions the veracity of this myth as broadly applicable to all non-industrial peoples and questions its embeddedness in environmentalist discourse since it limits our understanding of the ways in which people actually interact with their environment (1996, p. 133).

Religious environmentalism also relies heavily upon this 'myth of primitive ecological wisdom'. The existence of religious beliefs and practices within cultures across the globe that appear to suggest care for nature, supports this 'myth' and they provide the basis for two assumptions that are central to religious environmentalist discourse. Firstly, that religious traditions (particularly non-Abrahamic) are environmentally friendly and, secondly, that an 'ecogolden age' existed at some time when people treated the environment with respect because of their religious/ cultural traditions. These assumptions underpin religious environmentalist discourse, which often articulates the desire for a *return* to a mythic state of ecological harmony that is premised upon recognition of the sacredness of the Earth. In particular, the values and lifestyles of preindustrial communities are believed to embody such environmental wisdom, which disappeared from the West, following the rise of Christianity, and are increasingly threatened across the globe due to the spread of industrialisation and western values.

However, as indicated above, practices that involve the worship of nature are not necessarily concerned with environmental protection. Moreover, all religious traditions can submit themselves to environmentalist as well as non-environmentalist interpretations. Postcolonial critique of the romanticisation of the values and practices of non-industrial peoples has highlighted the ways in which the representation of certain communities as environmentally friendly silences indigenous voices. In particular, Native American groups have articulated strong opposition to the appropriation of their culture by well-meaning environmentalists in the USA (Taylor, 1997). Similarly, in India, both Guha (1989; 1990) and Baviskar (1995; 1997; 1999; 2004) have challenged the essentialisation of certain groups in India as 'close to nature' thereby removing their autonomy to make decisions about their own development. It is common for such critiques to view 'environmentalism' as having emerged from within a western context. In particular, it is argued that the idea of the *intrinsic value* of nature (which non-industrial people are presumed to uphold) has its roots in the European Romantic Movement (itself a reaction against industrialisation), which idealised nature as a realm of purity and intrinsic value. By contrast, this view of nature is difficult to find in developing countries, such as India, where the majority of people cannot afford to put the 'Earth first'. However, this is not to say that environmentalism is wholly a postmaterialist phenomenon, but instead suggests that in developing contexts people are likely to have different reasons for engaging in environmentalist activities. The distinction made by Guha and Martinez-Allier (1997) between the 'empty belly environmentalism of the South' and the 'full stomach environmentalism of the North' is useful here to account for the types of environmentalism that are more likely to arise in different contexts. They observe that in the South environmental movements and concerns are much more likely to be in response to local environmental problems that have a direct bearing upon people's lives. By contrast, ecocentric or 'deep ecological' thought, which is concerned to protect nature 'for its own sake', is much more prevalent within environmentalism in the developed world, where people are not directly dependant upon natural resources for their survival.

Religious environmentalists also invoke the idea of nature as intrinsically valuable and, as we have seen, tend to confuse instances of nature worship with an environmentalist attitude that considers nature to be in significant in its own right. Therefore, does the reliance of religious environmentalism upon a particular understanding of nature limit its relevance for non-western contexts? This is the key issue which this book seeks to address: does religion have a role to play in ecological thinking and action in a country such as India, or is religious environmentalism a narrowly focused, colonial, postmaterialist and romantic ideology that has limited relevance in a developing context?

## Postcolonial Critique and the Myth of Primitive Ecological Wisdom

The postcolonial critique of the idea of 'primitive ecological wisdom' poses a challenge to religious environmentalist discourse. The postcolonial critique of this position points towards concerns about the impact of the representation of non-western peoples in discourses invented by 'powerful outsiders'. It could be argued that such a critique often overextends itself, and that 'myths', such as the idea of primitive ecological wisdom, have a deeper symbolic significance that goes beyond concerns about their truth. For instance, as I will discuss in Chapter 5, within the environmental direct action (EDA) movement in the UK, the idea of 'getting back to nature' reflects 'an ethical expression of the desire and wonder we can still experience in relation to human and non-human others' (Smith, 2002, p. 422). For environmental direct activists, as well as other 'romantics' throughout history, this 'state of nature' is contrasted with the oppression, exploitation and alienation wrought by capitalist values and institutions. It is necessary to have a vision of an *Eden* to contrast with *Babylon*. While this 'myth' gives shape to the movement, it does nonetheless involve the representation of real people. The use of myths in the movement, as well as the symbolic value of key narratives, play an important role in maintaining people's involvement. This includes discourses about the Earth as sacred being an ancient view held by non-industrial peoples. How do we balance an appreciation of the symbolic significance of such discourses with a critique of their broader impact? This is a question that I will return to throughout the book. As we will see, scholars tend to emphasise one dimension or the other.

In thinking about this question, it is also relevant to note that Milton indicates that the 'myth of primitive ecological wisdom is not simply a notion imposed by romantic environmentalists on a sector of the world's population, it is an image which indigenous peoples accept and promote for themselves' (1996, p. 202). Brosius is critical of the (now often unreflective) tendency to portray as a 'myth', the idea that indigenous peoples live(d) in harmony with nature. He argues that this can undermine the integrity of indigenous communities who adopt this 'myth' as part of the process of securing their autonomy and defining their interests, since it plays into the hands of their opponents who can then easily dismiss indigenous people's environmentalist discourse as fabrication (1999). Similarly, in India we find that environmentalists and environmental groups may articulate their concerns within a religious framework. However, this does not get us off the postcolonial hook, since in many cases we still need be attuned to the manipulation of indigenous religious discourses by 'elites' within societies, who articulate a style of environmentalist thinking which has developed under the influence of western ideas and values, and which possibly has little relevance to the majority of the poor (Baviskar, 1997; Guha, 1989; 1990). Religious environmentalism in India has not only been critiqued for its romanticism but also because the 'Hindu civilizational response' to ecological concerns that it adopts, closely resembles discourses about the Hindu tradition employed by the Hindu Right (Baviskar, 1999; 2004; Mawdsley, 2005; 2006; Nanda, 2005). While other religious traditions are also to be found in

India, it has tended to be the Hindu tradition that has been most explicitly drawn into environmentalist discourse (see Chapter 6). As I will discuss in Chapter 7, some members of the Hindu Right have appropriated these ecological discourses, grounded in the Hindu tradition, as part of their opposition toward the Tehri Dam (which has been built on the sacred River Ganges). This suggests a blurring of the boundary between genuine concern for the ecological consequences of the dam and the fact that the Ganges is a powerful symbol of the Hindu nation (*Hindu rashtra*). Thus, the articulation of 'primitive ecological wisdom' as a Hindu quality, may mask concerns and interests that go beyond the ecological.

## The Aims of This Book

These criticisms notwithstanding, it seems premature to reject all forms of religious environmentalism in India as either harmful colonial rhetoric or supportive of the Hindu Right. My study is, nonetheless, critical of the tendency to romanticise Hinduism as environmentally friendly, since this is hardly useful as a general narrative capable of reflecting the actual environmental concerns of the poor. The Hindu tradition in India has no simple and predictable line on environmental conservation, it is a matter of interpretation. Mostly the tradition is indifferent to thinking about ecological issues, and religious belief and practice can even act against the interests of environmental protection. In this book I will argue that the relationship between Hinduism and the environment is more complex than religious environmentalist discourse typically suggests. The case studies discussed towards the end of this book will investigate the use of religion within 'empty belly environmentalism' in India. I will suggest that such uses of religion can be strategic and pragmatic in terms of achieving particular ends, rather than concerned with fundamentally transforming the relationship between humanity and the natural world in line with some version of deep ecological or ecocentric thinking. Thus, while many communities in the South do engage in forms of nature worship, or articulate their ecopolitics within a religious framework, the extent to which this indicates the same aims and motivations as western religious environmentalists is questioned.

This book investigates the myth of primitive ecological wisdom within religious environmentalism in Britain and India. However, as Milton writes

> the point of testing the myth is not to suggest that non-industrial societies have nothing to teach the industrial world about how environmental responsibilities might be defined and implemented. It is to demonstrate the value of a more sensitive awareness of how human societies understand and interact with their environments (1996, p. 112).

While this book will be concerned to address the factual basis for the myth, its primary focus is to examine the role and impact of this myth in religious environmentalist discourse in both contexts. Through comparing expressions of

*Book Outline*

*Genealogy of ecocentrism*

religious environmentalism in both a northern (Britain) and a southern (India) context my aim is to look at the different uses of the myth of primitive ecological wisdom and to assess the extent to which religious environmentalism is a narrowly defined postmaterialist, romantic ideology or whether it is more broadly relevant. In Chapters 2–4 I construct a theoretical framework from which to assess the later empirical chapters that present case studies from Britain (Chapter 5) and India (Chapters 6–7). I provide an analysis of understandings of religion and environmentalism, arguing that religious environmentalism is originally premised upon understandings of the nature of religion and of environmentalism that have their origins in the West. In Chapter 2 I argue that religious environmentalist discourse relies upon (or has as its foundation) a certain *type* of religion that is both modern and which has been typically associated with western religiocultural trends and preferences. This style of religiosity has a concern with ethics, specifically expressive or postmaterialist ethics (such as the intrinsic value of nature); it is a style of religiosity that is flexible and can be co-opted to accommodate and seek solutions to social problems; and it is optional (the believer can choose to belong or not). However, religious environmentalism not only relies upon a certain *type* of religion that is both modern and which has been typically associated with the West, but also upon a particular understanding of nature as *valuable in itself*. In Chapters 3 and 4 I trace the emergence of the idea of nature as intrinsically valuable back to the European Romantic Movement, which juxtaposed a vision of unspoilt nature against a natural landscape manipulated by industrialisation. This theme of reverence for nature, as a realm of purity and aesthetic value, has continued as a trend within western-influenced nature thought and informs the values and actions of many contemporary environmentalists, including those who draw upon religion. There has been criticism that the type of 'environmentalism' that has emerged largely reflects the interests and values of the wealthy industrialised nations (Baviskar, 1995; Guha, 1989): that it is postmaterialist.

Chapters 5–7 present case studies from Britain and India, which draw upon the earlier theoretical discussion for their analysis. In particular, the case studies aim to address the research question, which underpin this book. Does the reliance of religious environmentalism upon a particular understanding of religion and nature limit its relevance for non-western contexts? Chapter 5 is concerned with the emergence of environmental direct action (EDA) in the UK, since the 1990s, as a radical form of environmental politics that calls for a reorientation of human-nature relations in the form of environmentally sustainable lifestyles. There is a strong emphasis upon a radical 'do-it-yourself' (DIY) politics (McKay, 1996; 1998) and many emphasise an anarchic 'neo-primitivism', which looks back to (assumed) ecological affinities of preindustrial communities and forwards in terms of attempting to model contemporary ecolifestyles on the past (Smith, 2002). In the final two chapters, which will present case studies from India, my aim is to explore the use of religion in the Indian environmental movement. While most ecological initiatives in India are secular there are examples of religious environmentalism. In Chapter 6 I present two 'contrasting' case studies of religious environmentalism in India.

The first of these is an example that closely resembles the style of environmentalism and religiosity discussed in the previous chapter: radical environmentalism and deregulated spirituality. In July–August 1997 I attended a 'Rainbow Gathering' in India at Almora, in Kumaon region in the state of Uttarakhand. During this gathering both Indian and non-Indians assembled to discuss environmental issues facing India and to 'celebrate the sacredness of the Earth'. The second case study presented in this chapter is concerned with a different approach to religious environmentalism that is not radical or countercultural in outlook and which stresses the contribution that particular religious traditions or world religions can make towards environmentalist thought and action. This 'world religions' approach is clearly articulated by a UK-based organisation called the Alliance of Religions and Conservation (ARC). In this case study, I discuss an initiative in the sacred town of Vrindavan, North India, which is associated with the Hindu deity Krishna. ARC, together with another group called Friends of Vrindavan, have been instrumental is setting up a environmental project in Vrindavan, which employs the symbol of Krishna to encourage people to change their behaviour with regards to the natural environment.

While there are examples of religious environmentalism in India, most initiatives tend to be secular. One reason for this is the concern of secular commentators about the overt *Hinduisation* of any socio-political agenda, environmental or otherwise, and this is discussed in Chapter 7. The project in Vrindavan, for instance, has been criticised for employing similar symbols and discourses to the Hindu Right in India, a chauvinistic religio-political force in the country that has as its priority the establishment of a Hindu *rashtra* (nation). This raises questions about the blurring of the boundaries between genuine concern for ecological issues and an aggressive religio-nationalistic agenda that also employs religious environmentalist language. Thus, religious environmentalism in India faces the critique not only that it is an anachronism that can romanticise poor people's situation, but also that it is dangerous because of its co-option by the Hindu Right.

# Chapter 2
# The Religious Environmentalist
# Mode of Religion

## Introduction

Ecotheologians[1] have sought to *reinterpret* old traditions: finding and stressing passages in classic texts that help us face the current crisis. Thus we are reminded that the *Talmud* instructs us not to live in a city without trees; or that St. Francis's love of animals makes him a kind of early, Christian, Deep Ecologist. Thinkers have also tried to *extend* more familiar religious beliefs, especially ethical ones concerning love and respect for other people, to nonhuman nature. Nature becomes the Body of God, or the 'neighbor' whom we must treat as we would like to be treated. Creative ecotheologians *synthesize* elements of different traditions...some Christian thinkers unhesitatingly using Taoist images of humanity's integration into a natural setting, or Jews quoting Buddhist nature poetry. In particular, ideas from indigenous, or native peoples – communities whose relations to nature originated before the current model of domination of the earth – have been studied. Finally spiritual thinkers are *creating* new ideas, practices, and organizations (Gottlieb, 1996, p. 10).

Prior to the 1960s there was little widespread public concern about the destruction of the natural environment, the depletion of natural resources, environmental pollution and the consequences of this for future generations: there was no 'environmental movement', as such, and the worship of nature was less likely to be linked to issues about its preservation. Whilst 'nature religion', the belief in the sacredness of features of the natural world, is a very ancient feature of many religiocultural traditions, 'religious environmentalism' is fundamentally modern. However, religious environmentalist discourse not only tends to rely upon a particular understanding of nature (as valuable in itself) but also upon a certain *type* of 'expressive religiosity' that is both modern/postmodern and emerged within western contexts. This is not to say that expressive or 'modern' religion is today confined to western contexts, owing to global flows of culture and information that transcend geographical boundaries. Moreover, it is not the only style of religiosity and other religious forms may still dominate in other regions.

---

[1]   I would replace the word 'ecotheologians' here with 'religious environmentalists'. Whilst ecotheology does capture the nature of this phenomenon as a response to the contemporary 'eco' crisis, the term 'theology' implies a Christian approach.

*..ɔ ..ne Term 'Religion' a Viable Cross-cultural Tool?*

We can suggest that religious environmentalism maintains a comprehensive and coherent narrative through its blending of *expressive attitudes towards nature with an expressive style of religiosity*. While the notion of the 'environment' requires careful qualification before it is useful as a cross-cultural tool (see Chapters 3 and 4), the same is true for the idea of 'religion'. Thus, we must consider that the way in which religious environmentalists use religion reflects the particular history of religion in the West. The religious environmentalist understanding of religion reflects a specific orientation towards religion which is not universal either throughout history or within contemporary global society. Whilst there is much diversity of religious expression within western society, certain key trends have shaped and characterised western religious phenomena. In drawing comparisons with India, I suggest that definitions of religion, as well as how it relates to the life of the believer and its role in society, may be highly variable between different cultures (Bellah, 1964; Mandelbaum, 1966).

Some critics of the use of the term religion as a cross-cultural tool present a 'mild' critique and stress the importance of not imposing western, largely Christian understandings of what a religion should be onto non-western religious traditions. For instance, the Hindu temple does not perform the same function as a Christian Church, although they are both places of 'worship' (Nye, 1995). According to this mild critique, we might also wish to assess different understandings of 'worship': does it mean the same in Hinduism as it does in Christianity? Other scholars present a far stronger critique, arguing that the very word 'religion' is problematic, since it 'imposes on non-western institutions and values the nuance and form of western ones, especially such popular distinctions as those between religion and society, or between religion and the secular, or religion and politics, or between religion and economics' (Fitzgerald, 2000, p. 9). Fitzgerald argues, in fact, that scholars should abandon the term religion and that religious studies should be reframed as a form of cultural studies, concerned with institutions which are 'imbued with deep collective significance and that transcend any particular individual or time' (2000, p. 10). While I do not take this sort of critique to the same extreme, I do welcome the way in which it encourages us to be suspicious about the validity of the concept of religion as a cross-cultural tool and, as I will argue, this is particularly problematic when the idea of a universal notion of religion is put into the service of social or political movements which have a global reach. It is important to understand that the *type* or *mode* of religion that we find within religious environmentalism emerged within a specific context and is different in important ways to popular Hinduism in India or Theravada Buddhism in Thailand, for instance. I am not just drawing attention here to differences in doctrine, belief and practice found within various traditions, but that religion as a generic category can play a different sort of role and emphasise different functions dependant upon the context.

Thus, the blanket claim that Hinduism or Buddhism are environmentally friendly may become meaningless since it arguably only makes sense within the particular religious context from which the claim emerged: it is not necessarily possible to generalise this claim to other contexts. Just because religious traditions can be interpreted to support contemporary environmentalist thinking does not mean that this reflects the way in which the particular tradition is actually understood in other contexts. While environmentalist exegesis can be carried out on all religious traditions and ecological wisdom can be read into the lifestyles and values of indigenous communities, this does not mean that those traditions have ever been understood as concerned about environmental destruction or that such indigenous communities share any of the same concerns as modern environmentalists. Religious environmentalism is a movement situated in a particular sociohistorical context, and the way that it understands religion serves its 'ecocentric' ideology.

The shape that 'religion' takes reflects the political and social transformations that have occurred within different contexts. This is why it is problematic to extend a western (Christian-influenced) understanding of religion to other cultures, since the sociocultural context is different. Yet this model of religion tends to dominate global discourses about religion (and I am interested in this with respect to religious environmentalism). Probably the most important factor in shaping the style of religiosity that has come to define the cross-cultural category 'religion', is the distinction between the sacred and the secular. Religion is the domain of the sacred and is to be distinguished from all that is not sacred: the secular. However, the emergence of these two contrasting ontological structures (the religious and the secular, which tend to be seen as incompatible and in competition) is the product of particular sociocultural trends, emerging in the West following the Protestant Reformation. By contrast, in other contexts (India will be the example discussed in this chapter) the religious ontology often seamlessly merges with worldly concerns. This very distinction between the sacred and the secular, or the religious and the non-religious, has shaped definitions of religion and attitudes towards its role, with respect to both the individual and society. This distinction, which became most significant following the Protestant Reformation, has been a central factor in the shaping of western religiosity and is fundamental to an understanding of religious environmentalist model of religion.

## The Sacred and the Secular

In India the distinction between the sacred and the secular, or the religious and the non-religious, is less clearly marked that it is in the West. Within popular or village Hinduism, for instance, certain rituals and personal observances are performed with the aim of securing material or pragmatic ends. The making of *vratas* (vows) is common, whereby the deity is promised that if particular boons are granted, the devotee will do something in return (such as keeping a vigil at the deity's shrine or arranging a feast in his/her honour) (Weightman, 1978, p. 61). Similarly, illness is often attributed to supernatural causes that require the services of a specialist priest (*baiga*), who can exorcise a malicious spirit or suggest the performance of rituals (1978, pp. 61–4;

Babb, 1975). The description that Keith Thomas gives of the Church in Medieval Britain, as 'a vast reservoir of magical power, capable of being deployed for a variety of secular purposes', seems to suggest a similar style of religiosity (1973, p. 51), where 'the line between magic and religion is one which it is impossible to draw in many primitive societies; it is equally difficult to recognise in medieval England' (1973, p. 57). Through the worship of saints, the investing of material objects with supernatural powers or the belief in the direct efficacy of sacred utterances, the Medieval Briton aimed to control and influence the material environment.

However, the sixteenth-century Protestant Reformation resulted in a rejection of 'magic' both outside and within the Church (1973, pp. 304–5). The boundary between prayers and spells was clearly demarcated and the direct efficacy of ritual or the worship of relics was rejected. Whilst prayer and religious ritual were continued as an integral part of post-reformation religious life in northern Europe, there was no longer any guarantee that they would bring particular benefits; it was God's choice to listen or not. Thus, there arose a religion of faith and belief as opposed to practice. Suffering and misfortune were explained as divine providence and Christianity no longer provided the direct means to overcome them. The gaps left by the decline of magic were filled by the intellectual and technological changes accompanying the scientific and philosophical revolution of the seventeenth century. On the one hand, 'mental' changes 'saw the emergence of a new faith in the potentialities of human initiative' (1973, pp. 791–2) and, on the other hand, technological and scientific innovations meant that it was possible not only to explain but also to control and manipulate the material world through human effort (1973, p. 775). Rather than becoming redundant, religion became more rational and specialised in its field of action. It became divorced from the world (and eventually the state) as it turned its attention towards contemplating the otherworldly.[2] The emphasis had shifted from religion as a means of explaining and manipulating the world through recourse to divine powers, to religion that was concerned with the search for personal knowledge and experience of God.[3] Under the influence of Protestant values the 'pragmatic' use of religion was increasingly viewed as magic rather than religion.

---

[2]    There is a sense in which Protestantism is 'this worldly'. Max Weber ([1930]1985) argues that in contrast to Catholicism, the emerging Protestant faiths in sixteenth-century Europe emphasised the significance of worldly success as a sign of one's predestined salvation and as such is 'this worldly'. However, he stressed that 'it strode into the market-place of life, slammed the door of the monastery behind it, and undertook to penetrate just that daily routine of life with its methodicalness, to fashion it into a life in the world, but neither of nor for this world' (p. 154). Thus, whilst Protestantism can be seen as 'this worldly' in the sense that it gave religious significance to worldly affairs, this significance was firmly directed towards transcending the world. However, by this stage it had lost its power to directly influence both the material world and the achievement of salvation by the powers inherent within religion such as ritual, indulgences or good works.

[3]    Catholicism also underwent such a transformation but in many ways has retained some of the more magical elements lost by Protestantism: for example, the doctrine of transubstantiation or the cults of the saints still popular in southern Europe or southern Ireland.

**Pragmatic and Transcendental Dimensions of Religion**

By contrast, other forms of religion have not undergone this process of puritanisation and separation from the world. Village Hinduism, for example, is concerned with the material world, as well as the 'transcendental'. People live within a sacred cosmos, permeated by both benevolent and malevolent divine powers that need to be carefully managed in order to maintain a stable social environment. Mandelbaum (1966) suggests that it is useful to draw a distinction here between the 'transcendental' and 'pragmatic' aspects of religion, which find expression through two different and separate 'complexes' of belief and practice. The 'acts of the transcendental complex are directed toward such concerns as the proper fate of the soul after death and the proper maintenance of the social order, the pragmatic looks to the curing of a sick child, the location of a lost valuable, victory in a local tussle' (1966, p. 1175). While the Brahmin priest, who is associated with the higher castes and has knowledge of the Sanskrit texts, operates within the transcendental complex, the functionaries within the pragmatic complex are low caste ritual exorcists, *baigas*. Whereas the '*Brahmin* priest is the human instrument of access to the uppermost regions of the pantheon' (Babb 1975, p. 197), the domain of the important pan-Indian Gods, the *baiga* has the power to manipulate and communicate with local deities and spirits. The local deities and spirits may lack the power of the great Gods, but they are more closely connected with the material world and the concerns of day-to-day life: 'they are ritually more accessible than the great deities' (Babb, 1975, p. 240).

This pragmatic use of religion is a broad characteristic of many religious traditions outside the post-reformation West, where religion 'includes abstract cosmology as well as specific 'magical' devices used to cure or exorcise' (Mandelbaum, 1966, p. 1174).[4] While Mandelbaum's distinction between pragmatic and transcendental complexes has been criticised for oversimplification,[5]

---

[4] For instance, the Muslim veneration of *pirs* ('venerated saintly men, whose tombs become locally renowned shrines' (Mandelbaum, 1966, p. 1178)) and the Sinhalese Buddhist use of 'beliefs and rites through which they communicate with lesser supernaturals for immediate benefits' (1966, p. 1179) suggest a style of religion which is concerned with pragmatic ends.

[5] With respect to a Hindu context, Weightman (1978), for instance, introduces another complex, the 'dharmik', which is concerned with activities directed towards the performance of one's duty or *dharma*, and is hence intimately connected to social stability. He considers that 'the Dharmik Complex is essentially "group religion", the religion of man in the world, while the Transcendental Complex owes its inspiration to the world renouncer who seeks to obtain liberation from the worlds of society and existence through "disciplines of salvation"' (Weightman, 1978, p. 65). Other studies have suggested that a clear distinction between separate complexes and their religious specialists is difficult to discern in reality. Babb (1975), for example, found Brahmin priests in Chhatisgarh (Madhya Pradesh) to be involved with pragmatic religion, as well as transcendental, and Wadley's (1975) study in Karimpur (Uttar Pradesh) suggests that it is often not possible to distinguish between the two complexes.

it is nonetheless useful because it points to the existence of different styles or types of religiosity both historically and today. It is also useful as a starting point from which to think about one pattern of religious change as concerned with a gradual de-emphasis upon the pragmatic dimension and a corresponding elevation of the transcendental. I am not suggesting that this distinction is absolute, since it is clear that western (predominantly transcendental) religion does have a pragmatic function for believers. The point is that it is less marked and less fundamental, and official versions of the tradition would seek to downplay it altogether. However, this shift to a transcendental focus has also had an impact upon non-western religion. Although the pragmatic use of religion is still important in both India and Sri Lanka, for example, reform movements within these traditions 'parallel the developments that took place in Christianity from the time of the Reformation' (Mandelbaum, 1966, p. 1181) which have resulted in an emphasis upon the transcendental dimension of religion and a downgrading of the pragmatic.[6] In India in the nineteenth century a number of Hindu reform movements emerged which aimed to provide an interpretation of Hinduism that modelled a Christian image of what a religion should be, with key texts and doctrines. The thinking of intellectuals, such as Ram Mohan Roy, the founder of the Brahmo Samaj (Killingley, 1993), and Swami Vivekananda, the father of neo-Vedanta (Radice, 1998), was more concerned with the transcendental, ultimate goals of religion than the ways in which religious action can serve pragmatic ends. Neo-Vedanta, in particular, offered a version of Hinduism that more closely resembled the transcendental religion of the West (Knott, 2000, p. 29) or a 'world religion'. It is common to think about these transformations in Hindu thought as an outcome of the contact between educated Indians and the West, largely *via* the colonial British and the influence of Christian missionaries (Coward, 1991; O'Flaherty and Derrett, 1978). Thus, the shift to a more transcendental focus was one of the necessary steps taken towards Hinduism becoming a so-called 'world religion', one that could be compared with other world traditions.

---

[6] Apart from drawing our attention to the pragmatic function of religion, Mandelbaum is also concerned to demonstrate the various degrees of separation between these two complexes. His thesis suggests that the greater the degree of separation the less important the pragmatic becomes. He suggests that transformations in religion in India and Ceylon (Sri Lanka) have taken place under influence from the West – including, Christian missionaries: 'what these influences have done is to give rise to reformers whose program includes and expansion of transcendental beliefs and practices so as to make the pragmatic counterparts of no use of interest' (1966, p. 1181). See also Gombridge and Obeyesekere (1988).

**Is Hinduism a Religion?**

A number of scholars have taken this discussion a step further, arguing not so much that Hinduism underwent a transformation in the eighteenth and nineteenth centuries, but that prior to the late 1700s there was no such thing as a religion called Hinduism. In making the claim that Hinduism is an 'Orientalist' invention or construction the aim is not to imply that a new religion, as such, was formed in the eighteenth century, but instead to draw attention to the ways in which the colonial Orientalist scholars, missionaries and administrators gave a name (Hinduism) to the totality of diverse practices found in India that were associated with the priestly Brahmin caste. For instance, Klostermaier argues that the idea of a Hindu or Hinduism is not indigenous to India: 'the very name *Hinduism* owes its origin to chance; foreigners in the West extending the name of the province of Sindh to the whole country lying across the Indus River and simply calling all its inhabitants *Hindus* and their religion *Hinduism*' (1994, pp. 30–31). Similarly, according to Smith,

> The term 'Hinduism' is, in my judgment, a particularly false conceptualisation, one that is conspicuously incompatible with any adequate understanding of the religious outlook of Hindus...the classical Hindus were inhibited by no lack of sophistication or self-consciousness. They thought about what we call religious questions profusely and with critical analysis...they could not think of Hinduism because that is the name we give to a totality whatever it might be that they thought, or did, or thought worth doing (1964, p. 61).

Thus, according to this argument, the term 'Hinduism' is a category superimposed by outsiders (e.g. British colonialists, Christian missionaries and western 'Orientalist' scholars). As Richard King asks: 'is there really a single ancient religion designated by the catch-all term 'Hinduism' or is the term merely a fairly recent social construction of Western origin?' (1999, p. 146).

King argues that the term Hinduism is an invention by colonial orientalists, reflecting their colonial and Christian presupostions (King, 1999, p. 165; Fitzgerald, 1990). However, not only was a monolithic unity forced upon the totality of what 'Hindus' across India did and believed in, but this reflected a blending of a Christian model of what a religion should be with a Brahamical (upper caste) version of that tradition (Thapar, 1989). This new form of organised Hinduism

> seeks historicity for the incarnations of its deities, encourages the idea of a centrally sacred book, claims monotheism as significant to the worship of deity, acknowledges the authority of the ecclesiastical organization of certain sects as prevailing over all and has supported large-scale missionary work and conversion. These changes allow it to transcend caste identities and reach out to larger numbers (Thapar, 1989, p. 228).

This is part of the process, then, of Hinduism becoming a world religion, and in order not to 'erase the colonial subject from history and perpetuate the myth of the passive Oriental' (King, 1999, p. 146) the contribution of indigenous thinkers and movements to this process must also be acknowledged. For example, the Brahmo Samaj was formed in 1828 by Ram Mohan Roy who defined Hinduism by referring back to the 'golden age' of the elite Sanskrit traditions, to identify a religion which knew of one true god, *Brahman*, and foundational texts, the *Upanishads*. Christianity had presented a critique of the idolatry and polytheism of the religious practices associated with Hinduism, and it was Roy's intention to 'rehabilitate the Hindu identity scoffed at by the Europeans' (Jaffrelot, 1993, p. 518), albeit following the rational logic and Christian model of the western colonialists. Moreover, as Killingley notes, Ram Mohan Roy was (probably) the first Hindu to use the term Hinduism in the early nineteenth century (1993, pp. 62–3).

While there have been critiques of this position (Lorenzen, for instance, argues that although the term Hinduism may not have been used until the late eighteenth or early nineteenth century that a 'Hindu religion …was firmly established long before 1800' (1999, p. 631)) it is not my intention here to pursue this debate. Instead, I wish to sum up what it can offer to our understanding of the religious environmentalist's model of religion. The dominance of transcendental religion in the West has had an impact upon how non-western traditions have been understood and interpreted. The colonial Orientalist scholars, for instance, were far less concerned with the pragmatic religion of village Hinduism or indigenous Buddhism than they were with exegesis of the written texts and the isolation of foundational teachings directed towards the salvation of the individual. Pragmatic religion was generally regarded as an aberration, a corruption of an authentic religious tradition that reflected a golden age of human civilisation (e.g. the religion of the Aryan authors of the Vedas, the most ancient Hindu texts) or the original intention of the founder (e.g. the Buddha).[7]

---

[7] This is particularly marked within the study of Buddhism even today where a 'Protestant Buddhism' (Mellor, 1991; Almond, 1988), has taken hold, which emphasises, for instance, that there are no gods in Buddhism and its focus is primarily soteriological. By contrast, studies of indigenous Buddhism reveal a world where believers endeavour to accumulate merit through ritual observances or to express a belief in the efficacy of spirits or demigods. Thus, when scholars encounter pragmatic dimensions of indigenous Buddhism, they have, at times, had difficulty reconciling it with what they understand to be the transcendental core of the tradition. While reform Buddhist reform movements in Sri Lanka, for instance, have also been called forms of 'Protestant Buddhism' these are fairly recent, and continue to exist alongside what Gombrich and Obeyesekere call 'spirit religion' (1988).

## Characteristics of Modern and Postmodern Religious Forms

This shift within religious traditions to a concern with the transcendental is also captured in Robert Bellah's five stages of religious evolution (1964). According to this model, 'modern religion', which dominates in the West today (but is also found in non-western contexts, although with less pervasiveness), has evolved through a series of stages during which 'religious collectivities become more differentiated from other social structures and there is an increasing consciousness of the self as a religious subject' (1964, p. 358). In its 'primitive' stage religion is undifferentiated from other social structures, and 'the religious life is as given and as fixed as the routines of daily life' (1964, p. 363). By contrast, within the second type of religion, 'archaic' religion, we find the emergence of 'true cult with the complex of gods, priests, worship, sacrifice and in some cases divine or priestly kingship' (1964, p. 364). The third stage, the 'historic', includes the main scriptural religions and is distinguishable from the earlier stages because 'historic religions are all in some sense transcendental' (1964, p. 366). An emphasis upon the afterlife becomes more important than worldly concerns, traditions of world renunciation emerge and the gap between the pragmatic and the transcendental dimensions of religion widens. The stage that corresponds to the split between pragmatic and transcendental complexes is 'early modern religion', which was marked in Europe by the Protestant Reformation. In this stage, the role of the priestly mediator was curtailed and salvation became available to all. The focus of religion becomes a personal relationship between the individual and the divine, and a distinction is clearly made between religion and magic. The fifth and final stage, the 'modern', is the one that is most relevant to this study of religious environmentalism. Religion increasingly becomes something that people choose to be part of and while they are more likely to engage in critique of religious doctrines, they may also decide to reject religion altogether.

The shift to modern religion has also been marked by its privatisation, as sectors of society and culture were 'removed from the domination of religious institutions and symbols' (Berger et al., 1973, p. 113). While some scholars predicted that secularisation ('the diminution of the social significance of religion' (Wilson, 1982, p. 149)) would lead to the disappearance of religion altogether, others argued that we would see an increasing pattern of privatisation. Classical nineteenth-century sociology of religion had seen the role of religion in bolstering the status quo and in providing social cohesion within emerging industrial societies, but by the mid twentieth century the emphasis lay upon the ability of religion to offer a source of meaning and identity to individuals and groups in a world where industrialisation had taken hold and they increasingly felt alienated (Beckford, 1989, p. 12; Berger et al., 1973; Luckmann, 1967). People often continued with public religion, attending church or participating in religious sacraments, but this becomes primarily 'rhetorical' and instead an 'individual' or 'personal' religion takes hold within the private sphere where a meaningful 'life-world' is created (Luckmann, 1967). These theories of secularisation have, however, been criticised for implying that the same pattern of declining religious significance and privatisation is likely to occur in all societies as they modernise and industrialise. In terms of the West, this pattern has not been borne out everywhere: in North America, in particular, public religion continues to have a social presence that is absent in much of Northern Europe (Martin, 1990). It is also not surprising, therefore, that Indian sociologists have written little on the process of secularisation since religion still retains a strong public role, as well as pragmatic function.[8]

In addition to privatisation, another distinctive feature of this category of 'modern religion' is the reinterpretation of religious traditions in line with liberal values, such as human rights or religious tolerance. These correspond to what Woodhead and Heelas (2000) call 'religions of humanity', which are often 'characterized by a strong sense of the importance of the collective dimension of human existence and by active ethical and political concern' (2000, p. 71). Within this modern religiosity, 'the best deeds are those which aid one's fellow human beings, respect their rights, and exemplify kindness and compassion...Religions of humanity are characteristically optimistic both in their belief in the fundamental goodness of human nature and in the possibility of building the perfect human society here on earth' (2000, p. 72). However, Bellah's 'modern religion' prefigures what some have called a further type of 'postmodern religion', which Woodhead and Heelas have termed 'spiritualities of life' or 'inner spiritualities' (2000, p. 110). In contrast to 'religions of humanity' (which are expressed from with the context of the world religions), 'inner spirituality' (or 'self spirituality') is radically deregulated and detraditionalised, and the individual 'self' becomes the ultimate source of authority, rather than a transcendent deity or the teachings of any particular tradition. This is not to say that those attracted to this style of 'postmodern religion' reject the teachings of religious traditions and the worship of all forms of the divine, but that the individual chooses which teachings to follow (often drawing upon several traditions together) and the divine is normally conceived of as 'imminent' (frequently conceived of as identical to the 'self').

This 'postmodern religion', in its detraditionalisation and self-orientation, is markedly different in many ways from what we have called 'modern religion' and reflects the 'emergence of a multiplex reality, one filled with and constituted by different cosmologies and world-views grounded in subjective experience' (Szerszynski, 2005, p. 22). As Szerszynski suggests, this postmodern religion is also 'post-transcendental'. It is subsequent to, but a consequence of, the elevation of the transdendental since the Protestant Reformation in that the self and the subjective become the primary locus of moral authority rather that a transcendent external divine being. The 'transcendental arc' that we have been charting in this chapter descends and religion enters a new mode or phase with the sacralisation of

---

[8]     While the above patterns of secularisation and the privatisation of religion are not characteristic of modern India, Indian scholars have had a great deal to say about the idea of secularism, which as a political ideology has been promoted since the post-independence era. See Chapters 6 and 7 for a detailed discussion.

a ?

the self and the imminence of the divine (in both the individual and nature) (2005, p. 9). Postmodern inner spiritualities allow the individual to break down many of the dualisms established following the Protestant Reformation (e.g. divine/ self; sacred/secular; pragmatic/transcendent) and this is found to be particularly effective in orientating the individual towards engagement in causes on behalf of the natural world. While 'dependent' upon transcendental religion (in the sense of being subsequent to but a consequence of it), postmodern spiritualities in many ways reflect an attempt to reconnect with the pragmatic dimension of religion and 'the very plurality of the postmodern sacred also allows it to accommodate echoes of earlier orderings of the sacred' (Szerszynski, 2005, p. 23). This has been recognised as a quality of religious environmentalism by Deudney, who writes that 'Earth religion makes claims upon all aspects of life and asserts the need to subordinate the secular to the sacred…it calls into question the modern Western tradition of the separation of church and state' (1995, p. 284).

The shift to both modern and postmodern religiosity characterises much of the so-called alternative or expressive spiritualities that have emerged since the 1960s, particularly in the West. It is also from within this context that we can best understand much contemporary religious environmentalism, particularly styles that are radical and detraditional. From the 1960s onwards, the western public became increasingly attracted to various 'alternative spiritualities', reflecting disenchantment 'with institutionalised modes of identity provision' (Heelas, 1996, p. 158). As Bruce points out 'those who participated in these movements were typically from the more comfortable sectors of western societies, from social groups which had benefited from above-average education and incomes; the working-classes were absent from the new religions' (1996, p. 183). The suggestion that there is a 'postmaterialist' dimension to participation in alternative spiritualities will be discussed in more depth below. New Religious Movements (NRMs), such as Transcendental Meditation (TM), Krishna Consciousness[9] or Rajneeshism (Bruce, 1996), emerged against the backdrop of the 1960s counterculture, which marked a disaffection with the institutions and values of mainstream society amongst a section of the young and predominantly white, middle class youth. The attraction towards eastern spiritualities, in particular, indicated a (somewhat idealised) search for meaning within cultural traditions that were considered to have not (yet) been affected by the worse excesses of materialism. Some movements were 'world rejecting', such as the Moonies, and individuals retreated from the world and the trappings of contemporary technological and industrial society. By contrast, the 'world affirming' movements, such as TM, sought to secure and maximise worldly rewards (Bruce, 1996; Wallis, 1984).

One feature of these alternative spiritualities, that is relevant also to our discussion of religious environmentalism, is the shift towards what Charles Taylor

---

[9]    The Krishna Consciousness movement is directly descended from the sixteenth-century Bengali *Vaishnava* poet, *Chaitanya*. Its newness refers to its mass appeal to western members.

has called 'Romantic expressivism' as the locus of moral authority for the individual. Taylor identifies three primary moral sources for humanity: theism, disengaged reason and Romantic expressivism (1989, p. 495). While the theistic model reflects the way in which traditional religion exerted authority over the individual, this has become less pronounced in the modern era, giving way to an emphasis upon reason as a source of morality following the Enlightenment. More recently, however, a third approach to morality emerged (largely as a reaction towards the disengaged reason and scientistic thinking of the Enlightenment): Romantic expressivism. The Romantic expressive, found, for instance, in the original Romantic poets and artists of the eighteenth century, the North American Transcendentalists, such as Thoreau, or the 'human potential movement' of the 1950s, is typically concerned with the creative imagination, intuition and individuality as a source of morality and authority (Taylor, 1989). Other scholars have similarly attempted to chart this shift away from the external authority of the Church to a more individualised, expressive, internalised moral voice (Tipton, 1982; Heelas, 1996). While we should not think about this as the progressive replacement of one source by another (as Taylor (1989) points out his three domains continually influence and borrow from each other), such a schema is helpful in theorising contemporary, alternative styles of spirituality.

While the NRMs reflect a shift towards expressive values, they still retain (to varying degrees) elements of a more traditional authoritarian ethic, since they typically rely upon the authority of tradition and the leadership of spiritual teachers. By contrast, the so-called 'New Age' religions may be characterised by their radical detraditionalisation. A number of scholars have explained this as a 'turn to the self' (Heelas 1996; Sutcliffe and Bowman 2000) where the individual – more specifically the 'inner self' – becomes sacralised and serves as the ultimate source of meaning and morality, rather than the external authority of tradition. Whereas traditional religion exercised external authority over the individual, leaving little room for personal decision making (at least about the 'big' things in life), the impact of social and cultural changes, upon the relationship between the individual, society and religion (particularly since the Protestant Reformation), has thrown the individual back upon his/herself in all matters including religion. Drawing upon Taylor's 'Romantic expressivism' (1989) and Tipton's 'expressive style of ethical evaluation' (1982), Woodhead and Heelas suggest that 'expressive spirituality' is an appropriate term to capture the deregulated and individualised nature of this style of spirituality (2000, p. 113). Increasingly, scholars are choosing not to use the term 'New Age', since it has not generally been adopted in self-reference by those attracted to expressive or self spiritualities. The term has developed negative connotations, suggesting a shallow commitment to 'consumeristic, trivial, "Hollywood spirituality"' (Woodhead and Heelas, 2000, p. 112). Moreover, the term 'New Age Religion' suggests something rather more fixed and definite than actually exists.

Those attracted to 'expressive spirituality' (I shall use this term from now on) typically draw a range of resources and techniques, from esoteric traditions to modern psychology, which assist them in discovering and developing the 'inner self'. Sociologically this can be seen as the most radical expression of Luckmann's 'personal' or 'individual' religion where the individual self becomes sacralised as a spiritual focus and source of authority; it is a religion of the self. However, this style of spirituality often attracts individuals who are deeply concerned about sociopolitical issues, as with the 'religions of humanity': they link their personal development and transformation to broader concerns about human rights, the environment or gender issues. Therefore, the idea of a 'religion of the self' does not capture the social conscience of many who are engaged with different styles of expressive spirituality. As Woodhead and Heelas write, concerning expressive spirituality specifically, that

> it draws attention to the great importance attached by those pursuing the inner quest to freedom and self-expression: to expressing what one truly is; to living life as the expression of one's authentic nature; to affirming oneself as bound up with the natural or authentic order as a whole (2000, p. 113).

As we shall see, the radical environmentalists that I discuss in Chapters 5 and 6 are committed to individual freedom and self-expression but this is seen as connected to their broader political concerns.

In terms of the above discussion, very broadly speaking, religious environmentalism can be divided into two types. First, we find that which reflects upon the ways in which religion can be interpreted to support environmentalism from the point of view of a particular tradition (e.g. Hinduism, Islam or an Indigenous Religion): this is to be aligned with the 'religions of humanity'. Second, we also find a whole range of religious environmentalisms that more closely resemble the so-called 'inner spiritualities' that are radically detraditionalised, drawing upon a eclectic range of suitable beliefs and practices to express concern and respect for the natural world. In reality, this distinction can be difficult to maintain but it is useful to draw nonetheless, not least because there are differences in terms of the styles of environmentalist action that these two types engage in (this will be returned to below). Bron Taylor, in his most recent book, makes a similar distinction between 'green' and 'dark green' religion (2009, forthcoming, Chapter 1), where he argues that it 'is important to distinguish green religion (environmentally friendly behavior is a religious obligation) from dark green religion (nature is sacred and has intrinsic value therefore it is due reverent care) because these two forms are often in tension and sometimes in direct conflict' (2009, forthcoming). Dark green religion is 'generally "deep ecological," "biocentric" or "ecocentric," considering all species to be intrinsically valuable, namely, valuable apart from their usefulness to human beings' (2009, forthcoming). Moreover, it is radical and would include the *bricolagic* expressive spiritualities that attract the interest of radical environmentalist groups such as Earth First! and the EDA activists discussed in Chapter 5 of this book.

While there is overlap between 'green' and 'dark green' religion, another central difference is the importance of a distinction between religion and spirituality for many who are involved within forms of green religiosity outside the mainstream churches or the world religions. The term spirituality has a long history, but as Anna King writes 'it has acquired new associations from its use by New Age writers, by psychotherapists, by ecologists, by feminists, by gays, by black people…It has been linked with protest and with the creation of new paradigms' (1996, p. 354). In particular, the term is employed in distinction to the word 'religion', in order to reclaim that 'unity at the heart of religious traditions and the transformative inner depth of meaning of those traditions' (1996, p. 345). Following the theoretical discussion in this chapter, the juxtaposition of spirituality against religion can be seen as having come about in response to 'the rise of secularism in this century, and a popular disillusionment with religious institutions as a hindrance to personal experiences of the sacred' (Zinnbauer et al., 1997, p. 550).

## Why Distinguish between Religion and Spirituality?

In my interviews and conversations with religious environmentalists, in both Britain and India, many stressed that religion was different from spirituality. Spirituality was considered as a core belief in, or experience of, the divine and was frequently reduced to notions of living in the 'correct way' or appreciating the interconnections between all living organisms where 'simple, daily life actions to preserve the earth could be viewed as "spiritual" activities' (Bloch, 1998a, p. 59). Religion, by contrast, was described as the institutionalisation of such belief and experience, it is concerned with texts and dogma and the normative leadership of male authority figures. The idea of spirituality suggested the purity of transcendental/ultimate experience outside the social and political restraints of institutionalised religions: it is more about feelings, emotions and knowledge than about believing in particular doctrines, carrying out set practices or recognising hierarchies of authority. This use of the spiritual/religious distinction within religious environmentalism reflects broader public opinion, where '*religiousness* is increasingly characterised as "narrow and institutional", and *spirituality* is increasingly characterised as "personal and subjective"' (Zinnbauer et al., 1997, p. 563). Zinnbauer et al. carried out a survey of 346 individuals to find out if they considered themselves to be spiritual or religious. Their results suggest that those who saw themselves as 'spiritual but not religious' 'reject traditional organized religion in favor of an individualized spirituality that includes mysticism along with New Age beliefs and practices' (1997, p. 561). This correlates with my own findings. 'Radical' or 'dark green' religious environmentalists, who were not members of a particular tradition but more individualistic and syncretic in their religious identity, were likely to call themselves spiritual rather than religious. However, religious environmentalists who were members of particular traditions (i.e. 'green') also tended to refer to spirituality as that which cuts across different

traditions (Taylor, 2009, forthcoming). For example, the belief in the sa
of the Earth is commonly promoted as a core spiritual value.

For radical environmentalists, in particular, the distinction between ᵣₑₗᵢgᵢₒₙ
and spirituality has another significant dimension in supporting the view that
religion, specifically Christianity, is actually to blame for the environmental crisis
in promoting the 'dualistic distinction that is made between what is considered
sacred and what is considered secular' (Bloch, 1998a, p. 57). By contrast, those
radical environmentalists, who have adopted expressive spiritualities,

> assert that *all* aspects of life are sacred, both the sky-like 'heavens' and
> the 'matter' of earth. Drawing upon both contemporary environmentalist
> information resources and older spiritual traditions that honoured the earth as
> sacred…[they]…argue that activities involving the protection of the earth should
> be conceptualized as part of one's spirituality, and that an alternative spiritual
> network is needed to accomplish this' (Bloch, 1998a, p. 57).

Thus, such religious environmentalists typically consider Paganism or
the cultures of indigenous communities as 'spiritual' rather than 'religious'.
Another challenge to the distinction between the sacred and the secular, is the
'reintroduction' of magic: 'a rite that is enacted to bring about a certain condition
or change supernaturally, generally in response to a specific circumstance
perceived as crisis-like or unfavourable' (Bloch, 1998b, p.286). The performance
of *Earth magic* (for instance, involving channeling the energies of the Earth and
the person towards a healing process) is a feature of contemporary Paganism and
various New Age traditions, as well as radical environmentalism (Bloch, 1998b).
Thus, within this 'expressive' culture of radical environmentalists, Pagans and
New Agers there exists a range of strategies which seem to symbolically reverse
the transcendentalisation/secularisation/privatisation process that has provided the
theoretical backdrop to this chapter. Thus, individuals seem to be reacting against

both the privatisation and the puritanisation of religion. This is returned to in more
depth in Chapter 5 where I discuss the use of the word spirituality by radical
environmentalists who do not consider themselves to be what we would normally
think of as religious or spiritual. I suggest that this is a discursive strategy to
overcome the dualisms of modern society. This, I suggest further, is a characteristic
of millenarian movements.

However, the distinction between religion and spirituality was also made
by environmentalists that I interviewed in India. T.N. Prakesh, the editor of a
magazine called 'The Honey Bee', which promotes traditional farming practices
(which are often considered within a broad conception of traditional culture that
includes an emphasis upon the celebration of seasonal festivals or the propitiation
of nature spirits), was critical of mainstream or, what he called, 'elitist' definitions
of religion and drew a more general, universal definition of spirituality similar to
the expressive spiritualists above. He objected to the identification of religiousness
with particular activities, such as not eating meat or the observation of strict purity

laws, which are not followed by the lowest castes or those outside Hinduism, such as *adivasis* (tribals):

> So what is spirituality for them? How do you define spiritual attributes? Personal characteristics, vegetarianism, not taking meat, being very clean? I don't take spirituality on that level. Spirituality is for me what is not materialistic. It's more general. Very recently there was a conference in Ahmedabad, a farmers' grassroots level conference, international conference. There was a farmer, a labourer from Karnataka, a veterinary healer. He doesn't take one penny for his service. He says 'If I take it I will lose it, I will lose my capacity'. It is a belief, a strong belief, spiritual by nature. He's a labourer, every day he works in another's field for the rupees he earns and even for the medicine he won't take the money. If you go to Sanskrit scholars they take spirituality as eating vegetarian.[10]

In another interview with an environmental scientist in Delhi this distinction was also drawn with respect to the idea of the sacredness of the Earth as a spiritual value which cuts across religions, 'let us not confuse sacredness with religion, sacredness has nothing to do with religion. Sacredness is something which pervades across religion, it is a belief system'.[11]

In important ways the idea of spirituality in this context serves to symbolically reverse dualisms between sacred and secular; private and public; and transcendental and pragmatic. Moreover, alternative spiritualities frequently engage with sociopolitical issues through their affiliation to various social movements. Whereas the privatisation of religion in the West signalled to earlier theorists, such as Berger and Luckmann, that religion had lost its publicly influential role, more recently, scholars have argued that religion has a renewed sociopolitical role in postindustrial or advanced industrial society (Beckford, 1990; Beyer, 1990, 1992, 1994, 1998; Hannigan, 1991). While some argue that the sociopolitical significance of religion is more likely to be found within the new or alternative spiritualities, which have attracted increasing numbers of participants as membership of traditional religion has declined (Beckford, 1990), others consider that there is also a resurgence of religious activity within world religions ('religions of humanity') (Beyer, 1994; Hannigan, 1991). In non-western contexts, where secularisation has been less marked, it may of course be difficult to see a resurgence of religious activity *per se*. While this chapter has looked at shifts in the relationships between the individual, religion and society in the West, the new religious forms that have emerged (and which have been discussed at length in this chapter) have become globalised. Thus, even in places such as India, where traditional forms of religion are still strong (i.e. where one is born into a tradition rather than choosing to belong to it; where the external authority of tradition is the dominant source of morality; and

---

[10]   Interview University of Agricultural Sciences, Bangalore, 27/2/97.

[11]   Interview Jawaharlal Nehru University, New Delhi, 24/4/98.

where the distinction between sacred and secular is less marked, if at all), these globalised religious forms may also shape people's religiosity. I will show below, however, that participation in New Religious Movements, such as Rajneeshism (which would correspond to Bellah's 'modern religion') is not that widespread in India. The case study presented in Chapter 6, which will include a discussion of the involvement of Indian followers of Rajneesh in 'expressive spiritualities' and radical environmentalism, will suggest that what we are witnessing here is an example of what Baviskar has called 'bourgeois environmentalism' (2003). Participants are educated, relatively affluent and are well versed in the themes and theories of global environmentalist thinking. They are producers of religious environmentalist representations that are dependent upon the European Romantic Movement and transcendental religion.

**Religion/Spirituality and Social Problems**

Theories about the secularisation of society and the privatisation of religion might seem to suggest a reduced role for religion in the public sphere, its main sphere of action is now to provide a meaningful life-world for an increasingly alienated individual. However, it is also possible to demonstrate the ways in which individuals employ religious/spiritual resources to make sense of and deal with contemporary social problems: the creation of a meaningful life-world moves beyond individual concerns and issues and includes attention to the solution of social problems. For instance, the sociologist Peter Beyer, author of the influential book 'religion and globalization' (1994), agrees with Berger and Luckmann (who were largely responsible for the privatisation thesis) that the functional sub-systems, which characterise modern global societies, 'concentrate on specialized means of communication and not on the total lives of the people that carry them, they leave a great deal of social communication undetermined, if not unaffected...Different aspects of what remains have been variously called the private sphere, the life-world, or the domain of expressive action' (1992, p. 4). However, he is rather more optimistic about the role of religion within this social framework, and argues that 'the globalization of society, whilst structurally favoring privatization in religion, also provides fertile ground for the renewed public influence of religion' (Beyer, 1994, p. 71). Beyer's discussion is confined to what he calls 'systemic religion' ('world religions' as opposed to 'expressive spiritualities' and New Religious Movements). Under conditions of globalisation religion also takes on the characteristics of a globalised functional sub-system. 'Systemic religion' (which is created by and has a structural function within the global system) manifests itself in the forms of the various world religions – they are, according to Beyer, a product of globalisation, 'standard sub-systems of the global religious system' (1998, p. 7). Thus, like Tim Fitzgerald, he sees world religions as a modern phenomenon, yet, unlike Fitzgerald, because they are central to the way in which religious practitioners perceive their religiosity, he does not conclude that they are a 'fallacy' (Fitzgerald, 2000; Beyer, 1998, p. 26). He suggests that the world religion category only becomes problematic when talking about religions in the past.

For Beyer, while religion is a functional sub-system, like the economy, science or medicine, its function (i.e. communing with the divine) has been marginalised or privatised in contemporary global society (1994, p. 78). However, in contrast to the other sub-systems, the religious way 'of relating to the world is too broadly based to allow the sort of instrumental specialization typical of functional subsystems like economy, polity and science' (1992, p. 7). He suggests that because religion is 'totalizing' (concerned with providing meaning for all aspects of an individual's life) and does not operate in clearly defined specialist areas, it 'can and does serve as a kind of system specializing in what, from the perspective of the dominant functional systems, are residual matters' (1992, p. 8). Thus, the privatisation and marginalisation of religion means that it is well placed in modern global society to address the gaps left behind by sub-system specialisation in the public sphere.[12] In particular, there arises a conflict in the global system between the 'systemic values' of equality and progress, and the 'systemic effects', such as the consequences of poverty and environmental degradation, which contradict these core values of modernity. Whilst the global sub-systems are all encompassing in their field, the high degree of specialisation they achieve does not enable them to deal with such systemic effects or 'residual matters' (1992, p. 5).

Beyer suggests that this public influence of religion takes two directions: first, an 'ecumenical' or 'liberal' approach which looks to global problems and their solution; and, second, a 'particularist' or 'conservative' approach which stresses local, cultural and religious distinctiveness (1990; 1994). The former corresponds to what Woodhead and Heelas call 'religions of humanity' (2000). Beyer argues that the ecumenical or liberal religion is particularly suited to dealing with environmental problems because global environmental issues point to holistic solutions and the 'holism of religious communication…offers a logical social perspective from which to address this aspect' (Beyer, 1992, p. 10). By contrast, particularist religion, which would include, for example, different forms of religious nationalist and fundamentalism, is less orientated towards a shared concern about global issues and universal freedoms. The case study in Chapter 7 of this book is concerned with the involvement of the Hindu nationalist movement in environmentalist campaigns, particularly that concerned with the River Ganges. In this case, as we might expect from a 'particularist' religious response, the environmentalist rhetoric that is used must be seen within the context of specific

---

[12] He is using marginalisation and privatisation here to refer to the relationship between systemic religions and the global system. This does not seem to be the same as saying that 'religions' in general are marginalised within local contexts. For instance, one example he discusses is Iran and the Rushdie affair, which stems from a reaction against the margnalisation of Islam within global system, which has no respect for religion. However, Islam itself is not marginalised within Iran.

Hindu nationalist aims and symbols. And we find a blurring of the boundaries between a concern for the ecological health of the river and the promotion of the Ganges as a symbol of the Hindu nation.

## Ecumenical/Liberal Religion and New Social Movements

Much of this book, however, is concerned with various expressions of the ecumenical (liberal 'religions of humanity') approach, since this has shaped the sociocultural context within which we find religious environmentalism. While Beyer's discussion focuses upon the systemic world religions, the expressive spiritualities and many of the New Religious Movements also adopt an 'ecumenical' or 'liberal' approach to dealing with the problems caused by globalisation. People choose to participate in these styles of spirituality often from disaffection with mainstream religion and society. Beyer and others have noted that these liberal religious movements often adopt the aims and strategies of the so-called 'New Social Movements' (NSMs) in the West. It is no coincidence that during the 1960s, when religions of humanity, New Religious Movements and expressive spiritualities begin to emerge, there was also a shift within the aims and strategies of social movements. Whereas the class-based movements of the early twentieth century were concerned with 'articulating claims to fundamental political and human rights (voting rights, freedom of speech, freedom of the press) or with the social distribution of economic benefits' (Hannigan, 1991, p. 320), the NSMs were interested in 'what may be termed cultural rights: the right to one's own life-style, the right to be different, the protection of the individual against new kinds of risks (e.g. nuclear, biotechnological)' (1991, p. 320; Beckford, 1990, p. 7). Beckford considers that the nature of these new concerns are more suited to religious contribution and that 'these changes have helped to precipitate a new form of increasingly *visible*, if not church oriented, religiosity or spirituality that favours synoptic, holistic, and global perspectives on issues transcending the privatized self and the individual state' (1990, p. 9). He suggests that we need to look outside the established religions for the focus of religious influence. It is the privatised, individual religion of Luckmann, where 'the individual may choose from the assortment of "ultimate" meanings as he sees fit' (Luckmann, 1967, p. 99) and where the themes of 'individual "autonomy", self-expression, self-realization...have some claim to "sacred" status' (1967, p. 113), which are significant.

Beckford draws our attention to the process of *bricolage* (Levi Strauss, 1962; Roof, 1999; Campbell, 2002)[13] in which individuals select, borrow and interpret diverse religious symbols and ideas for novel purposes. In particular,

---

[13] The term *bricolage* was originated by the anthropologist Levi Strauss. For a discussion of its use in social movements see Hetherington (1998, p. 28; 2000, pp. 98–9).

symbols of the oneness of all human beings fit equally well into the logic of arguments against capital punishment, the destruction of the natural environment, and the exploitation of the South by the North. The flexibility of some religious discourses permits these provisional and shifting constellations of symbols and causes. This makes some religious constituencies more 'cooptable'...by activists in social movements (1990, p .9).

Such religious movements are able to operate like new social movements because they have shifted from a doctrinal-centred approach to a problem-centred approach: the motivation to act arises from issues concerning certain practical problems rather than disputes over doctrine and orthodoxy (Beckford, 1990, p. 8). Beckford identifies what he describes as a 'global ethic' underlying this new spirituality in the West:

this new spirituality conveys such a strong sense of urgency about global problems. It is so remarkably inclusive in scope that it should be called the 'global ethic'...There is more than a hint of reluctance to tie the new global spirituality to any kind of fixed principles. Instead, there is a strong respect for the view that social reality is overwhelmingly complicated, emergent, changeful and consequently, not amenable to interpretation in terms of fixed principles (1990, p. 8).

Many of the environmentalists discussed in the following chapters similarly engage in such a process of *bricolage*, they 'co-opt' a range of religious and cultural symbols to express their environmentalist commitment and to argue that religious values provide a model from which to re-orientate humanity towards the natural world. This is particularly prominent within the expressive spiritualities adopted by the radical environmentalists discussed in Chapters 5 and 6. Moreover, in contrast to traditional religious systems where considerations of orthodoxy and dogma dominate the types of discourse religions turn their attention to, religious environmentalism (both that expressed from within the world religions, as well as the alternative spiritualities) is 'problem centred'. The shift from a doctrine-centred approach to a problem-centred approach is again a characteristic of Beyer's publicly influential religion, a style of religiosity, which, under modern global conditions, no longer focuses upon the specialised, privatised function of religion to commune with the divine and instead turns outwards to address the systemic problems generated by the global system (1992, p. 1994). In common with the NSMs, such religious movements are concerned with controlling the interruption of the private sphere by the rational mechanism of public institutions but, at the same time, we find that 'the secular world is being "sanctified" by elements associated with the religious domain' (Hannigan, 1991, p. 322).

*can this still apply in catastrophist discourse?*

*Bluhdorn post-sustainability / post-ecological.*

## The Postmaterialism Thesis and the Shift to Expressive Values

It is helpful at this point to reconsider the above discussion in terms of a global view of the nature of social problems, since this study is concerned with an investigation of religious environmentalism in the UK and India. The next chapter will explore this concern more fully, when I look at the social movements that have coalesced around environmental concerns in both contexts. However, at this stage it is important to ask whether the same pattern of social movement change has occurred in India? Has there been a 'shift from politico-economic issues of inclusion in the benefits of industrial society to more cultural concerns with the quality of like and the image of the good society' (Beyer, 1994, p. 98)? In the next chapter I will discuss the work of a number of scholars who argue that such a shift is much less prominent in developing countries, such as India, where social movements continue to reflect more immediate concerns associated with security, income and basic freedoms, rather than so-called 'quality of life issues'. In particular, it is argued that modern environmentalism, particularly of the sort that romanticises about returning to an ecogolden age, is reflective of a shift to expressive values since the 1960s. Bernice Martin, for example, argues that whilst the material prosperity of advanced industrial societies frees the individual from pursuit of 'the immediate disciplines of survival' (1981, p. 16) it has taken away 'natural social rootedness and automatic structures of belonging' (1981, p. 16). Thus, 'whole populations are enabled to discover layers of "expressive" needs – self-discovery and self-fulfilment, richness of personality, variety and depth of relationships' as a mechanism for confronting what Durkheim called *anomie* (1981, p. 16). This 'expressive revolution' has impacted upon how people construct and approach social issues in late twentieth/early twenty-first century society, particularly within prosperous nations or prosperous sections of poor nations. Although not all social problems are unrelated to the identification of material needs, it is often the case that people are also concerned to secure their individuality, their rights and those of others, or the pursuit of values rather than material outcomes.

Inglehart has famously (and controversially) referred to this shift in terms of the emergence of a postmaterialist society: 'the basic value priorities of Western publics seem to be changing as their societies move into a post-industrial phase of development. This process of value change is likely to bring new issues to the fore' (1977, p. 21). He argues that by the early 1970s there had been a shift

> from an overwhelming emphasis upon material well-being and physical security toward a greater emphasis on the quality of life…Today, an unprecedentedly large proportion of Western populations have been raised under conditions of exceptional economic security. Economic and physical security continue to be valued positively, but their relative priority is lower than in the past (1977, p. 3).

He also suggests that the pursuit of 'spiritual needs' or 'personal betterment' are more likely to become important once more basic or material needs are satisfied. He is not arguing that previous generations or other cultures are not 'religious'. Instead, religion has undergone a number of transformations. He is referring here to the modern and postmodern styles of religiosity we have been discussing in this chapter, and he employs the idea of postmaterialism to argue that they are both contemporary and more likely to arise in western contexts. The postmaterialism thesis may be useful in accounting for key differences between modern/ postmodern religiosity/spirituality and more traditional religious forms. I suggest four transformations of religion that are important in illuminating differences between modern/postmodern and traditional religiosity (e.g. Hinduism), and in understanding the religious environmentalist approach to religion.

Firstly, religion has become more a matter of personal choice for most in the West. In the past, people were born into a religious culture, and involvement with a religious tradition was more an expression of collective cultural identity rather than individual identity. This is still the case for the majority of people in India, for instance. However, in the West religion is increasingly becoming more of a personal issue where the individual chooses his/her own spiritual path rather than accepting the authority of traditional religious systems. Alternatively, one can choose not to affiliate to any religious tradition at all. Secondly, as the discussion of inner or expressive spiritualities indicated, people may embark upon a spiritual path today as an expression of their desire for personal development, to become a happier or more fulfilled person, rather than from obedience to the external authority of the religiocultural tradition, as is predominantly the case for most Hindus. Whilst there is provision for personal development in all religious traditions, increasingly in the West the 'therapy' aspect is becoming more prominent.

Thirdly, the shift to expressive, or postmaterialist, values has influenced the role of religion in some contemporary societies. For example, religious environmentalists' search for environmental values within religious traditions, as guidelines for how humanity ought to relate to the natural world. Whilst religion/ spirituality also provides other functions in the face of environmental disaster, such as solace or reassurance through prayer and ritual, or direct methods such as the performance of Earth magic, the overwhelming emphasis is upon how humanity ought to behave and is therefore an ethical issue. On the one hand, this emphasis upon the ethical dimension may be linked to the 'expressive revolution' in the West, where issues about the rights of humans, nature or animals are primary concerns. On the other hand, it may be traced back to the emphasis since the Protestant Reformation upon individual salvation, where adherence to divinely sanctioned ethics has soteriological significance. Finally, the postmaterialist is more likely to respond to a religious message that relates to personal values, particularly so-called 'postmaterialist values'. All religious traditions provide systems of ethics, which have both a religious and a social dimension. On the one hand, they offer the individual an opportunity to do something in this life towards the next life, be it securing a place in heaven or a better rebirth. On the other hand, ethical provision

seeks to maintain social stability and continuity. Although all religious tradit
sanction materialist values, such as sexual or dietary regulations, the religious
sanction of values such as global human rights or care for nature are more likely
to emerge in a postmaterialist context.


## Conclusion

Religious environmentalist discourse not only relies upon a particular understanding
of nature (as valuable in itself) but also upon a certain *type* of religion that is both
modern and which has been typically associated with western religiocultural trends
and preferences. While Bellah's model was useful in enabling us to distinguish
different types of religion it is nonetheless problematic and some caveats should be
drawn. Firstly, in talking about 'five stages of *evolution*' Bellah's model could be
criticised for suggesting that there is something superior about 'modern religion'
*vis-à-vis* earlier forms and to imply that this is the goal towards which they will
progress. This is rudely ethnocentric and becomes particularly problematic in a
study such as this, which is concerned to juxtapose different types (or according
to Bellah 'stages') of religion in order to think through the different ways that
they respond to modern social problems (e.g. the environment in this case). It is
important not to imply that the modern religions of humanity and postmodern inner
spiritualities are superior religious forms to traditional 'Hinduism', for instance.
This brings us to a second limitation that arises once we begin to think about where
contemporary Hinduism fits into these different stages of evolution or types of
religion. There are elements of the so-called 'primitive' stage (in, for example, the
pragmatic religiosity discussed above); we find the 'archaic', for example, in the
still existent elaborate sets of reciprocal relationships between complexes of gods,
priests, worship and sacrifice at the core of the Hindu temple; we find the historic
where Hinduism is seen in terms of its textual traditions; we find 'early modern
religion' in the medieval devotional *bhakti* traditions, as well as more recent Hindu
reform movements; and, finally, we also find 'modern religion' in the application
of Hindu ideas to humanistic concerns and the postmodern in self-religiosities that
draw upon aspects of the Hindu tradition. Thus, it is difficult to see how Bellah's
'stages' are steps in an evolutionary process. On the one hand, this implies that
some styles of belief and practice within contemporary Hinduism are inferior to
others and, on the other hand, it fails to adequately account for diversity in religious
forms that exist across Hindu belief and practice today: Bellah's stages would seem
to co-exist rather than to be successive and progressive stages.

As we have discussed above, some scholars have argued that this diversity
within contemporary Hinduism makes it very difficult to consider it as a single
'world religion' (and that when it is seen as a world religion this favours Christian
and Brahmanical priorities). However, my interest here is to emphasise that the
religious environmentalist model of religion, as outlined above, is not compatible
with Hinduism as a whole, only with some parts of it: i.e. that which is 'dependent'

upon the transcendental dimension of religion and the pursuit of postmaterialist expressive ethics. Both 'religions of humanity' ('modern') and 'life spiritualities' ('postmodern') are concerned with universalisation: with building links across cultures or looking for similarities in religious traditions with respect to an 'ethic of humanity'. Having established that religious environmentalism seems to rely upon a particular mode of religion that does not reflect styles of religiosity that are widely found in India, we are now in a better position to begin to assess the validity of the claim that 'Hinduism is environmentally friendly'. This chapter has focused upon the claim that Hinduism as it is widely practised in India today does not resemble the religious environmentalist mode of religion (modern and postmodern; expressive and postmaterialist). In the next two chapters I will take this argument further by looking at claims that the religious environmentalist attitude towards the environment (as intrinsically valuable) is also premised upon a particular understanding of nature that has its roots in the European Romantic Movement and is again reflective of postmaterialist values.

# Chapter 3
# The Prehistory of Contemporary Environmentalism

## Introduction

> The Age of Ecology opened on the New Mexican desert, near the town of Alamagordo, on July 16, 1945, with a dazzling fireball of light and a swelling mushroom cloud of radioactive gases. As the world's first atomic bomb went off and the color of the early morning sky changed abruptly from pale blue to blinding white...For the first time, there existed a technological force that seemed capable of destroying much of the life on the planet (Worster, 1994 [1977], p. 342).

Writing in the late 1970s, the historian Donald Worster pinpointed this apocalyptic event as heralding the 'Age of Ecology'. It marked the juncture of the scientific, technological and Industrial Revolutions of the preceding centuries and presaged the onslaught of environmental worries that began to attract the concern of scientists and activists during the late twentieth century. From the early 1970s onwards, attention was increasingly drawn to the environmental consequences of human activity, particularly regarding the overuse and the misuse of natural resources within industrialised economies (Hannigan, 1995, p. 23ff). Moreover, it was realised, as with the example of the first atomic bomb, that the environmental consequences of such human activities could not be contained locally. By the early 1970s, emissions from large-scale industry had been linked to the problem of acid rain (Hannigan, 1995, p. 128ff) and, in the 1980s, the connection between CFCs and global warming created a climate of moral panic (Yearley, 1996, p. 26). The idea of a 'global environmental crisis' has become the subject of television documentaries, films and newspaper articles, and government leaders meet at international conferences to discuss ways of collectively reducing environmental damage. People have joined environmental organisations and campaigns, and are encouraged to adopt more 'environmentally friendly' lifestyles: the 'Age of Ecology' has been marked by passionate calls for limits to human interference within the natural environment. It has become taken for granted that a global problem exists and that remedial measures, such as reducing $CO_2$ emissions, to mitigate the consequences of the greenhouse effect, or individuals recycling their household waste, are all essential in order to deal with this crisis facing humanity. Nevertheless, despite good intentions, a certain irony beleaguers rich nations in their attempts to promote international regulations on $CO_2$ emissions or to prevent the felling of rainforests, since it is these regions that produce the most greenhouse gases and whose consumers devour non-renewable resources.

There has been criticism that the type of 'environmentalism' that has emerged to confront these concerns largely reflects the interests and values of the wealthy industrialised nations (Baviskar, 1995; Guha, 1988). It is the aim of this chapter to reflect upon the historical and cultural context that has shaped understandings of environmentalism in the West. For instance, some scholars have argued that (western) 'romantic' understandings of nature as having intrinsic value have been imported to poor countries across the globe in various forms of environmentalism, yet are not rooted in indigenous ways of relating to the natural world. There is also often a degree of resentment and apathy towards environmentalism within developing countries where environmental priorities may compromise economic development (Baviskar, 1997). Many are suspicious that the identification by the North of certain 'global' problems as reflective of 'global' interests is selective. This bias can often be difficult to prove, since, as Yearley suggests, the reliance of environmental discourse upon scientific findings makes it appear objective and universal (1996, p. 85). However, 'the conviction that science speaks objectively and disinterestedly means that one need have no qualms about excluding other people from decision-making since they would, in any event, have arrived at the same conclusions as oneself' (Yearley, 1996, p. 118).

Although in Chapter 4 I will argue against the claim that environmentalism is a western, postmaterialist 'luxury', I do suggest that the types of environmentalist concerns people have and how they express them are likely to be affected by their culture and socioeconomic context (Guha and Martinez Alier, 1997). In Britain, for instance, environmental concerns are rarely survival issues, whereas in India, environmental problems (such as the contamination of water supplies in urban centres or the effects of rural deforestation on farming practices) are also direct life and death issues. A recent study in the journal *Nature* (Patz et al., 2005) predicts that although the world's poorest countries produce less greenhouse gases than wealthier nations, it is within these regions that dramatic rises in disease and malnutrition, as a result of climate change, are likely to have a devastating impact: 'the regions with the greatest burden of climate-sensitive diseases are also the regions with the lowest capacity to adapt to the new risks' (2005, p. 315). Thus, context is important in thinking about the ways in which different communities might be affected by ecological change as well as how they identify and approach environmental concerns.

An awareness of the importance of context upon the construction of environmental knowledge did not attract scholarly attention until the mid 1990s (Cronon, 1992; Eder, 1996; Evernden, 1992; Macnaghten and Urry, 1998). Prior to this, the sociological study of environmentalism had concentrated upon investigating the causes of environmental destruction or providing explanations for the rise of environmental awareness and movements (Hannigan, 1995, pp. 13–29). However, such approaches did not 'adequately account for the manner in which environmental problems are defined, articulated and acted upon by social actors'

(Hannigan, 1995, p. 30). A social constructionist approach is useful for this study since it will allow me to trace the historical, social and cultural influences that have shaped the model of environmentalism adopted by religious environmentalists. A social constructionist approach to interpreting environmentalism could be criticised for denying the realism of environmental problems and that there is any value to various (constructed) approaches to dealing with ecological concerns. While it is the aim of this book to reveal the contingency of religious environmentalism to particular ways of thinking about the relationship between humanity and the natural world (as well as to a particular historically situated style of religiosity), this analysis does not lead me reject religious environmentalism as a potentially valid style of ecopolitics.

This chapter will investigate the ways in which nature has been 'socially constructed' in the West, since 'there are multiple ways of representing nature and the environment from scientific to mystical. Rather than a fixed entity, the environment is a fluid concept which is both culturally grounded and socially contested' (Hannigan, 1995, p. 109). Because environmentalists are responding to what they identify as global problems they typically portray their solutions (i.e. their particular type of environmentalism) as universally relevant, as totalising and all encompassing. However, the identification of something as an environmental problem and the way in which it is approached is in itself 'a social construction that rests in a range of negotiated experiences' (Bird, 1987, p. 260). Thus, as Hannigan suggests 'how we construct environmental knowledge subsequently becomes the basis for contesting claims as to basic rights, responsibilities and responses towards technology, nature and society' (Hannigan, 1995, p. 109). This is a theme which has also been taken up within anthropology (Douglas, 1972; Milton, 1993; 1996), where concepts of nature and the environment are relativised and contextualised, and also within environmental history where it has been realised that 'the environment is and has long been a contested site at an ideological as well as material level' (Arnold and Guha, 1995, p. 16). Chapter 4 will investigate the impact of this upon the construction of the environment and environmentalism in the late twentieth and early twenty-first centuries. While this discussion will suggest that ideas of nature and environment have been socially constructed over time in particular contexts and are not universal across the globe, it could be argued that such a particularist argument is invalid in an age of globalisation.

This study does not deny that certain styles of environmentalism, which have their origin in the West, are now globalised. Indeed, as Beyer suggests, once we get to the postcolonial period, it is perhaps more useful to think about globalisation instead of westernisation (1998, p. 4). What I want to emphasise, however, is that certain global ideas have their origins in the West: while global society is not to be 'understood simply as the imperialistic spread of Western society around the globe…globalization still bears the marks of its origins' (Beyer 1998, p. 4). The persistence of this mark of origin may mean that certain ideas about nature that were socially constructed within a western sociocultural context are not that relevant to local cultural and socioeconomic interests in other places. Thus, one aspect of this study is the suggestion that religious environmentalism is a largely western creation that has been globalised. It is a version of 'romantic' environmentalism that has little relevance to the poor in developing countries. However, the situation is not so straightforward, since alongside different globalised discourses we also find indigenous/local versions or responses. Thus, while globalisation does imply a certain level of uniformity and homogeneity, it can also foster diversity where local culture interacts with global discourses to produce strategic localised versions. The hegemony of globalised discourses that represent other cultural systems, may stamp out diversity and silence voices, but it may also encourage the agency of different cultures to shape these globalised discourses to their own ends (Brosius, 1999).

## Nature as a Social Construction

The idea of 'nature' as a social construction has been taken up in a number of studies (Eder, 1996; Evernden, 1992; Macnaghten and Urry, 1998). Evernden is interested in the way that environmentalists construct an idea of nature as normative, where 'nature as the ultimate basis of moral standards is admirably suited to the advocacy of a new and more generous treatment of the natural environment' (1992, pp. 18–19). However, drawing upon the work of C.S. Lewis, he points out that, whilst the idea that there is something which exists called *nature* may seem obvious, it was the pre-Socratic Greek philosophers who first conceived of such an entity (Evernden, 1992, p. 20): that the 'great variety of phenomena which surrounds us could all be impounded under a name and talked about as a single object' (Lewis, 1964, p. 37). Thus, 'the possibility of having a *thing* called nature is as significant a development as a fish having a 'thing' called water: where there was once an invisible, preconscious medium through which each moved, there is now an object to examine and describe' (1992, p. 20). Macnaghten and Urry (1998) also develop this theme, arguing that 'there is no singular 'nature' as such, only a diversity of contested natures: and that each such nature is constituted through a variety of socio-cultural processes from which such natures cannot be plausibly separated' (1998, p. 1). They suggest that by the Medieval period in Europe, the idea of 'nature as everything' had undergone an important shift. God was now the creator of 'nature' and nature was considered as one of the 'two books through which God revealed himself: through the Bible (the ultimate book of revelation), and through the book of nature (through which the work and artisanship of God could be revealed)' (Macnaghten and Urry, 1998, p. 9). They suggest that humanity's intervention in the natural world (for example, clearing forests for agriculture or mining stone for building cathedrals) was understood in spiritual terms, as 'discovering God's providential design and in constructing artifacts designed to express the perfectibility of God's order' (Macnaghten and Urry, 1998, p. 9; Merchant, 1992).

Although nature is seen as God's creation (and beneath God) it is considered as a living organism where

> The Spirit, descending from God in the heavens and beyond, mingled with the ether and the ambient air, to be imbibed by plants, animals, and humans on the earth's surface. The living character of the world organism meant not only that the stars and planets were alive, but that the Earth too was pervaded by a force giving life and motion to the living beings on it (Merchant 1992, p. 42).

However, the new sciences of the seventeenth century transformed nature from a living, organic entity into an inert mechanical process which became the subject of scientific enquiry, to be discovered and understood according to rational, mathematical laws: 'God no longer had to be conceived *within* nature, but could now be detached from nature, placed in the heavens overlooking 'His' mechanical creation' (Macnaghten and Urry, 1998, p. 10). This mechanistic view of nature also served to hasten the separation of humanity from the natural world. The human mind was that which observed and analysed nature according to rational principles. Thus, a shift had occurred since the pre-Socratic philosophers whereby nature was no longer seen as everything but became defined in relation to and as separate from humanity and God (Merchant, 1992).

Thus, by the Enlightenment period, God was no longer conceived of as within nature, the laws of physics were considered to be God's laws and hence provided a moral basis for massive interference within nature; the discovery of and use of God's laws, during the Industrial Revolution could be legitimated. As Merchant writes 'the mechanistic worldview continues today as the legitimating ideology of industrial capitalism and its inherent ethic of the domination of nature. Mechanistic thinking and industrial capitalism lie at the root of many of the environmental problems' (1992, p. 59). Oelschlaeger sums up this transformation:

> The Industrial Revolution involves a coalescing of so many variables that it appears almost a coincidence: but for the Renaissance there would not have been the growth of trade; but for the growth of trade there would not have been the wealth of the British Empire (extracted from colonial nations through imperialism); but for wealth there would not have been capital; but for industrial technology there would not have been the machines to engender mass production; but for the Reformation there would not have been the religious justification for pursuing world success; but for the market there would not have been the division of labor; but for mass production there would not have been mass product; and so on (1991, p. 91).

This 'triumph' over nature has, however, generated different responses. The Enlightenment view considered that progress rests in the transcendence of and mastery over a presocial state of nature. Hobbes famously characterised this primitive state as marked by 'continual fear, and danger of violent death; and the life of man, solitary, poor, nasty, brutish and short' (1960 [1651], p. 82). By contrast, Locke described the 'state of nature' as one of 'peace, goodwill, mutual assistance and co-operation' (1963 [1698], p. 19) and argued that the foundation of a just society lay in uncovering so-called 'natural laws' (Smith, 2002). This interest in 'natural law', as well as the writings of Rousseau (which stressed that the 'state of nature' represented original innocence rather than original sin), fed into the emergence of a radically different attitude towards nature than that found within the mechanistic view of the Enlightenment. By the late eighteenth century, the Romantic critique of incipient industrialisation provided an alternative way of thinking about nature: 'from work-houses, to smog-filled factories, from child chimney sweeps to the destruction of the countryside…these processes rapidly became criticized as inhumane, unjust and, most relevant here, unnatural' (Macnaghton and Urry, 1998, p. 12). However, while it is not surprising that English Romantics, such as Wordsworth and Ruskin, have been viewed as 'early environmentalists', the post-Enlightenment industrialisers and colonisers were not unconcerned about the protection of the natural environment.

Before I discuss the Romantic legacy of contemporary environmentalism, I will first outline what I am calling the *managerial approach*, which sought to manage and conserve natural resources for practical, instrumental reasons. This will be contrasted with the *Romantic approach*,[1] which prized the aesthetic value of an unspoilt wilderness away from the influence of humanity. I will suggest that although environmentalism did not emerge until the middle of the twentieth century that it has its antecedents in these approaches to natural resource use and upon particular social constructions of nature.

## The Managerial Approach

*Early Conservation Interest: British Forests*

There is often a tendency within contemporary environmentalism to imply that both the depletion and conservation of natural resources are relatively recent phenomena. With respect to Britain, for example, this ignores nearly six thousand years of human alteration of the natural environment. Furthermore, the effects of human activities upon nature did not go entirely unnoticed and unchecked. Within western nations, and their colonies, there is a long history of resource depletion and conservation, which predates contemporary concerns about the natural environment (Evans, 1997; Grove, 1998a; 1998b; Oelschlaeger, 1991; Worster, 1994). For example, by 1086 only 15 per cent of Britain remained wooded. Whilst

---

[1]    I use *Romantic* with a 'capital' to distinguish it from the often-derogatory use of 'romantic' to imply a naïve, idealistic or impractical position. I intend *Romantic* to imply that this approach towards nature pertains to or is embedded within the eighteenth- and nineteenth-century European Romantic Movement.

the Anglo-Saxon system of open-field farming had been largely responsible for this decline in forests, tree clearance had begun much earlier; by the end of Bronze Age (500 B.C.E.) England had been stripped of half its trees (Evans, 1997, p. 14). The first sign of state-led conservation, however, resides in the Royal Forests established by William the Conqueror to preserve game for hunting, the violation of which was punishable by death. Yet, as Evans points out, although the Royal Forests encouraged the regeneration of a 'varied flora and fauna any benefit to wildlife was incidental to the interests of the huntsmen and outside the Royal Forests and parks the decimation of wildlife went on unabated' (1997, p. 15). Whilst by 1350 a rising population and thirst for agricultural land had reduced tree cover to only 10 per cent of the British landscape, the Black Death in 1348 provided 'a respite – of some 500 years – from the attentions of a devastated human population' (Evans, 1997, p. 15). However, by the fifteenth century awareness had emerged of the need to conserve forests, following their unprecedented rate of depletion to service the growing ship building industry. Evans writes that the Tudors were keen to control the felling of trees 'though not for the sake of the wolf or any other wildlife. Timber was a valuable resource for housing, shipbuilding and iron smelting and had been "managed" since Norman times' (1997, p. 16). Although previous generations were not blind to the effect of human depletion of natural resources and the need to periodically enforce prudential measures, it was not until the expansion of trade during the Renaissance that the plenitude of natural resources became a subject for concern.

The following centuries saw developments in technology, which sought to harness natural resources for the expanding economies that eventually allowed the emergence of the Industrial Revolution. However, at the same time, industrialising nations became aware that the depletion of natural resources threatened increasing economic progress and industrial development. For example, in the United States, in 1907, President Roosevelt organised the Governor's Conference, an event sometimes cited as dating the emergence of conservation as a public philosophy influential at the highest levels. In a letter to the governors, Roosevelt wrote that 'it is evident the abundant natural resources on which the welfare of this nation rests are becoming depleted, and in not a few cases, are already exhausted' (Oelschlaeger, 1991, pp. 282–3).

In contrast to Britain, the United States of America had a shorter history of large-scale human intervention in nature but at the same a larger territory to exploit. However, by the early twentieth century it became a central theme of American economic policy that natural resources ought to be utilised and managed for their maximum economic benefit to the whole society. Roosevelt appointed Gifford Pinchot as Chief Forester and he became the 'major architect of the "Progressive conservation ideology"'; to protect the 'nation's economy' rather than 'nature's economy' (Worster, 1994, p. 266). As Worster writes, Pinchot

> saw the world as badly in need of managing…he would insist that all renewable resources, especially forests and wildlife, be approached in the future as crops

to be planted, harvested, and cultivated by skilled experts. And like any good American farmer, he could see value in the land chiefly where it could be turned to profit (1994, p. 267).[2]

## Indian Forests and the Colonial British

However, an additional and crucial economic resource for many western nations was a dependency upon their colonies. Whilst it is true that colonial powers exploited the natural resources of their colonies, often with ruthless effect, Grove argues that 'current preoccupations with a "global" environmental crisis about pollution, climate change and resource over-use...were foreshadowed in the early days of empire by the dramatic globalisation of economic and natural transformations that was enabled during the colonial period' (1998a, p. 4). Whilst the ecological impact of westernisation and the empire, beginning in the fifteenth century with the expansion of trade in western Europe, is felt almost everywhere, there is an ironic twist to this tale which is often overlooked. On the one hand, colonial expansion of western Europe, to all corners of the globe, created the conditions for the exploitation of natural resources and ecological decline; on the other hand, it was from within this context that the colonial powers first became aware of the potentially devastating effect of human interference within the natural world and, in particular, of ideas linking deforestation with climate change emerged. Thus, whilst the British colonial government in India, for instance, was primarily inclined to manage forest resources in order to maintain economic growth, it also became aware that the destruction of forests had climatic consequences.

Following the earliest days of colonial exploration and expansion, deforestation and major rainfall decline were linked, and by the mid-eighteenth century, the 'increasingly complex infrastructures of colonial rule under the British and French...provided the basis for the kinds of information networks needed to systematically collate environmental information on a global basis and to respond to perceived environmental crises with effective forms of environmental control based upon unitary climate theories' (Grove, 1998a, p. 7). Another arena that allowed the emergence of global knowledge was the creation of botanical gardens since the fifteenth century, both within Europe and the colonies, which had encouraged exploration of the 'interactions between botany, ecology and colonizing societies' (Grove, 1998b, p. 192). This created knowledge about the interactions between various plant species, a 'global knowledge of plants', which was then exported to the colonies to analyse their ecological impact and which contributed to the management of natural resources.

By the beginning of the nineteenth century, the colonial government in India began to experience pressure from 'the scientific lobby' to consider the consequences of continuing with massive deforestation and, instead, to resort to

---

[2]   There were a number of critics of this position, for example John Muir, Henry David Thoreau and Aldo Leopold (Oelschlaeger, 1991).

plantation programmes. In particular, the links between dwindling forests and the decline in rainfall patterns had alerted scientists to the need for radical measures. However, the colonial government was reluctant to encourage 'a severe reduction in large short-term revenue income in favour of high expenditure on long-term and unquantifiable conservationist benefits' (Grove, 1998a, p. 75). A process of vigorous lobbying, combined with the high esteem with which such scientists were held by the colonial elite, eventually resulted in the formation in 1847 of the Bombay Forest Department, which, as Grove argues, was formed from fear of the consequences of continued deforestation – both climatic and 'the threat of famine and unrest' (1998a, p. 85), rather than just concern over timber shortages.

Following this period, however, the colonial government did become increasingly concerned about preserving forest resources for economic reasons, particularly since the building of the railway network in the mid nineteenth century had resulted in massive deforestation. The establishment of a National Forest Department in 1864 saw the emergence of a series of forest acts, 1865 and 1878, which sought to 'exclude the activities of private capital from the forests' (Grove, 1998a, p. 81). The 1878 act 'was a comprehensive piece of legislation which, by one stroke of the executive pen, attempted to obliterate centuries of customary use by rural populations all over India' (Gadgil and Guha, 1993, p. 134). The act distinguished between two main types of forest: 'reserved forests' and 'protected forests' (Gadgil and Guha, 1993, p. 208) and for the first time there was a national classification for forests and other previously communally owned lands:

> The Indian Forest Act, as is well known, provided for the constitution of 'Reserved' and 'Protected' forests. Reserved forests were State property in the full sense of the word. Before any area was declared Reserved Forest, it was surveyed, demarcated and subjected to a regular settlement carried out by a Forest Settlement Officer. Access to these forests was restricted, and no one could use their products unless under official privilege granted by the government. These forests (which, as a rule, were of high commercial value) could only be exploited commercially by the Forest Department itself. The Protected Forests were Government forests which remained to be surveyed and settled, and which were temporarily left open to public use with certain restrictions, particularly regarding the felling of any valuable timber, any class of tree being liable to be declared as reserved (Pouchepadass, 1990, p. 10).

The effect of such legislation has been the subject of much critique of the British colonial state, particularly by Indian scholars and activists. As Gadgil and Guha write 'by around 1860, Britain had emerged as the world leader in deforestation...Upon occasion, the destruction of forests was used by the British to symbolize political victory' (1993, p. 118). However, Grove suggests that such 'anti-colonial environmental discourse' ignores the fact that the 'scientific lobby' were instrumental in constructing an environmental critique of colonial forestry practices, 'often as a surrogate for more direct but less politically palatable social commentaries on colonialism itself' (1998a, p. 41) and that there had been a process of state forest control and significant deforestation stemming from precolonial times (1998a, p. 55). What this disparity in emphasis and detail suggests is that the construction of environmental history itself is a crucial element in defining the environmentalist narratives that come to shape various environmentalist positions within contemporary global society. Nevertheless, the British legislation did mean that land was effectively 'stolen' from the Indian people, in order to preserve the interests of the colonial government, and forest policy since independence has done little to reinstate traditional rights. As the above discussion suggests, at first, the desire to conserve India's forests emerged from the concerns of the 'scientific lobby' about the links between decreased rainfall and deforestation. The management of natural resources soon, however, became essential if the colonial government was to maintain sufficient resources for economic expansion.

## Game Sanctuaries and National Parks

Another concern for the colonial government, by the turn of the century, was the decline in fauna, which threatened the hunting pastimes of the colonial elite. Increasingly, measures were undertaken in many states to restrict access to game for only the 'royal visitor and viceroy, senior administrator and army officer, wealthy tourist and Indian prince' (MacKenzie, 1988, p. 172). The Indian Forest Act of 1878, discussed above, included the skins, horns, tusks and bones of animals within the Act and thus had the impact of also curtailing the largely subsistence hunting activities of the indigenous population (1988, p. 283). The Forest Department began to create game sanctuaries, which either restricted hunting, until the 'head of game' had increased sufficiently, or required the closure of areas of forest for a number of years (1988, p. 285). By the 1920s there had been a shift from the conservation of game to the preservation of wildlife in general, and the gradual introduction of legislation banning trophy hunting. However, it was largely the post-independence government who took on the cause of preservation of wildlife, passing a number of wildlife protection acts in the 1950s. India is perhaps best known for its moves to preserve the tiger, popularised through the World Wildlife Fund's 'Operation Tiger' (1969); 'ironically the vanquishing of the tiger, which had been seen as an imperial obligation and vital social rite of British India, had been transformed into the rescue of the tiger as a symbol of the independence and environmental awareness of modern India' (MacKenzie 1988, p. 291).

Thus, there has been a shift from the conservation of game to satisfy the hunting pursuits of the colonial elite, to the preservation of species for their own sake. However, such conservationism has been criticised for not serving the interests of local populations. Guha argues that the creation of national parks and wildlife sanctuaries in India is a result of the transportation to India of a western Romantic idealisation of nature, of the Deep Ecological variety, and the contention of such environmentalists that 'sustainability' equates to the preservation of wilderness (1989). The creation of wildlife sanctuaries and national parks has meant that people have been displaced and evicted from their land in the interests of conserving natural areas and wildlife. Violent disputes have become common as people have endeavoured to reclaim their traditional land rights (Guha, 1994). For example, in 1984, sixteen peasants, who had been engaged in disputes with the management of the Bharatpur Wildlife Sanctuary, were slaughtered as they grazed their cattle on 'sanctuary' land (Grove, 1998a, p. 211). In 1972 the Indian Wildlife (Protection) Act was introduced, with the numbers of national parks and wildlife sanctuaries rising from 131 in 1975 to 496 by 1995. However, as Kothari et al. point out, this Act

> severely curtails human activity…Within parks, no human activity is permitted unless it is 'in the interest of wildlife'; in sanctuaries, some activities – such as the collection of fruits, fodder, fuel and other forest products, and land-based production activities including agriculture – are permitted, but only at the discretion of the wildlife and civic authorities (1995, p. 189).

In the next chapter I will discuss in more detail debates about different types of *environmentalisms* and will particularly address the concern that the *Romantic* style of environmentalism that values nature for its own sake, is a postmaterialist phenomena. However, before this debate is returned to, I will look more closely at the emergence of a Romantic response to nature. It is necessary to describe and explain the shift that occurred from a situation where 'all types of natural wilderness…were regarded with scorn, while agriculture on the other hand, was a wonderful improver of the landscape' (Evans, 1997, p. 17), to one where:

> Even the rude Rocks, the mossy Caverns, the Irregular unwrought Grottos, and broken Falls of Waters, with all the horrid Graces of the Wilderness itself, as representing Nature more, will be the more engaging, and appear with a Magnificence beyond the formal mockery of princely Gardens (Shaftesbury, *The Moralists*, 1709, cited Evans, 1992, p. 20).

Evans argues that between the seventeenth and nineteenth centuries attitudes towards the natural world 'changed in two ways – a more caring and responsible attitude towards animals and a new appreciation of wild landscape – and for two reasons: a reappraisal of our place in the world and a new isolation from nature' (1997, p. 18). By the end of the nineteenth century, in England, we find the beginnings of a preservationist movement. One that is not concerned with nature for instrumental or managerial reasons, but that seeks to elevate nature as significant in its own right. Lowe suggests that this 'profound shift of opinion arose from a reassessment of the social and economic changes of the nineteenth century…the source of the nation's economic and political power was coming to be seen as destructive of the moral and social order, human health, traditional values, the physical environment and natural beauty' (1983, p. 338). However, this 'new evaluation of the features being obliterated and a new orientation towards the forces and motives which wrought these changes' (1983, p. 337) began earlier with the European Romantic Movement, and it is this *Romantic approach* which forms the second of the responses to humanity's interference in the natural world.

The *managerial* response to humanity's relationship with the natural world had been born from within the Enlightenment climate, where nature was considered as a collection of parts which could be empirically observed, explained and manipulated to serve social and economic improvement. This model of the natural world, and the scientific approach that it entailed, was further sanctioned by recourse to religion; the discovery and manipulation of the laws of physics were considered to be according to God's plan. However, the unpredictable and uneven effects of industrialisation had, by the nineteenth century, cast doubt upon the social benefits of the Enlightenment paradigm. The Romantic Movement emerged in response not only to the social consequences of industrialisation but also the consequences for the humanity of the individual. The Enlightenment world-view was seen as dehumanising; it had desacralised creation and at the very least God was the remote divine-controller of the universe, no longer imminent and accessible through nature. The Romantics sought to reinvest both the individual and creation with the 'spirit' and spontaneity, which had been all but destroyed in both the laboratory and upon the factory floor.

## The Romantic Approach

### The Wilderness Aesthetic

A reaction against the mechanisation of nature and industrialisation coalesced within the European Romantic Movement, a collection of writers and artists who responded to the problems, such as inhumane working conditions and the destruction of the countryside, which the Industrial Revolution had created: 'in regard to nature Romantics preferred the wild. Rejecting the meticulously ordered gardens at Versailles, so attractive to the Enlightenment mind, they turned to the unkempt forest. Wilderness appealed to those bored or disgusted by man and his works. It offered an escape from society but was also an ideal stage for the Romantic to exercise the cult that he frequently made of his own soul' (Nash, 1973 p. 47). The poetry and prose of William Wordsworth, for example, expresses a rejection of the scientific attitudes towards nature, which he considered robbed it of its moral and aesthetic significance. As the following poem, from *Poetical Works*, reveals, nature was to be 'encountered individually, immediately, and spontaneously...he sought Enlightenment, not power' (Oelschlager, 1991 p. 118):

> My heart leaps up when I behold
> A rainbow in the sky:
> So was it when life began;
> So is it now I am a man;
> So be it when I grow old,
> Or let me die!
> (cited in Oelschlaeger, 1991, p. 118)

For the Romantics, the wilderness became hallowed as the antithesis of an industrial landscape, both in terms of its 'naturalness' as an environmental space and also as a metaphor or model for healing society. Again as Wordsworth wrote in his preface to the *Lyrical Ballads:*

> For a multitude of causes unknown to former times are now acting with a combined force to blunt the discriminating powers of the mind, and unfitting it for all voluntary exertion to reduce it to a state of almost savage torpor. The most effective of these causes are the great national events which are daily taking place [i.e. war with France], and the increasing accumulation of men in cities, where the uniformity of their occupations produces a craving for extraordinary incident which the rapid communication of intelligence hourly gratifies…I should be oppressed with no dishonourable melancholy, had I not a deep impression of certain inherent and indestructible qualities of the human mind, and likewise of certain powers in the great and permanent objects [i.e. Nature] that act upon it which are equally inherent and indestructible (William Wordsworth, 1800, pp. xviii–xx).

Whereas the Enlightenment tendency considered that human societies should rise above a presocial nature, the Romantics prized wild nature. For Rousseau (1712–78) 'wild nature was idealized as an oasis free of the ills of civilization, a retreat to which the harried and battered, the suppressed or oppressed, might turn for relief' (Oelschlaeger, 1991, p. 111). The path to social harmony lay in a return to a natural or primitive existence (Smith 2002).[3] Beyond this, however, the Romantics sought to critique the mechanistic idea of nature. On the one hand, they 'addressed themselves to the idea of nature-as-an-organism' (Oelschlaeger, 1991, p. 113) and, on the other hand, their creative output sought to re-invest nature with the qualities available to the senses which had been erased by the mechanistic approach. Nature had become 'devoid of taste, sight, sound, and feeling; it was known only through mass, velocity, position, and repetition of invariant patterns' (1991, p. 113).

---

[3]  This 'anarchic primitivism' becomes a feature of contemporary environmentalism within green anarchist groups or the green primitivism movement (Smith 2002). This style of environmentalism is discussed in Chapter 5.

*The Popularisation of Romantic Attitudes towards Nature*

Whilst Romanticism was the creation of and largely the preserve of a select group of intellectuals, these ideas of nature and the elevation of nature to a model for social rejuvenation were also reflected at the level of public consciousness as well as within more contemporary attitudes towards nature and the environment. By the end of the nineteenth century, attitudes within British society had begun to express 'a moral and aesthetic revulsion to the contemporary industrial city' (Lowe, 1983, p. 339) and a number of voluntary organisations had formed which aimed at protecting the natural environment from industrial encroachment. For example, in 1865 the Commons Preservation Society was formed to protect the London commons from industrial development and in 1885 the Selborne Society for the Protection of Birds, Plants and Pleasant Places was established (Macnaghten and Urry, 1998, p. 35).

However, another influence upon the emergence of the preservationist movement in Britain was the Victorian interest in natural history, and the collection of rare species in particular. By the late nineteenth century, enthusiasm for this pastime was blighted by the gradual dwindling or disappearance of certain species and field clubs and natural history societies were established to curtail the damage. As Evans argues, it was the emergence of these 'amateur' societies, which, although often short lived, had thrust natural history and the conservation of wildlife into public consciousness, whereas 'it might have become a purely scientific discipline, as inaccessible to the amateur as many other branches of science have become' (1997, p. 34). In fact, the earliest natural history society was formed as early as 1689. The Temple House Botanic Club was established for the purposes of the study and collection of plants, for their medicinal use and to maintain the botanical gardens, which had become so popular during this period. However, such groups were interested in 'the study – though not the conservation – of nature as an end in itself' (Evans, 1997, p. 34).

It was not until the last decades of the nineteenth century that any groups were established with conservationist goals at the forefront of their agenda. This was, however, not out of a sense of protecting nature for itself but to conserve specimens for scientific study (Lowe, 1983, p. 333; Evans, 1997). It was clear that the threat to species, both at home and in the colonies, was not only a result of over-collection, but hunting and industrialisation also had a part to play, and 'the once-stalwart objects of nature seemed vulnerable and fragile' (1983, p. 337). However, a shift had occurred by the late Victorian period whereby the conservation of species for collection was overtaken by the preservation of nature as a realm of purity away from urban centres, where 'nature, untamed and primitive, also stood in stark contrast to the rigid and stultifying social conventions of Victorian society' (Lowe, 1983, p. 339). Thus, such early preservationism was not only a response to material conditions but had a more important cultural dimension.

The Romantic Movement had spearheaded a transformation in the intellectual climate. The social philosophers and scientists of the Enlightenment period, trusting in reasoned analysis and empirical investigation of a mechanistic material world, were challenged by a new paradigm which valued the organic and aesthetic qualities of nature and the extension of this model to the social sphere. In fact, many aspects of and sources for contemporary environmentalism are a product of the amalgamation of these two broad worldviews. Ruskin, for example, 'criticises the ways in which industrial society produced forms of social organisation that were not organic and functional as in nature, but involved competition, individual achievement and the division of labour' (Macnaghten and Urry, 1998, p. 12). For Ruskin, and other Romantics, the industrial psyche was not only of consequence for its social significance but also had an effect in undermining the spontaneous, creative human spirit. Consequently, their art and poetry reflects an attempt to discover and express such a 'creative imagination'.

However, at the popular level, this Romantic tendency was perhaps most strongly reflected in the idealisation and preservation of relics of an English past. As Adams suggests 'idealised myths of the rural at the end of the Victorian period were particularly persistent' (1996, p. 75). Whilst they emerged in response to the effects of the Industrial Revolution, and were no doubt strongly influenced by the antecedent Romantic Movement, they were also supported by the fact that agricultural decline at the end of the nineteenth century meant that the significance of the countryside need no longer be predominantly economic. The countryside 'was ripe for appropriation as a cultural symbol', and recurrent rural 'myths' emphasised a countryside which was conceived of as 'anti-urban, anti-industrial, anti-mechanised and anti-chaotic' (Adams, 1996, p. 75). Following the First World War, the countryside increasingly became associated with the leisure pursuits of the middle classes, away from the metropolis, and by 1949 the National Parks and Access to the Countryside Act was passed, which led to the creation of ten national parks in England and Wales. This is not to say that economic motives for such preservation were absent, but that, overall, 'concerns about nature were perceived as largely distinct from...broader economic considerations of progress and modernisation...nature was seen to exist away from cities and sites of production' (Macnaghten and Urry, 1998, p. 44; Lowe, 1983, p. 340). However, this drive to discover and experience a pure and undefiled natural realm was also seen by many as an antidote to the causes and consequences of the First World War. As Webb argues, within European society the social and economic consequences of the First World War had encouraged 'a myriad of plans for the reform or replacement of the materialist system...they shared two characteristics: a revulsion against "materialism", which had caused the war, and a longing for some more cohesive society to replace the loose, anarchic "individualism" that had contributed to the crisis' (1976, p. 82).

By 1921 a book by Edward Carpenter, 'Civilisation: Its Cause and Cure', (1889) had been reprinted fifteen times. He advocated both vegetarianism and a return to rural life as an antidote to the alienation of the individuals from their 'inner and undying' selves, which had created 'a wretched feeling of isolation, actual or prospective, which man [*sic*] necessarily has when he contemplates himself as a separate atom in this immense universe' (cited Webb, 1976, p. 82). A range of movements emerged, both within Europe and America, which organised camps for children to immerse them in the outdoor life. In America the Woodcraft League of America was formed in 1917 by the naturalist and artist Edward Seton. Since 1900 he had been experimenting with camps which were based upon the model of the so-called 'Red Indians' [*sic*]: 'the Redskin [*sic*] "was the great prophet of the outdoor life", a "master of woodcraft", "taught the sacred duty of reverencing, beautifying and perfecting the body", "sought for the beautiful in everything"... and "he was the world's great historic protest against avarice"' (cited in Webb, 1976, p.84). Similarly, in Britain, Ernest Westlake and his son Aubrey, both Quakers, founded the Order of the Woodcraft Chivalry, for which Seton was the Grand Chieftain. There was a strong religious element to their ideas, a desire to create a social religion which integrated every aspect of life and which recognised that 'in order to become spiritual one must first be natural' (1976, p. 86). This represented a reaction against the values of the 'civilised' world, civilisation had been won at a price and it was time to turn back and to 'regain paradise', 'a state of harmony with all creation' (1976, p. 86).[4]

These movements are frequently called the 'back to nature movements', which indicates that they consider that humanity has lost something through its increasing separation from the natural world as a result of the scientific attitude towards nature and the industrialisation of the landscape. There is a yearning after a 'golden age' when humanity was considered to have been in harmony with nature; people are seen as having become dehumanised through their separation from nature and there is an attempt to re-establish a connection with the natural world. As Webb writes 'no generation since the Industrial Revolution has lacked dreamers and destroyers, its quota of Luddites, or those in search of a Golden Age' (1976, p. 81). However, this quotation reveals a fundamental difference between reactions to the colonisation of nature during the Industrial Revolution. On the one hand, we have groups, such as the Luddites, who responded to the mechanisation of nature from their pragmatic position as workers whose livelihoods were under threat (Thompson, 1963). On the other hand, we have the Romantics who are in search of a 'golden age'. An element of this search is the recourse to groups, such as the 'Red Indians' [*sic*] above, who are thought to epitomise the last remnants of such a golden age. There is often also a tendency for the *Romantic* approach within environmentalism to interpret the struggles of groups, such as the Luddites or the Diggers, as being movements to preserve their traditional way of life from industrialisation and as a struggle to preserve the 'natural' from corruption, when this 'ideological' factor is rather less important than more fundamental issues over

---

[4] This 'illuminated approach' with its ideas of 'race betterment', also provided the ideological foundations for the fascist movement in Italy and the Nazi movement in Germany, with their 'emphasis upon blood and soil, the improvement of the race, and the revival of national tradition' (Webb, 1976, p. 125). See Chapter 7 for a discussion of claims that certain neo-pagan groups have formed alliances with neo-fascist organisations.

land rights and sustaining a basic living. This romanticisation of such groups and communities is a feature of contemporary environmentalism, both within India and Britain, where there is often tendency to idealise the lifestyles and values of preindustrial or contemporary small-scale communities who are dependent upon the land, who have more of a direct connection with nature.

Thus, whilst the Romantic Movement owes its origins to an extraordinarily talented group of artists and poets, its ideals and visions have come to permeate public consciousness throughout much of the western world and beyond. Although other factors were involved in the creation of a preservationist culture in Britain, such as the interest in natural history and the increasing use of the countryside as a focus of recreation, the Romantic worldview presents a stage from which to contextualise certain modern attitudes towards nature and the environment, which have since become globalised.

**Defending the Use of Dichotomies as an Analytical Tool**

In this chapter I have emphasised two sets of dichotomies: first, the *managerial* and *Romantic* responses to industrialisation and, second, the distinction between western and non-western ideas about the natural world. Below I will indicate some limitations to these dichotomies, since, in practice, these distinctions are difficult to maintain absolutely. They are nonetheless methodologically useful in terms of allowing us to identify and challenge bias within contemporary environmentalism that favours certain models of nature and modes of action.

*Managerial and Romantic*

Contemporary environmentalism has been influenced by both the *managerial* and *Romantic* approaches to industrialisation, and, whilst I have presented these as separate paradigms or worldviews, the actual situation is more complex. Whilst theoretically they appear to be mutually exclusive, in reality they are often difficult to separate. For example, they are both premised upon the gradual distancing of people from direct dependency upon the natural world. One factor in explaining the success of the *Romantic* attitude is that it was only possible due to the changes that the Industrial Revolution eventually brought in terms of both economic and social improvements. For example, the rise in leisure time and pursuit of countryside activities was only possible once the urban poor became more prosperous and had both the time and financial means to make such excursions. Increasingly, large sections of western publics became more economically secure and their day-to-day needs were met more remotely; by municipalities, in terms of water and electricity, or bought in, rather than individually produced, in the case of food. On the one hand, the remoteness that many individuals feel from the natural world is a product of the Enlightenment and Industrial Revolution. On the other hand, the means of becoming reunited with the natural world was incumbent upon the rising expectations and economic prosperity enabled by industrialisation.

Therefore, whilst people may aim to treat nature as though it is intrinsically valuable, this can be seen as being as much of a product of the Enlightenment as the mechanistic view of the natural world. Furthermore, the idea that nature is intrinsically valuable is not necessarily always held consistently by individuals. For instance, a person may be more likely to express or value this attitude when faced with an example of natural beauty than when driving their car along a newly constructed motorway, cutting through an ancient woodland. Thus, the *Romantic* attitude towards nature may often be held more as a cultural sentiment than as a practical value. It represents an ideal, a perfect vision which our society is largely incapable of accommodating. It is perhaps for this reason that it has become the subject of comment from within religious traditions.

*Western and Non-western*

The second dichotomy, which is not always easy to maintain, is between western and non-western. Whilst I have argued that both responses to the Industrial Revolution originated within the West, they are now found across the globe as features of contemporary environmentalism. Even prior to the modern era there was interchange between West and East. For example, Hutton, the father of modern geology, was influenced by Hindu cycles of time in creating his theories of the age of our universe (Driver and Chapman, 1996). Ruskin was as influenced by eastern ideas, as Mahatma Gandhi was impressed by the writings of Ruskin. Fischer writes that it was upon reading Ruskin's *Unto This Last*, whilst in South Africa, that marked a turning point in his life and he decided to put Ruskin's 'teachings' into practice (1982, p. 90). Gandhi established a self-sufficient farm near Durban in 1904, which was to be the beginning of his famous ashram and freedom movement that he established when he later returned to India. Like Ruskin he abhorred the way in which people lost their traditional livelihoods and dignity to industrialisation. He championed the cause of the 'hand loom', which had become contentious because India had begun to export the raw materials but to re-import the cloth back from the Lancashire cotton mills. The 'hand loom' became a symbol of the Indian struggle for independence, both economic and political. Gandhi established a number of ashrams throughout India, where he stressed simple living and vegetarianism as basic 'spiritual' disciplines. Furthermore, his more active, and ultimately successful, political campaign was waged non-violently according to the ancient Indian tradition of *ahimsa*, or non-harm.

In turn, however, the teaching and example of Mahatma Gandhi has become an important resource within contemporary environmentalism. Environmental direct activists may justify their non-violent protests in terms of an appeal to the example of Gandhi and he is often cited as the 'forefather' of the modern environmental movement. Whilst Gandhi certainly had respect for the natural world, and the land was a central feature of his emancipatory vision, he was not an environmentalist.

Gandhi was a social reformer; his primary allegiance lay with the *svaraj*, self-rule, movement and the upliftment of the socially and economically disadvantaged. Just as Gandhi interpreted Ruskin to suit his own political ideology, so western environmentalists are interpreting Gandhi to suit theirs.

Another way of thinking about the interaction between 'East and West' is in terms of globalisation. As I suggested at the start of this chapter, in the current era, it can be more productive to think about globalisation instead of westernisation. For instance, as the above example of Gandhi and Ruskin belie, the idea of westernisation implies a one-way process, with no impact or influence from the non-West. However, many aspects of globalisation still bear 'the masks of its origins' (Beyer 1998, p. 4) and this is what I wish to draw attention to in emphasising the western origins of the *Romantic* approach to nature, in particular. Moreover, it is also important to be attuned to the power hierarchies within global systems (global spread does not mean the flattening of inequalities). So it is important to draw attention to the origins of Romantic ideas about nature since they tend to be portrayed as an attitude that is inherent to many non-western cultures, and they influence the way in which those cultures are represented to the broader global community. While globalisation does imply a certain level of uniformity and homogeneity, and serves to mask power differentials, it can also encourage diversity where local culture appropriates global discourses to produce strategically placed localised versions. The strategic use of global representations (such as the myth of primitive ecological wisdom) may be employed by those seeking to elevate and transform their marginalised position within the global system: it can serve as a method of resistance and assertion of power.

## Conclusion

The purpose of presenting this discussion as a prehistory of contemporary environmentalism was to make two points. Firstly, the history I have presented is western. Although I have concentrated upon Britain, North America and much of Europe can tell a similar story about industrialisation and responses to it. In the following chapter, it will become clear just how dependent contemporary environmentalism is upon these antecedent transformations in attitudes towards nature. Whilst environmentalism is a global phenomenon, I am suggesting that it owes its origins to a particular history of ideas about nature and humanity's relationship to it. Therefore, although contemporary environmentalism is global in focus it is not necessarily global in relevance. Through a discussion of environmentalism in India I will show how there is often a tension between western style environmentalist ideology and Indian attitudes towards the natural world. For example, I will discuss the apparent paradox that, whilst Indian religious traditions appear to support contemporary environmentalist thinking, many Indians are antagonistic towards or at least apathetic with regard to the environmentalist's goals.

The second point that this discussion has made is that environmentalism proper is a very recent phenomenon. The preceding discussion has shown how ideas about nature have changed throughout western history, and that there have been moves to protect the natural world from human interference at least since the Norman period. However, I have also shown that until the end of the nineteenth century the motivation to conserve nature was more a reflection of human interests; for example, to maintain economic growth or to conserve specimens for study. By the late Victorian period, and certainly since the Second World War, nature had come to represent something quite different. The remarkable, but often taken for granted, idea that nature is significant in its own right was born. This is not to say that nature ceased to have other functions. For example, the natural environment is the source of basic human needs and is also meaningful in terms of its leisure potential; both economic and utilitarian uses of the natural world. However, western society increasingly viewed the natural world in a way that was either mediated by or seen in contrast to the idea that it has its own integrity and is not only significant in terms of its usefulness to humanity. It was not until the 1960s that environmentalism began to emerge as distinct from the earlier more Romantic preservationist concerns about the protection of wildlife and the wilderness, or conservationist measures to manage natural resources. By contrast, environmentalism is marked by the awareness that the destruction of the natural environment threatens human survival, where the emergent environmentalists 'aimed their campaigns at *social* practices which were thought to be environmentally destructive rather than seeking the preservation of threatened *natural* sites and species' (Macnaghten and Urry, 1998, pp. 48–9).

# Chapter 4
# Environmentalisms:
# A Comparative Approach

## Introduction

It was the publication of Rachel Carson's famous book 'Silent Spring' in 1962 that brought to the attention of the American public the devastating effects of pesticides upon the countryside and the food chain. Other writers, such as Paul Ehrlich (1968) and Barry Commoner (1971), respectively drew attention to concerns over population growth and the inability of the Earth to deal with the effects of mass technologies. These authors, and others, served to popularise scientific concepts of ecology (Rubin, 1994). As Hannigan writes, Rachel Carson, in particular, 'brought the concepts of ecology, food chains, the "web of life" and the "balance of nature" into the popular vocabulary for the first time. Using ecology as the explanatory linchpin, she simplified a variety of problematic human/nature relationships into one "environmental crisis"' (1995, p. 118). Problems that had seemed to be local were united as related issues and questions about humanity's interaction with its environment, and hence its responsibility as an actor within nature, were becoming salient: 'what environmentalism added to those fertile ideas of human ecology was a sense of urgency, bordering at times on apocalyptic fear' (Worster, 1994 [1977], p. 353).

As Macnaghten and Urry write

> Through the 1970s and early 1980s a succession of 'issues' emerged which became constituents of an 'environmental agenda'. These were the proliferation of chemicals in the 1960s, resource and energy scarcity in the early 1970s, nuclear power and motorways in the late 1970s, agriculture and countryside issues in the early 1980s, and more recently acid rain, ozone depletion, biodiversity and global warming (1998, pp. 50–51).

What this list suggests is that the 'environmental agenda' became more directed towards increasingly global aspects of environmental destruction, issues which affected the global environment rather than isolated and localised natural spaces. A global environmentalism emerged as environmental 'disasters' within particular countries were also being recognised as part of a wider global problem: for example, the 1967 Torrey Canyon oil spillage off the Cornish coast, which contaminated hundreds of miles of coastline, was just one of a number of similar disasters occurring across the globe. In response, governments began to formulate global responses, and in 1972 the first international environment conference was held in Stockholm, Sweden. The Indian Prime Minister Indira Gandhi attended this event, amongst others. This response has also included a number of reports from bodies that aimed to represent international interests. In 1970, the 'Club of Rome', a group of politicians, industrialists and scientists, developed a computer-simulated model to predict the effects of environmental problems such as population growth and industrial expansion. Their report, *The Limits to Growth,* predicted, for example, that famines and resource depletion would pose serious threats to life on the planet by the end of the century. The production of other reports during the 1980s helped to publicise the idea of a global environmentalism: the Brandt Report in 1980 and the Bruntland Report in 1987. More recently, the United Nations Earth Summits, held in Rio de Janeiro in 1992 and Johannesburg in 2002, brought together world leaders in an attempt to discuss the social and economic inequalities between North and South, as well as to approach the issue of 'sustainable development'. Both events also hosted an 'alternative summit' which aimed to give an opportunity to individuals, other than those from international governments and environmental agencies, to discuss more 'grass roots' approaches towards saving the environment. This reflected the feeling amongst many grass roots activists and environmentalists that the interests of the vast majority of the world's population were not being represented by the 'official' global bodies. For example, at the Rio summit there was participation from various NGOs, representatives from Native American Indian communities, the Dalai Lama and a range of religious groups, including 'Lutherans...Brazilian spiritualists. Hindu groups...and Tibetan Buddhists' (Fernandes, 1992, p. 7) who all attended to discuss their approach to environmental issues.

Although it is possible to give materialist explanations for the rise of environmentalism, commentators have also argued that the emergence of an environmental movement must also be seen within the context of the socioeconomic conditions that gave rise to a range of 'new social movements' (NSM) in the West during the 1960s and 1970s. In particular, attention is drawn to the expressivism and radicalism of the countercultural and student movements of the late 1960s in the USA and Europe. It is no coincidence that the environment became a central theme within the counterculture, in particular, indicating both concern over real environmental problems and also a wider expression of dissatisfaction with the structures and values of mainstream society. Below I will outline the main themes within new social movement theory and will discuss its benefits and limitations as an explanatory model for forms of discourse (both rhetoric and action) concerned with the environment. Moreover, to what extent does NSM theory help us think about environmentalism globally or is its explanatory power confined to the postindustrial West? Advocates of new social movement theory argue that NSMs reflect a new phase in social movement formation that is related to the emergence of postmodern, postindustrial or postmaterialist societies. How do we therefore explain the existence of the environmental movement, in contexts that are still in relatively 'early' phase of capitalist/industrial development?

**New Social Movement Theory**

The so-called 'new' social movements, which emerged in the 1960s (including, for instance, the feminist and peace movements, as well as environmental movements), have been distinguished from 'older' class-based social movements whose struggle was refined to work relations or direct participation in the political process (Beckford, 1990, p. 7). By contrast, it is argued that the ideological nature of NSMs represents a fundamental break with movements of the past and that participation in new social movements is linked to identity and culture rather than the pursuit of discrete goals with material or social benefits. They are more concerned with quality of life issues than materialist goals alone (Dalton et al., 1990; Offe, 1985). Pichardo (1997) outlines four areas in which NSMs are typically considered to differ from movements of the past. Firstly, and most fundamentally, the emphasis upon ideology and identity reflects a shift from 'economic redistribution' to 'quality of life and life-style concerns' (1997, p. 414). Secondly, the tactics of NSMs reflect an 'anti-politics of identity' (Kauffman, 1990) or 'an apolitical withdrawal from politics' (Pichardo, 1997, p. 414). They typically, but not always, resist formal participation in politics often 'employing disruptive tactics and mobilizing public opinion to gain political leverage' (1997, p. 415), and using 'highly dramatic and preplanned forms of demonstrations replete with costumes and symbolic representations' (1997, p. 415; Tarrow, 1994). This mirrors strategies employed within the British environmental direct action movement discussed in Chapter 5 (see also Hetherington, 1998; Maffesoli, 1996; Szerszynski, 1999).

Thirdly, the structure of NSMs tend to be anti-authoritarian and anti-institutional: 'they tend to rotate leadership, vote communally on all issues, and to have impermanent ad hoc organizations' (Pichardo, 1997: 416; Offe, 1985). Finally, commentators have emphasised that the nature of participants is a defining feature of NSMs. While some studies emphasise that the support base for NSMs is the 'new' middle class ('a recently emerged social stratum employed in the nonproductive sectors of the economy' (Pichardo, 1997, p. 416; Cotgrove and Duff, 1981; Lowe and Goyder, 1983; Rudig, 1988)), others argue that NSM participants are tied by a shared concern for social issues rather than by class. Pichardo suggests, however, that neither view can completely account for the evidence. He draws attention to studies which reveal that the environmental movement is comprised of two types of participant: 'the 'new' middle class is one; the other is geographically bound communities that are being directly affected by the negative externalities of industrial growth' (1997, p. 417). However, he hints that the 'more ideologically committed' middle class has quite different reasons for involvement to other participants and that 'the participants of environmental movements do not draw significantly from outside the white middle class unless there is some motivating, geographically based, grievance' (1997, p. 417).

*Are 'New Social Movements' Really New?*

However, the extent to which there is enough here to actually warrant the description 'new', has been questioned, particularly since there are so many exceptions. Moreover, NSM theory underestimates the scale of middle class protest in the past and not all NSMs are non-heirarchical or avoid political participation (Pichardo, 1997, p. 418). Others have also challenged the distinction between old and new social movements, arguing that older movements also exhibited a cultural or 'symbolic' dimension. As Doherty et al. write 'culture and symbols were important to nationalist, fascists and workers movements in the nineteenth and twentieth centuries. Almost all the empirical features said to be distinctive about the new movements can be found in some historical precursor' (2000, p. 11; Calhoun, 1993; D'Anieri et al., 1990). Similarly, as Eyerman and Jamison argue, the older social movements of the nineteenth century should not be conceived of as purely a response to the socioeconomic changes brought by industrialisation, but, like the so-called new social movements, they were domains of 'cognitive praxis': 'for us, the movements of the nineteeth-century are not primarily significant as responses to social change, but as (epistemological) creators of industrial society' (1991, p. 80). Thus, overlap between the empirical features of new and old social movements (e.g. goals, tactics, structure and types of participants) suggest to some commentators that continuity exists between them.

   However, Doherty et al. argue that for theorists who defend the newness of NSMs, the empirical differentiation of new from old social movements is not what matters most: 'almost all the empirical features said to be distinctive about the new movements can be found in some historical precursor' (2000, p. 11). Instead, such theorists are interested in the ways in which new social movements are a response to changes in the structures of modern societies that could not have provided the backdrop to the concerns and actions of older social movements. A number of scholars have drawn attention to the ways in which the shift to postmodern, postindustrial (Touraine, 1981) or advanced industrial (Beckford, 1989) society has meant the intrusion of the state into the civic sphere. Pichardo summarises this view: 'with the advent of a service/technical economy with its emphasis on growth and information management, capital accumulation necessitates social as well as economic domination. Social domination involves controlling dissent and knowledge (ensuring conformity) and therefore requires an expansion of the state's coercive mechanisms into the civic sphere' (Pichardo, 1997, pp. 419–20; Habermas, 1987; Melucci, 1984; Sassoon, 1984; Touraine, 1971). As discussed in Chapter 2, processes of individualisation and detraditionalisation have led 'to the emergence of less institutionalised forms of identity and social arrangement. Institutions such as science, the church, the monarchy, the nuclear family and formal structure of government are appearing to be delegitimated, and increasingly seen as part of the problem rather than the solution' (Macnaghten and Urry, 1998, p. 27; Beyer, 1994). These changes have lead to increasingly diverse forms of social and political organisation, including the formation of new social movements, 'non-party-based and self-organising affiliations and associations, often in the form of self-help groups, community groups and voluntary organisations' (Macnaghten and Urry, 1998, p. 27).

The nature of modern societies has, on the one hand, created a situation where individuals are thrown back upon themselves, without previous security of familiar institutions such as the church and the family, but, on the other hand, it has created a vantage point from which the failings of society become the subject of critical reflection. As both Offe (1985) and Beyer (1994) emphasise, contemporary political and economic institutions are unable to solve the problems that they create and require action from external social movements to attend to their defects. Giddens, for example, argues that modernity is marked by this radicalised style of reflexivity. All societies at all times have reviewed their worldviews and practices as they came to acquire new information. For example, traditions are never static but develop and change in response to changing circumstances. However, 'only in the era of modernity is the revision of convention radicalised to apply (in principle) to all aspects of human life, including technological intervention into the material world' (1990, pp. 38–9). Beck develops this idea of reflexivity arguing that there has been a transition from industrial to risk society. During the industrial phase 'the incalculable threats of pre-industrial society (plague, famine, natural catastrophes, wars, but also magic, gods, demons) are transformed into calculable risks in the course of development of instrumental rational control, which the process of modernisation promotes in all spheres of life' (1996, p. 30). However, risks in contemporary society, such as those created by the chemical, nuclear or arms industries, cannot be explained, predicted or contained by the rational logic that was suitable during the industrial phase. This, he argues, is the point at which risk society is born, and that 'recognition of the incalculability of the hazards produced by technical-industrial development compels self-reflection on the foundations of the social context and a review of prevailing conventions and principles of "rationality"...risk society is tendentially a *self-critical* society' (1996, p. 32).

*The Symbolic Nature of Participation in New Social Movements*

Thus, the problem is that society can no longer make sense of itself and a new critical discourse has emerged which aims to illuminate and accommodate the failing structures of contemporary (post)industrial society. Many authors have stressed the affective dimension of this critical discourse. The above discussion on the 'symbolic' nature of participation in new social movements suggests that it is as much about expressing who you are, your values and ideologies, as it is about creating a space for direct political intervention. Firstly, rather directly affecting the political process, they were a response by individuals to protect identity and self-expression from the encroachment of the technocratic state, 'they claim for real the bogus priority the day-to-day experience, affective relations, and the deep motivations of individual behaviour have received in a society that intervenes in the very roots of individual life' (Melucci, 1996, p. 106). Secondly, participation in the movement itself has a 'symbolic' effect upon the individual and wider society:

> The message of such movements is their action itself – not what they state for record or claim as its content...This, then, represents a completely different way of challenging the institutional powers. Sometimes these movements, as it were, present the society with cultural gifts by their action: they reveal new possibilities, another face of reality. When they act, something has already been said by this very action; at once, the message has been incorporated into the social arena and the debates may commence. Whether or not the issues then become topics for political contestation depends on the extent to which they can be taken up by politically relevant agents or otherwise translated into political agendas for the public (Melucci, 1996, p. 183).

Eyerman and Jamison's interpretation of social movements as 'cognitive praxis', 'also seeks to grasp the symbolic, or expressive, significance of social movements' (1991, p. 48). However, they consider that the significance of social movements is not only in their ability to upset the dominant systems of meaning, but that they also play a crucial role as 'producers of knowledge' (1991, p. 55) in society. Social movements open up or create new cognitive spaces, in which social knowledge is constructed and contested, *via* 'social encounters, within movements, between movements, and even more importantly perhaps, between movements and their established opponents' (1991, p. 57). In particular, they argue that whilst the environmental movement of the 1960s began as a reaction against modern industrial society, it became a 'movement' once it adopted ecology as a basis for its political orientation. Ecology was thus transformed from a scientific discipline to 'a way of life' or a 'set of beliefs', 'the movement provided, we might say, the social context for a new kind of knowledge to be practised' (1991, p. 73). This emergence of the movement corresponds to the shift discussed above from the 'conservation' or 'preservation' of nature to concerns about the global environment. Thus, Eyerman and Jamison are suggesting that the environmental movement was not only a response to material conditions, but that, in itself, it created new forms of socially constructed knowledge with which to conceive and articulate concerns for the natural world. The movement itself created the discourses and frameworks that are now taken for granted by environmentalists, both ideological and cultural, 'it carved out a new conceptual space, giving the 'environment' and ecology political and economic significance that, in the course of the 1980s, have affected the political cultures of almost every nation' (1991, p. 77).

In terms of creating a sense of identity and belonging for members beyond instrumental aims, or in terms of opening up cognitive space for new forms of public discourse, there does seem to have been a shift in the identification and articulation of social problems. As Pichardo writes, 'what seems to be unique is their ideological (identity) orientation – the one hypothesized characteristic that seems truly to mark a break from the past' (1997, p. 425). Increasingly, social movements have articulated issues concerning the quality of life, rights and values of the individual, other people, and even animals. For example, the expression of environmental concerns includes such issues as the right to live in a clean, healthy and pleasant environment and even the right of the Earth to be treated with respect. Alongside the idea that the NSMs are a unique feature of postindustrial society, an attempt to carve out a domain of affective or symbolic meaning, against the totalising tendencies of the technocratic state, we must also consider another argument put forward to explain this shift. The 'postmaterialism thesis' states that since the Second World War there has been a 'value shift' amongst western publics (specifically the 'new' middle class) that is a product of increased economic affluence and security. This argument is particularly significant for our discussion, since it has been one of the theories employed not only to explain the advent of NSMs but also the rise in interest in environmental issues (Ingelhart, 1995).

We will return to the postmaterialism thesis and new social movements below, when we discuss some of the limitations of this line of thought. In particular, I will ask: how do we account for the existence of environmental movements in contexts that are not 'postmaterialist' or that do not have movements that conform to the typical NSM type? Moreover, can an economic explanation fully account for the emergence of the environmental movement? Is there a clear distinction between 'old' and 'new' social movements? These questions are key to the themes raised in this book, and, before we investigate them, I first want to look more closely at the different styles of environmentalism that have emerged since the 1960s – in both the West as well as other regions (the country that will interest us here is India). I will then move on to look at some of the critiques of 'western environmentalism', as a foreign import to developing countries, that have both a material and an ideological component. On the one hand, how effective is an environmentalist message that requires 'poor' people to put the 'Earth first'? On the other hand, what ethical issues are raised by the portrayal of the poor in developing contexts as inherent environmentalists, as 'close to nature' by virtue of their religiocultural traditions?

*Styles of Environmentalism: Ecocentric and Technocentric*

While we do not really find anything resembling modern environmentalism until the 1960s, responses to environmental problems have not been uniform. Environmentalism has become an arena of fiercely contested ideologies about humanity's relationship to nature and the degree to which humanity should limit its impact upon the natural world. This book identifies two broad attitudes that are found within contemporary environmentalist thinking which, I will argue, mirror the legacy of the *managerial* and *Romantic* responses to nature discussed in Chapter 3 (O'Riordan, 1981; Pepper, 1986; Merchant, 1992; Oelschlaeger, 1991). The *Romantic* approach is the forebear of an *ecocentric* attitude towards nature, which maintains that humanity should not disrupt the 'natural balance': human activities should mirror natural processes in order to avoid adverse consequences. This position assigns *intrinsic value* to the natural environment and maintains that it should be prudently preserved for its own sake rather than because of its usefulness to humanity. Thus, the natural world should be protected because this is the right thing to do rather than for any material benefits this will bring for humanity (Merchant, 1992, pp. 74–80; Pepper, 1986, pp. 27–30). Any material benefits, such as a cleaner healthier environment are of course a motivating factor in adopting this position, but even if a particular activity would entail some sort of hardship or loss to humanity then it ought to be pursued in the interests of the Earth. This position is critical of forms of environmentalism which mirror the *managerial* attitude (Pepper calls this the 'technocentric' approach (1986, pp. 27–30)), which consider that it is only necessary to be prudent with regard to resource exploitation because of the consequences for humanity and the interests of economic growth. This position assigns a *use value* to the natural world and is criticised by ecocentrics for being anthropocentric. They argue that, under such conditions, the environment will only be protected to the extent that this does not interfere with human needs, and that ultimately this will not go far enough in reducing damage to the environment.

Ecocentrism shares the values and aesthetics of the European Romantic Movement but was also articulated as part of the vision of a number of North American thinkers, including, Henry David Thoreau (1817–1862), John Muir (1838–1914) and Aldo Leopold (Taylor 2008; 2009). Bron Taylor writes that many consider Leopold (1887–1948), in particular, to be the 'greatest ecologist and environmental ethicist of the 20th century' (2009, forthcoming). In 1949 Leopold published 'The Sand County Almanac', in which he advocated his famous 'Land Ethic': 'a thing is right when it tends to preserve the integrity, stability, and beauty of the biotic community. It is wrong when it tends otherwise' (1968 [1949], pp. 224–5). Representations of nature as an 'ecosystem' or 'organism', which emerged from within the discipline of ecology, supported an alternative perspective from which to view the relationship between humanity and the natural world. Instead of standing above and separate from nature, humanity was reduced to another species subject to the same relationship of interconnections and dependencies found between non-human species. As Leopold pointed out, an acknowledgment of this relationship suggested that there were limits to the extent to which humanity could interfere in nature without consequences. It is the interpretation of the significance of this acknowledgment that forms a major division between different types of responses to environmental problems in contemporary society.

The ecocentric sentiments behind Leopold's 'Land Ethic' also influenced the Norwegian philosopher Arne Naess, who in 1973 wrote an article in which he first contrasted 'shallow' with 'deep ecology'. The former corresponded with the *managerial/technocentric* approach and the latter with the *Romantic/ecocentric* approach to nature. The name 'deep ecology' was subsequently attached to an environmentalist ideology that seeks to fundamentally transform human/nature relations through recognition of the interconnectedness of all species. By contrast, 'shallow' ecology might deal, for example, with reducing industrial emissions or creating taxes on pollution, but, it is argued, is unlikely to have any lasting impact upon reforming human nature relations. In particular, the publication of a volume edited by Devall and Sessions, 'Deep Ecology' (1985), popularised what had hitherto been confined within academic circles and deep ecological ideas gradually became more pervasive within mainstream society, providing a conceptual framework from within which more radical environmentalist groups could express their concerns. This style of ecological thinking underpins the values of Earth First!, one of the most well-known and influential radical environmentalist groups.

Where ecocentrism takes an extreme view about the types of activities which humans should ethically engage with, tending to be radically opposed to industrialisation and the mechanisation of nature, and favouring instead the retention or revival of economies based upon the minimum interference in the natural world, the *managerial* approach accommodates environmentalist concerns as long as they do not seriously hinder continued economic growth or other human interests. The *managerial* approach ignores the radical ecocentric interpretation of ecology and instead uses the science of ecology to develop an understanding of how best to maintain natural resources so as to continue with economic and industrial development. Radical environmentalists identify this position as underpinning the values and activities of global multinational corporations, which are considered to show very little regard for social justice or the ethical implications of their actions. As I will discuss in Chapter 5, there is an increasing overlap between radical environmental direct action and the anti-globalisation/anti-capitalism movement that has grown in size and notoriety particularly since the anti-World Trade Organisation protests in Seattle in 1999.

As Pepper writes, these two modes (*technocentric/managerial* and *ecocentric/ Romantic*) are 'eminently recognisable in almost any public debate about modern environmental issues' (1986, p. 30). However, in reality the picture is not simple, and in between these two 'extremes' fall actual expressions of contemporary environmentalism, which variously attempt to mitigate levels of technological development with recognition of the environmental consequences of such human activity. Where such expressions differ is the extent to which they regard the tenability of continued large-scale industrial and technological expansion, as well as the extent to which they present a critique of the values and practices of contemporary industrial society. Appropriate technologists, for example, are closer to radical ecocentrics, disagreeing in principle on the extent to which the Earth ought to be prioritised above human needs. They are not, however, as radical in their thinking and actions as so-called neo-primitivists, who favour a 'return' to simple, hunter-gather style lifestyles. By contrast, international reports such as the Brandt Report (1980), which first raised sustainable development to the international agenda, are often considered to be (i.e. by ecocentrics) closer to the *managerial* or *technocentric* approach. Although the Brandt Report addressed the issue that present levels of industrial development seriously threaten not only the stability of the environment but were creating conditions of intense human suffering, particularly in the global South, it is still considered by more radical activists to reflect the priorities of large-scale global industrial and technological development. Thus, discussions about the effect of $CO_2$ emissions have not resulted in the banning of the burning of fossil fuels, as the radical ecocentrics would advocate. Instead, for them, it has centred upon ways of reducing emissions so as to overcome the worst negative consequences, whilst still pursuing a form of economic growth that is otherwise potentially damaging to the environment.

Apart from those individuals who have deliberately adopted environmentalist positions, and actively participate in environmental groups or forms of direct action, many other people are concerned about environmental issues but do not directly engage in environmentalist activities. Environmental discourse has become a part of public consciousness. Few people in Britain, for example, would disagree, if asked, that environmental degradation or global warming were serious issues facing contemporary society. However, the degree to which they undertake any practical measures or consider it a priority in their day-to-day lives varies. To the exasperation of many radical environmentalists, concern for the environment has arguably become a trend, a fashion, another manifestation of consumer culture, with an increased demand for environmentally friendly clothing and cleaning products, or ecotourism and hydrogen powered vehicles.

## The Place of Religion

So where does religious environmentalism fit within this characterisation of different approaches to the 'environmental crisis'? The debates that emerge within religious environmentalism call for a deep and significant transformation in personal behaviour (as an authentic expression of one's religious or spiritual orientation). This is the first level that needs to be addressed in order to reverse the damage that is being done to the environment. This would suggest values that are at the 'radical' end of the environmentalist spectrum. However, not all religious environmentalists are radically ecocentric. Various expressions of a 'stewardship' ethic are common which maintains that humanity should act as steward of creation rather than as an equal partner within creation. This is popular within religious traditions that are doctrinally strict in their view of humans as having a higher moral value than creation and enjoying a special relationship to the divine. For instance, Christianity, Judaism and Islam are not as amenable to an ecocentric ethic as Buddhism or Hinduism, for instance. Moreover, the Abrahamic religions are doctrinally strict about the transcendence of the divine above humans and nature, and hence the ecologically attractive notion of an imminent form of the divine (which renders nature itself divine/sacred) is not possible. Instead, within these traditions the Earth is sacred by virtue of being the creation of the divine. For strict ecocentrics this position does not go far enough since it still posits human interests over those of the natural world (see below for a discussion of ecocentrism as anthropocentric). Nevertheless, the stewardship ethic is clearly *more* ecocentric than the *technocentric* and *managerial* responses, which, it is argued, shape mainstream, international responses to concerns about the environment.

In addition to challenging individual behaviour, religious environmentalists also present a critique of broader social, economic and political processes that are considered to be environmentally damaging. The radical direct activists discussed in Chapter 5 are critical of the entire trajectory of global industrial capitalism and seek to create alternative communities based around 'ecological principles'. While some are radical ecocentrics, or 'deep ecologists', promoting wilderness preservation and forms of 'anarchic primitivism', others are less radical, suggesting instead various alternative, 'appropriate technologies' that would permit modified yet modern styles of living. As I will discuss, these direct activists are typically not attracted to participation in one of the major institutionalised world religions, and have a particularly strong critique of the Christian tradition. Instead, they have adopted a 'deregulated' religiosity that draws upon eastern spiritualities and Indigenous Religions. By contrast, those religious environmentalists who belong to one of the world religions, tend to be less radical in their critique of capitalism and the extent to which individuals should transform their behaviour, advocating instead the benefits of changing individual behaviour within the confines of existing lifestyles (e.g. recycling, ethical consumerism and reducing car use rather than withdrawing from society and becoming self-sufficient). I will refer to these environmentalists as 'weak' ecocentrics, since their view of the human-nature relationship does not prioritise nature over humans (as in the radical or 'deep ecological' approach), yet it does require a greater nature-centredness than technocentric environmentalism. And, more importantly, mirroring Romanticism and Leopold's land ethic, it invests the natural world and human relationships to it, with a moral significance.

However, if, as I am suggesting, ecocentrism (both radical and weak) is part of the legacy of *Romantic* attitudes towards nature that emerged after the Enlightenment and Industrial Revolution in Europe, can we assume that it reflects the ways in which non-western cultures deal with environmental risk and vulnerability? While ecocentrics frequently claim that non-western cultural traditions inherently support an ecocentric ethic, others have described this as a 'myth of primitive ecological wisdom' (Milton, 1996) or a 'new traditionalist discourse' (Sinha et al., 1997), which is a form of 'Orientalism' that silences the voices of the poor (Baviskar, 1997). Alternatively, as Milton (1996) indicates, some indigenous peoples actively portray themselves as ecologically wise, they have appropriated the 'myth of primitive ecological wisdom'. Brosius (1999) argues that the deconstruction of this 'myth' by academics becomes morally questionable, since it effectively provides the adversaries of indigenous peoples (e.g. mining or logging companies) with the means to undermine their position. Moreover, in India we find environmental organisations and publications that have adopted a religious environmentalist position. Thus, on the one hand, the representation of particular cultures through discourses shaped by more powerful groups is (as the discussion below will argue) an important consideration in reflecting upon religious environmentalism in India. However, on the other hand, religious environmentalist discourses have been appropriated by individuals and groups in India. The aim of the case studies presented in Chapters 5–7 is to look at different examples of religious environmentalism. Is it the case that these discourses have been adopted by various elites in India, a product of a 'bourgeois environmentalism', that has little relevance to the majority of the population? Or do they have relevance at the grass-roots level? How does this fit with our earlier discussion about NSMs and postmaterialist values?

Before, we move on to look at empirical examples of religious environmentalism and to address the above research questions, I first want to look more closely at some of the criticisms of environmentalism, particularly the ecocentric version, as a western creation that makes demands upon and idealises the lifestyles and cultural traditions of non-western peoples. The next section will discuss some criticisms of ecocentric/deep ecological thinking (e.g. Bradford, 1989; Guha, 1989; 1990; Jackson, 1995; Lewis, 1992). The first criticism is philosophical and the second is sociological (see also the essays in Katz, Light and Rothenberg 2000).

*Nature as Normative?*

The first criticism argues that while ecocentrism and deep ecology claim to be non-anthropocentric, this position is actually incoherent. As Bradford writes:

> Deep ecology claims to be a perspective taken from outside human discourse and politics, from the point of view of nature as a whole. Of course, it is a problematic claim, to say the least, since deep ecologists have developed a viewpoint based on human, socially generated, and historically evolved insights into nature, in order to design an orientation toward human society...any vision of nature and humanity's place in it...is by definition going to be to some degree 'anthropocentric', imposing as it does a human, symbolic discourse on the nonhuman (1989, p. 9).

He suggests that the idea that all species have an equal right to 'live and blossom', is an imposition of a 'legalistic and bourgeois-humanist anthropocentrism' (1989, p. 9) upon nature. (Interestingly, Bradford was one of the early proponents of deep ecology and only later became doubtful about its consistency.) Other scholars have pointed out that the model borrowed from the ecological sciences (of all species living in natural, interconnected harmony) rests upon a very selective reading of 'ecology'. As Evernden argues, 'terms like competition, exclusion, exploitation, and survival...are less likely to be seized upon by those aspiring to establish the groundwork for an ecological ethic or an environmentally benign life-style, yet they are every bit as much a part of ecology' (1992, p. 9). He suggests that

Persons with contrasting viewpoints can draw upon this discipline, one group regarding it as revealer of the natural and proper, the other as a source of power and control (which it is natural for us to use). Each group believes its stance to be correct, and each expects endorsement from ecology (1992, p. 10).

Similarly, as Jackson suggests, ecology can just as easily reveal to us a scenario where 'we confront a nature populated by rugged individualists, eager opportunists, and self-seekers. There is no integrated community in nature, no enduring system of relationships; no deep interdependence' (1995, p. 132). Thus, both Evernden and Jackson argue that ecocentrism relies upon the construction of a particular 'scientific' model to support its claims. Recourse to the power and authority of science seems to legitimate this position and allows environmentalists to make the claim that living in harmony with nature is 'natural' human behaviour. However, the contingency of notions of 'natural' is clearly exposed when we consider that the scientific model that is employed to support such claims is itself socially constructed. It is the very fact that ecology has science as its basis that this rather selective reading can pass as a neutral and authentic description of nature. The application of a particular reading of ecology shapes how nature is perceived. This has had a lasting impact upon the way in which many environmentalists perceive what are natural and unnatural forms of human behaviour and social organisation.

Thus, the idea that 'nature is normative' (that particular norms for behaviour can be read from nature and that an ecological model of the interconnectedness of all species is non-anthropological) has been challenged. However, I am less concerned that this undermines the deep ecological/ecocentric project than I am with the fact that appeals to ecological science and assurances that the position is 'non-anthropological' suggest that deep ecology and ecocentrism are universal. I am using universal in two senses here: that this environmentalist philosophy can be put into 'practice on a worldwide basis' (Guha 1989, p. 72) and that this is possible not only because it is considered to be a desirable position, but also because many non-western philosophies are 'convergent in their structure with deep ecology' (Guha 1989, p. 77). As Guha suggests, it is important to 'examine the cultural rootedness of a philosophy that likes to present itself in universalistic terms' (1989, p. 72).

## Deep Ecological and Ecocentric 'Bourgeois' Environmentalism

The second criticism that I will discuss has two dimensions. Firstly, that ecocentrism does not reflect a universal value about nature since it is part of the legacy of the European Romantic Movement and, more recently, North American thinkers such as Aldo Leopold or Ralph Waldo Emerson and Henry David Thoreau. Secondly, the 'back-to-nature' aesthetic, prized within the writings of such *Romantics*, reflects a style of environmentalist thinking that is only tenable for those who are not directly dependent upon 'nature' for their survival. While the philosophical criticism presented above (concerning 'nature as normative') undermines deep ecological and ecocentric thinking in itself, this sociological criticism becomes most forceful when this style of environmentalism is assumed to be universally valid. Within the literature this is taken up in two ways. Firstly, we find critiques which argue that deep ecologists and ecocentrics often assume that their position reflects the way in which various indigenous people, tribal communities or non-industrial societies think about their relationship to the natural world (Baviskar, 1997; Milton, 1996). This view typically shapes what Milton calls the 'myth of primitive ecological wisdom' (1996) and often relies heavily upon the assumption that religiocultural beliefs and rituals inform ecocentric relations. Secondly, deep ecological and ecocentric thinking are criticised because it is suggested that they have often influenced the ways in which policy makers and environmentalists approach natural resource management in the developing world (Baviskar, 1997; Guha, 1989; Leach, 2007).

With respect to the first critique, Guha is concerned that there is a 'persistent invocation of Eastern philosophies as an antecedent in point of time but convergent in their structure with deep ecology' (1989, p. 76). He criticises this as an inherently Orientalist discourse where 'Eastern man [*sic*] exhibits a spiritual dependence with respect to nature…[and which has] the characteristic effect…of denying agency and reason to the East and making it the privileged orbit of Western thinkers' (1989, p. 77). Guha argues that this deep ecological romanticisation of eastern traditions is part of a broader process of western Orientalist construction: this appropriation of eastern cultural resources by the West tells 'us far more about the Western commentator and his desires than about the "East"' (1989, p. 77). However, this type of 'new traditionalist discourse' (Sinha et al., 1997) is also considered to have become part and parcel of a particular type of Indian environmentalism, of the 'bourgeois' or middle class variety. Within this 'new traditionalist' discourse, Baviskar locates what she calls the 'Hindu civilizational' response of middle class scholars and activists who appropriate the Hindu tradition as a source of ecological ethics and wisdom (1999). She points to critiques of this as a form of 'inverted Orientalism' for 'positively valorizing a mythical Other created by Western environmentalists' (Baviskar, 2004; Guha, 1989; Inden, 1986). Mawdsley similarly locates 'religion and ecology' as one strand of middle-class concern with the environment in India, alongside 'civic indifference' and 'environmental activism' (2004, p. 87).

The second critique of the universalisation of deep ecological and ecocentric thinking (*Romantic* attitudes towards nature) that has been voiced within India, concerns the extent to which they inform the values and actions of policy makers and environmentalists with respect to natural resource management (Baviskar, 1997; Guha, 1989; Jackson, 1993a; 1993b; 1994; Leach, 2007). Guha, one of the earliest proponents of this critique, has argued that the deep ecology inspired North American system of national parks has been transplanted 'onto Indian soil' (1989, p. 75). Since it maintains 'that intervention in nature should be guided primarily by the need to preserve biotic integrity rather than by the needs of humans'

(1989, p. 74), people have been evicted from the land upon which they depend: 'wildlands preservation has been identified with environmentalism by the state and the conservation elite; in consequence, environmental problems that impinge far more directly on the lives of the poor – e.g. fuel, fodder, water shortages, soil erosion, and air and water pollution – have not been adequately addressed' (1989, p. 75; Saberwal and Rangarajan, 2003; Saberwal et al., 2000). He draws attention to the example of 'Project Tiger', 'a network of parks hailed by the international conservation community as an outstanding success' but is critical since it 'sharply posits the interests of the tiger against those of poor peasants living in and around the reserve' (1989, p. 75). Thus, the same 'imagined communities' (Anderson, 1991), who have been valourised for their primitive ecological wisdom, are considered to be a threat to the natural environment. More recently, participatory approaches to conservation and environmental resource management have gained in popularity, but many remain critical that there is an underlying lack of commitment (Mawdsley, 2004; Jeffery and Sundar, 1999; Rangarajan, 2001; Sundar et al., 2001).

Baviskar also juxtaposes what she calls the 'bourgeois environmentalism' of the middle and upper classes in India, against the survival related ecological concerns of the lower class peasants and tribals (1997). The 'bourgeois environmentalist' has typically been exposed to western, globalised environmentalist discourses (including deep ecology/ecocentrism), is affluent and is more likely to be concerned with nature for its leisure potential and aesthetic value. She describes how this *Romantic* style of environmentalism has resulted in a situation where it is considered that tribal communities in India ought to remain close to nature regardless of their own considerations and interests. Drawing upon her work amongst tribal, *adivasi*, communities in Madhya Pradesh, Baviskar describes how conflicts have emerged in the region within a local organisation, the Sangath, which is concerned with land rights, forest management and ensuring that state funds reached the local 'tribal leaders' (1997, p. 203). The *adivasis* wished to gain control over their land from the state forest department, which had increasingly curtailed their traditional practice of *nevad*, where patches of land are cultivated within the forest. *Nevad* represents a crucial element of the local subsistence economy, but the rate at which the forests are being destroyed is likely to have repercussions in the near future. Although a balance between cultivation and protection of the forest would be the ideal situation, 'people feel an urgent need for agricultural land that overrides all other considerations…people are being forced to choose between the two and necessity compels them to choose land over forest' (1997, p. 206).

The Sangath was comprised of a mixture of middle-class urban youth, who had settled in the area, and local *adivasi* people. Whilst initially these middle-class 'activists' were motivated by a sense of social justice, rather than environmentalist ideology, Baviskar explains that the

> Sangath's ideological horizons expanded towards sustainable development only when it entered the nascent anti-dam movement, a struggle that sharply articulated a challenge to the modernisation-industrialisation-urbanisation

paradigm of development. Participation in the *Andolan* [movement] enabled the
Sangath activists to relate their work to a wider, analytically more sophisticated,
political framework' (1997, p. 212).[1]

Increasingly, there were conflicts within the Sangath between the middle-class
activists and the *adivasi* leaders. The former believed that sustainable development
was the way to improve their situation, whereas the latter were more concerned
about gaining control over resources so that they 'would be masters of their own
destiny' (1997, p. 217). Whereas the activists adopted the belief that it was best
if the *adivasis* remained close to nature in the forest, the *adivasis* themselves
regarded the relationship of economic dependency with the forest as having been
forced upon them rather than chosen, and felt that if they had access to good
land that their lifestyle would improve. Thus, although they wished to remain
on the land, the image that the activists had of the *adivasis*, as the guardians of
the forest, was not shared: 'for these *adivasis*, both ecological sustainability and
cultural dignity remain somewhat remote concerns' (1997, p. 220). Baviskar
points out that although they did benefit from the emergence of the Sangath, which
secured land 'for cultivating *nevad* and harvesting forest produce' (1997, p. 220),
the Sangath did not take up other crucial issues, such as the problems associated
with migration, which is eroding the tribal economy, because they were attached
to a *Romantic* idea of ecological sustainability and this shaped their selection of
relevant causes.

Another area that has received attention, with respect to the influence of the
*Romantic approach* upon styles of environmentalism in India, concerns the ways in
which thinking about women's relationship to the environment within mainstream
development policy and practice has also been informed by 'new traditionalist
discourse' (Sinha et al., 1997) under the guise of 'ecofeminism'.

### Ecofeminism and Neo-traditionalism

While there are many strands within ecofeminist thinking (Warren, 1996),
the underlying position is summed up by Green et al. (1998). They write that
ecofeminists critique the

> dominant model of development which is perceived as a male construct which
> has promoted economic development in ways which have been harmful both
> to women and to the environment by trampling alternative, local knowledge,
> especially women's knowledge, associated with organic concepts of people
> and nature as interconnected; by disregarding the spiritual and sacred in

---

[1]   Baviskar is referring here to the popular socio-political movement against the
construction of the Narmada dam in Maharashtra, which became a high profile campaign,
attracting the interest of internationally minded activists. This had the effect that concerns
about the dam became embedded within globally oriented environmentalist discourses.

people's attitudes to their environment and women's special role therein; and by overriding holistic and harmonious practices...[Ecofeminists] insist that the feminine principle is not quite extinct in the environmental context but still manifest in a residual, near instinctual wisdom which some women have been able to retain in the face of developmental pressures... '[Third] world women' are portrayed as the last bastion of feminine environmental wisdom and they provide the key to its retrieval (Green et al., 1998, p. 273).

Within this passage Green et al. allude to an important theme within ecofeminist thinking that emphasises the idea that women have a spiritual connection with the natural world. This spiritual connection is part of what is lost when environments are destroyed, yet it is this spiritual bond that is considered to have contributed to women's inclination to protect nature. In India, the fact that nature is gendered within Hinduism has proved to be a convenient resource for such 'spiritual' or 'cultural' ecofeminists and is taken as evidence of women's inherent closeness to nature. Within the Hindu tradition we find the idea that there are two fundamental principles within the universe. *Prakriti* (the feminine principle) is the source of all material existence within which *purusha* (the masculine principle), the unchanging divine person or 'self' within each individual, is enmeshed. The most famous exponent of this position is Vandana Shiva and she argues that, whereas western attitudes towards nature rely upon dichotomies between divinity/nature, human/nature and man/woman, in Hindu thought such dualities are overcome. First, divinity and nature are united since *prakriti* (the divine feminine force or the goddess) and the natural world are identical in essence. Second, she considers that *prakriti*, the 'feminine and creative principle of the cosmos' (1988, p. 38), is the source of all inanimate and animate creation, and that this implies the 'connectedness and inter-relationship of all beings...[and the]...continuity between the human and natural' (1988, p. 40). Finally, in Shiva's reading of the Hindu tradition, *prakriti* is not separate from *purusha*, the masculine principle, since 'in Indian cosmology, by contrast, person and nature (Purusha-Prakriti) are a duality in unity...[They] are inseparable components of one another in nature, in woman, in man...this dialectical harmony between male and female principles and between nature and man becomes the basis of ecological thought and action in India' (1988, p. 40). Hence, she concludes that the

ontological shift for an ecologically sustainable future has much to gain from the world-views of ancient civilisations and diverse cultures which survived sustainably over centuries. These were based on an ontology of the feminine as the living principle and on an ontological continuity between society and nature – the humanisation of nature and the naturalisation of society. Not merely did this result in an ethical context which excludes possibilities of exploitation and domination, it allowed the creation of an earth family (1988, p. 41).

While Shiva considers that these dualisms, which, she argues, have informed the socioeconomic values that have given rise to environmental problems across the globe, are absent in 'ancient civilizations and diverse cultures', her version of ecofeminism relies heavily upon a sacred ontology drawn from the Hindu tradition. A number of scholars have questioned this reading of the Hindu tradition and hence its basis as a reflection of ancient Hindu attitudes towards nature, as well as the foundation for a contemporary ecological ethic (DasGupta Sherma, 1998; Nelson, 1998b). DasGupta Sherma points out that Shiva's interpretation is at odds with that provided by the schools of Hindu philosophy of *Samkhya*, *Yoga* and *Advaita Vedanta*, where *prakriti*, the manifest universe, is seen as entirely separate from *purusha* and where the aim of spiritual practice is to overcome attachments to the material world, to life itself. For example, within *Advaita Vedanta*, the manifest universe is considered to be an illusion, *maya*, in the sense that it does not represent reality. Reality, by contrast, is the realisation that the divine self (*atman* or *purusha*) within the individual is identical with the impersonal absolute (*Brahman* or *Purusha*) and has nothing to do with material creation. She argues that Shiva's interpretation 'is only viable from the standpoint of Tantra, where the Goddess as *prakriti/shakti* is... identified with the highest spiritual principle, and there is, ultimately no dualism. Without this qualification, however, Shiva's praise of the *purusha/prakriti* doctrine is somewhat misleading' (1998, p. 105). It is within Tantra that various bodily techniques, including sexual, are utilised in order to realise the unity between the changing and creative feminine principle and the static godhead, the masculine principle (DasGupta Sherma, 1998; Pintchman, 1994, p. 108ff).

Thus, critics argue that Shiva's interpretation of Hinduism reflects contemporary environmentalist thinking, and although these ideas exist within the Hindu tradition, they are being reinvented as *the* conception of the relationship between the divine, nature and humanity rather than just *one* conception. Furthermore, even within Tantrism, the idea of the interconnectedness of humanity, nature and the divine does not imply environmental values or that people in the past were environmentally aware. It is interesting, moreover, that Shiva talks about her interpretation of Hinduism as 'Indian' cosmology, thereby obscuring the contribution of other forms of religiocultural tradition within the subcontinent. The cautious attitude that many commentators in India show towards religious environmentalism, because of its parallels to *Hindutva* ('Hinduness') rhetoric, would suggest that in the current climate it is important for Hindu inspired activists and writers to careful modify their use of language and symbols. Thus, it is argued that Shiva's interpretation of traditional 'Indian' ecological consciousness tells us more about her positionality than whether or not Hinduism is (or ever has been) environmentally friendly. In particular, she wishes to draw a distinction between western Christian influenced views about nature, where there is a distinction between the person and nature, and a 'traditional' Indian cosmology where nature and the person are considered as intimately connected and infused with divinity. This forms part of a broader critique of British colonialism in India and modern processes of globalisation/ westernisation as causing India's environmental problems. For Shiva the 'death of the feminine principle' is equated with 'maldevelopment', particularly the introduction of western modes of development into the 'Third World'. Many ecofeminists, thus, re-evaluate what they see as a 'myth of patriarchal progress' and instead envisage a 'return' to small-scale, agricultural communities which worship the Earth Goddess and where women's 'natural' inclination to work with nature rather than against it is permitted to flourish. This anti-colonial discourse is a strong theme within Indian environmentalism (see, for example, Gadgil and Guha, 1993) but has been criticised for limiting debate and over-simplifying complex historical processes and events (Grove, 1998b). However, the 'Hindu civilizational' response of Shiva and other middle-class writers and activists in India has also been influenced by deep ecological, ecocentric and *Romantic*-inspired ideas of nature that (although now globalised and reflecting the sociopolitical context of different locations) have their origin in the West.

To return to the specific example of ecofeminism, it is also important to consider the social implications of this restricted and partial representation of women's interaction with their environment. As Leach writes, these images of women as natural environmentalists have influenced and informed developmental policy and practice:

> The woman head-loading firewood across a barren landscape has become an environment and development icon. Reproduced in policy reports, NGO glossies and academic books alike, her image encapsulates powerful and appealing messages... These material dimensions were bolstered by fables about women's natural, cultural or ideological closeness to nature; varieties of Earth Mother myth which could be, and were, used to justify women's roles, as well as to give cultural and political appeal to the notion of global environmental sisterhoods (2007, p. 67; Dankelman and Davidson, 1988; Rodda, 1991).

However, women have not only been represented in a particular way, but this representation has informed policy and practice. Leach suggests that, from the 1980s to the mid-1990s, development donors and NGOs came to see women as allies in natural resource management. Jackson (1993) discusses the emergence of an emphasis upon women-centred environmental/conservation projects, which tended to accept traditional gender roles as natural and rarely involved women in decision-making processes. Popular initiatives have included social forestry, agroforestry, soil and water conservation projects, fuel-efficient stoves and solar cookers. However, as Jackson (1994) points out, these projects tend to treat women's time and labour as flexible and inexhaustible and often just add to their other tasks. Fuel-efficient stoves, for instance, may create more work for women as they need tending and are unsafe for small children (Jackson, 1994, p. 119). Moreover, there is an assumption that women are naturally in favour of 'sustainable development', when women in many cases have benefited from the 'green revolution'.

While Leach considers that such myths are receding, it is no longer *de rigueur* to depict women as natural carers, this view has permeated development thinking to such a large degree that it is still evident in policy and programmes to this day. For instance, UNEP's manual 'Women and Environment' (2004) promotes the tapping of women's and local people's productivist and participatory potentials to ensure efficient and supposedly sustainable use of resources (see also Mosse, 2003). Although this type of development discourse does not directly invoke the religious/spiritual symbolism that underpins such 'cultural' ecofeminism, it is uncritical about the extent to which portrayals of poor women as having shared concerns about 'sustainable' resources, for which they are inherently inclined to collectively mobilise or co-operate, are myth or fact. However, the virtual normalisation of the notion of women as natural carers is arguably a product of the cultural ecofeminist tendency to embed this blatant biological determinism within (vague and decontextualised interpretations of) eastern or Pagan religiocultural traditions. 'New traditionalist discourse' tends to homogenise communities and to ignore the ways in which caste, gender or ethnicity might actually inform people's use of natural resources as well as their interaction with modernity. It assumes an inherent desire on the part of poor rural communities (particularly women) to remain 'close to nature' rather than to participate in modernity: this is arguably a reflection of a bourgeois positionality. The struggles that poor communities face do involve a negotiation of the inequalities inherent within modernity, yet in opposing aspects of modernity their causes can risk being captured by new traditionalist discourse (see the discussion of the 'Chipko Movement' below).

The above discussion has presented some critiques of western 'ecocentric', *Romantic*-inspired environmentalism as not only inappropriate for but also as damaging to India. While it is argued that this style of environmentalism has its roots in the West, commentators also identify it amongst the elite in countries such as India: an elite which is relatively materially prosperous and which has been exposed to the language and culture of global environmentalism. For instance, as Baviskar writes, 'bourgeois environmentalism has emerged as an organised force in Delhi, and upperclass concerns around aesthetics, leisure, safety, and health have come significantly to shape the disposition of urban spaces' (Baviskar, 2003, p. 90). This would seem to suggest also, therefore, that religious environmentalism in India is also a predominantly 'middle class' phenomenon. If religious environmentalism is a middle class phenomenon in India then what role does religion play in the environmentalism of the lower classes, the urban poor and rural peasantry?

**Revisiting the Postmaterialism Thesis**

Inglehart (1995), and others, have applied the 'postmaterialism thesis' to explain the rise in environmental awareness, particularly within western societies since the 1960s. The postmaterialism thesis states that economic growth since the Second World War led to the satisfaction of people's basic material needs and that they then began to turn their attention to the pursuit of various postmaterialist leisure activities and the adoption of values that were directed towards improving the quality of life. This has included the desire for a clean and healthy environment, and the ideal of an unspoilt and natural environment. Inglehart suggests that individuals who experience material security during childhood become socialised to respond to postmaterialist values, and that they do not then adopt materialist values even if they experience a reversal of fortunes. Thus, during periods of widespread economic depression, large sections of western society would continue to hold postmaterialist values. Therefore, whilst external environmental factors have played a part in the rise of the contemporary environmental movement, it is argued that the way in which concern for the environment was expressed has been mediated by this transformation in people's attitudes.

A number of authors have argued that the isolation of postmaterialist values as the most significant variable in determining environmental concern ignores the importance of other factors. Cotgrove points out that environmentalists are more likely to come from backgrounds where parents are employed outside the market sector in jobs such as teaching, social work or medicine (1982, p. 52). He argues that individuals who are socialised within such an environment are more likely to challenge the dominant structures of industrial society. This suggests a social as well as an economic explanation for environmentalism. Individuals, who come from backgrounds where either they or their parents pursue professions on the periphery of the major institutions which support the market, are more likely to be able to identify and present a critique of the dominant structures of contemporary society. Similarly, Eckersley argues that 'Inglehart's thesis can at best provide only a partial account since it pays little heed (apart from material security) to the objective environment in which such values were formed' (1989, p. 219). She argues instead that

> new technologies (nuclear, genetic, chemical), the international communications revolution (computers and television), the considerable expansion in higher education, and the growth in our biological and ecological knowledge and understanding...have not only helped to produce new information about our social and physical environment, but have also helped shift social perceptions of old issues (1989, p. 221).

Explanations for the adoption of environmental values clearly require a more sophisticated rationale than economics alone. My aim in the remainder of this section is to examine a further critique of Inglehart's application of the postmaterialist thesis to account for environmentalism. Inglehart's thesis suggests that as poorer nations develop, more affluent members are likely to express postmaterialist values. This would seem to fit with evidence from India, where we increasingly find, for example, advertisements for holiday destinations in 'natural' environments or accommodation complexes which boast 'natural' surroundings, the proliferation of 'health food' shops or environmentally friendly consumer items, and recycling projects in middle-class neighbourhoods: or a 'bourgeois environmentalism'. This would seem to indicate that the more affluent sectors of society are expressing environmental concerns as a product of postmaterialist values. However, the postmaterialism thesis has been criticised because it implies that only postmaterialists are environmentalists. As Brechin and Kempton point out

> Among the most potent manifestations of environmental concern among the citizens of the poorer, developing nations has been the explosive rise and activities of local environmental groups and actions...There are the well-known cases such as the Chipko movement in India where village women stopped loggers from cutting down nearby forests upon which they depended (1994, p. 247).

They draw upon findings from two surveys,[2] which suggest that people in developing countries are concerned about both local and global environmental issues. They conclude that the information provided by these two surveys indicate that 'concern for the environment is not valued only by wealthy nations. Most convincing are the high rankings by most countries, and the lack of any statistically significant differences for global environmental concerns such as global warming, loss of biodiversity, and destruction of the ozone layer. From these data we would conclude that concern for the environment has become a global phenomenon' (1994, p. 253).

In the remainder of this section, I will suggest that the arguments put forward by both Inglehart and Brechin and Kempton have validity and are useful in understanding the ways in which environmentalism has become a global phenomenon. Inglehart's thesis does not deny that 'materialists' are environmentalists, but instead it is useful in indicating that materialists and postmaterialists are likely to be concerned about the environment for different reasons and in different ways. As Inglehart writes

> Postmaterialist goals are certainly not the only factor motivating concern for the quality of the environment. In a setting in which air and water pollution posed a direct threat to one's health and survival, this concern by itself leads people to take an active interest in the environment. But in advanced industrial societies where the immediate threat to one's survival has been receding rather than advancing, a simple stimulus-response model of this kind is less plausible. Increasingly, environmental concern may be motivated by concern for the quality of life, rather than by survival needs (1995, p. 64).

This distinction between 'quality of life' and 'survival needs' as motivating factors can be seen as indicating different sources of environmental concern.

---

[2]  The first was carried out by Louis Harris and Associates between 1988 and 1989 in sixteen countries. The second was a Gallup survey in 1992, which investigated environmental concerns in 22 countries (Brechin and Kempton, 1994).

A number of scholars have 'argued that ecological concern and activism in developing countries has emerged from a different source than in the more economically secure developed countries' (Brechin and Kempton, 1994, p. 261). For example, Martinez-Alier and Hershberg (1992) viewed environmental protests by poor and rural peoples as emerging from '(1) defending traditional methods of resource management; (2) preserving local control over and access to essential resources; (3) fighting to maintain more ecologically sound resource use patterns; or (4) experiencing a deterioration of living conditions' (Brechin and Kempton, 1994, p. 262). Guha and Martinez-Alier make a further distinction between the 'full-stomach' environmentalism of the North and the 'empty-belly environmentalism' of the South (1997, p. xxi), arguing that there are 'many varieties of environmentalism' and it is possible to show 'with reference to different individuals, communities and nations, which variety attracts and which repels' (1997, p. xx). They suggest that 'environmental movements in the North have...been convincingly related to the emergence of a post-materialist or post-industrial society' (1997, p. 16). The irony is that postmaterialists are more likely to live within a context where the effects of environmental degradation are less serious, or have less direct impact upon their lives, but at the same time they are more likely to respond to environmental issues.

Quoting Huxley's essay 'Wordsworth in the Tropics', Guha and Martinez-Alier note that

> Huxley deems it a pity that Wordsworth himself 'never travelled beyond the boundaries of Europe'. For a 'voyage through the tropics would have cured him of his too easy and comfortable pantheism. A few months in the jungle would have convinced him that the diversity and utter strangeness of nature are at least as real and significant as its intellectually discovered unity' (1997, p. xi).

Thus, Huxley considers that this type of romanticisation of nature could only emerge in benign climates and geographical regions, where nature had been subdued and controlled by humanity. Similarly, they quote the social historian G.M. Trevelyan, writing in 1931, who expressed this difference as follows:

> Modern Aesthetic taste for mountain form, is connected with a moral and intellectual change, that differentiates modern civilized man [*sic*] from civilized man in all previous ages. I think that he now feels the desire and need for the wildness and greatness of untamed, aboriginal nature, which his predecessors did not feel. One cause of this change is the victory that civilized man has now attained over nature through science, machinery and organization, a victory so complete that he is denaturalizing the lowland landscape. He is therefore constrained to seek nature in her still unconquered citadels, the mountains (cited in Guha and Martinez-Alier, 1997 pp. xii–xiii).

Thus, once humanity has become 'separated' from nature, in terms of no longer directly relying upon it for basic needs, or has managed to control/tame it, only then is it possible to sit back and reflect upon wishing to return to nature. This is a strong theme within ecocentric environmentalism. Additionally, the freedom that the materially secure enjoy from the vagaries of nature makes it possible to consider and respond to more abstract ethical issues that do not directly affect them. By contrast, 'nature-based conflicts...are at the root of the environmental movement in countries such as India...They are played out against a backdrop of visible ecological degradation, the drying up of springs, the decimation of forests, the erosion of the land' (1997, p. 17).

Thus, what I am suggesting is that although ecocentric environmentalism (in both its radical and less radical manifestations) is a postmaterialist phenomenon, which emerged within the new social movements of the 1960s, not all environmentalist activity is of this type. This explanatory model does not capture totality of environmental activity. Moreover, social action or mobilisation for environmental reasons is not modern: struggles over land rights or political activism to mitigate the consequences of environmental change are nothing new. Not all environmentalism takes place in postindustrial or postmaterialist context: on the one hand many environmentalist struggles do show a link with the aims and strategies of 'old' social movements (they can be class based, are directed towards political ends etc.). However, what is substantively 'new' about modern environmentalism is its strong ideological and identity component: there is a strong moral content that transcends material aspects (it is *more* ecocentric than anthropocentric). This is not to say that expressive or postmaterialist environmentalism does not have a material dimension but that this is more-or-less trumped by a moral vision about how one should treat an ethicalised nature.

Thus, what is new, and what is found in modern social movements, is a qualitatively different type of environmentalism that is concerned with global inclusive humanity, with expressive values and with quality of life. This should not lead us to claim, however, that premodern or contemporary 'subaltern' struggles over natural resources or with respect to environmental problems can only be explained by material, survival-based concerns. Issues of identity, morality, local culture or religious affiliation do become drawn into such environmentalisms. It would be incoherent to claim that because people are poor they are *only* motivated by material factors and that culture, religion, ethics or identity concerns are secondary or essentially unimportant. Moreover, the picture has been become more complex since 'historically marginalized communities have begun to recognize the political potency of strategically deployed essentialisms' (Brosius 1999, p. 281), such as various expressions of the 'new traditionalist discourse'. However, I am suggesting that in order to understand religious environmentalism and its potential as a global ecopolitical tool, it is necessary to make the methodological distinction between different types of environmentalism. In many places they overlap, yet there are distinct features.

## Indian Environmentalisms

My aim in this section is to look more closely at evidence for the diversity of styles of environmentalism in India and to begin to sketch out a framework for understanding the case studies presented later in the book. The above discussion suggests the existence of a style of environmentalism that does not fit either of the environmentalist paradigms I have identified as being prominent within 'western' environmentalism: the *managerial* approach and the *Romantic* approach. It is not really a response to conserve resources for the sake of global economic expansion or concern about the consequences of destroying the global environment. Neither is it to be characterised as a response to preserve the natural environment for its intrinsic aesthetic and moral qualities. Instead, we have a third approach, what I will call the *local pragmatic* response, that is concerned with the destruction of the environment from a perspective of basic survival, rights over access to resources and concerns about health and disease, for example, caused by pollution. This style of environmentalism, I argue, shares more in common with older social movements than the NSMs discussed above. While all three styles are found across the globe, evidence suggests that the 'empty belly' environmentalism of the south is more likely to be of the *local pragmatic* type. This is not to ignore or deny overlap between the different styles, but instead to make an important methodological point with respect to our understanding of the ability of religious environmentalism to 'cross borders'. What I am suggesting is that religious environmentalism is predominantly an orientation towards nature that is postmaterialist and *Romantic*. In this book I am interested in investigating the role that religion might play in *local pragmatic* environmentalism, since I do not see evidence of the relevance of *Romantic* religious environmentalism within much of the environmental movement in India.

Hannigan suggests that claims about the environment make use of two main rhetorical tactics 'which vary according to the nature of the target audience' (1995, p. 35). The first of these is the 'rhetoric of rectitude', which 'justifies consideration of environmental problems on strictly moral grounds' (1995, p. 47) and the 'rhetoric of rationality', where 'ratifying a claim will earn the audience some type of concrete benefits' (1995, p. 36). As I will discuss below, the 'ideological' rhetorical device is less often used in India by NGOs, for instance, to encourage environmental concern and changes in behaviour, whereas it is quite common in the UK. While not all UK environmental rhetoric is ideological, however, groups such as Friends of the Earth or Greenpeace do routinely employ moral language to express the notion of responsibility to future generations or the idea that the extinction of species is an ethical issue. This would seem to indicate the presence of different audiences likely to respond to different types of environmentalist message. In India the environmental message is more often couched in terms of *what you have to gain materially if you change your behaviour* whereas in the postmaterialist contexts it is *what you have to lose morally if you don't.*

This difference in approach is also related to the extent of available knowledge about this way of articulating environmental issues. Knowledge about global environmental issues is limited amongst the majority of the Indian population because of the lack of practical access to such ideas, for example via the mass media (Chapman et al., 1997). Hence, the means to articulate problems in this way and to be understood by the public is limited. It is more appropriate to express these issues in terms of their local relevance. It is by no means the case that global environmental rhetoric is absent from all articulations of India's environmental problems. India's environmental movement is diverse, and is made up of groups and individuals from different social and economic backgrounds, who may have competing interests and articulate their concerns according to their particular situation or knowledge (Gadgil and Guha, 1995). We do find global concepts within environmental writing in India, particularly in English language publications. Whilst these form part of the understanding of environmental issues amongst the better educated, middle class intelligentsia, in their written form, they are unavailable to the majority of the population. Environmentalists, to whom I have spoken, do not deliberately avoid the use of global environmental language, and endeavour to educate people about issues, such as global warming. However, the overall approach of environmental education pulls more in the direction of local and short-term benefits to communities rather than the global or long-term consequences.

Gadgil and Guha analyse India's population and its relationship to the environment in terms of three categories. They point out that four-fifths of India's population are 'eco-system people', India's rural people; one-third are 'ecological-refugees', for example, migrants or farm labourers who can no longer make a living from their land; and one-sixth are 'omnivores', big land owners, entrepreneurs or urban workers (1995, pp. 4–5). They argue that the irony is that the smallest sector, the omnivores, both consume most resources and benefit most from economic development, whereas the other sectors are the casualties of modern progress. They suggest that the omnivores are more likely to support and benefit from 'environmentalist' initiatives, such as the creation of national parks for recreational purposes, whereas the other sectors may be seriously disadvantaged (1995, p. 94). Therefore, for Gadgil and Guha, both the *global managerial* and the *Romantic* approach to environmentalism are more likely to be adopted by the omnivore.

As discussed, with reference to Baviskar's work, there has arisen a *Romantic* or bourgeois wing within the Indian environmental movement. In contrast to the peasant struggles, this wing tends to be motivated by ideologies beyond those which may concern the majority of 'eco-system people' or 'ecological refugees', either because they are not seen to be relevant or they do not have access to the ideas behind them. They are often the domain of an elite, educated group of social activists. As Baviskar (1997) reveals, such individuals often have a romantic image that sustainable development means that rural people should remain close to nature, rather than pursuing alternative sources of income. In particular, this style of environmentalism draws heavily upon the teachings and example of Mahatma

Gandhi. Guha calls this type of environmentalist, the 'crusading Gandhian' (1988). Gadgil and Guha write that 'it relies heavily on a moral/religious viewpoint in its rejection of the modern way of life...Crusading Gandhians argue that the essence of 'Eastern' cultures is their indifference to, even hostility, to economic gain' (1995, p. 107). Following Gandhi, they argue that India should retain its village culture of sustainable dependency upon the land and forests. They uphold a vision of a return to precolonial village communities as a reaction against the ills created by western forms of development and 'frequently cite Hindu scriptures as exemplifying a "traditional" reverence for nature and lifeforms' (1995, p.107). However, was Gandhi an environmentalist?

*Was Gandhi an Environmentalist?*

A strong theme within Indian environmentalist is the recourse to antecedent movements and traditions: many environmentalists turn to the example of Gandhi and 'traditional' Indian values to support contemporary environmentalist thinking. Whilst Guha points out that 'Mahatma Gandhi provides the environmental movement with both a vocabulary of protest and an ideological critique of development in independent India' (Guha and Martinez-Alier, 1997, p. 15), he is careful not to say that Gandhi was an environmentalist *per se*, but to stress that he has provided resources which contemporary environmentalists use. By contrast, many environmentalists in India uncritically consider that Gandhi was an environmentalist. As Khoshoo argues, 'the importance of Gandhi*ji* lies in the fact that he talked in his lifetime about many of the foregoing issues now being discussed under environment. He was no doubt a profound environmentalist, like Mahatma Buddha and Ashoka the Great' (1995, p. 14). The ecologising of Gandhi closely mirrors the way in which religious traditions have been reinterpreted in order to reflect environmental concerns. As discussed at the end of Chapter 3, whilst simple living was a central feature of Gandhi's vision, he was first and foremost a social reformer. Human rights came before ideologies about nature. By contrast, the environmentalists who have appropriated Gandhi's message, for example, Baviskar's well-meaning middle class activists, hold an environmentalist ideology that was absent from Gandhi's teachings. As Guha argues, Gandhi did not show any high esteem for the wilderness, a strong theme within contemporary *Romantic* environmentalism; 'there was nothing of the romantic in Gandhi' (Guha and Martinez-Alier, 1997, p. 167). His emphasis was firmly upon improving the practical village scenario. However, as Guha suggests, these ideas within Indian environmentalism owe their origins to the West, in particular to deep ecology (1997). Thus, whilst *Romantics* are drawn to Gandhi, and indeed Gandhi was drawn to the Romantic literature of Ruskin, in particular, there is little to indicate that he drew a sharp dichotomy between the urban and the wild. His focus was upon the village and the countryside and not the urban areas, which are so central to any evaluation of India's environmental situation today.

Gandhi drew a more crucial distinction between the colonial and the indigenous, which shapes his attitude towards the natural environment, rather than the distinction between the urban and the wild. One of the central elements to the abiding appeal of Mahatma Gandhi within Indian environmentalism is his condemnation of colonial rule. As one activist states:

> Our forefathers who fought to get rid of the foreign yoke thought that our country would become a land of milk and honey once the British were driven out. But now we see our rulers joining hands with the monopolists to take away basic resources like land, water and forests from the (village) people who have traditionally used them for their livelihood (cited in Guha and Martinez-Alier, 1997, p. 15).

Another dichotomy that is used by Gandhian environmentalists is between Gandhi and Nehru. Nehru, India's first prime minister following independence, is criticised for having ignored Gandhi's vision for independent India, which was based upon the village economy. Instead, Nehru took the path of state interventionist economic development. Many environmentalists blame this route for India's environmental problems. However, as Guha points out, this demonisation of Nehru is more a reflection of a contemporary need to account for India's environmental problems. He points out that both men were influenced by western ideas, Gandhi by Ruskin and Tolstoy, for example, and Nehru, by the 'statist, modernising tradition of the British Fabians and the Russian Marxists' (Guha 1997, p. 163). He also argues that both men aimed to implement their ideas to reduce poverty. Guha argues that Nehru in no way reflects the contemporary environmentalist's criticism of him that he sought to expand India's economy at the expense of the poor underclass, rather he was convinced that their improvement 'could be achieved only through rapid industrialisation and the use of modern technology' (Guha, 1997, p. 164). It is only with hindsight, now that an environmentalist discourse exists which challenges and rejects industrialisation, that Nehru is cast in an uncertain light. In fact, Guha argues that at times Nehru expressed an almost mystical and spiritual affiliation to India's natural environment, which was virtually absent from Gandhi's writings (Guha, 1997, p. 167).

However, as Guha points out 'the urge to demonise Nehru comes from a 'cowboys and Indians' vision of history, in which the world is divided into good and bad guys' (1997, p. 166). Such 'black and white' accounts of history are frequently encountered within the construction and expression of ideology, where certain assumptions underlie the narratives used to legitimate ways of seeing the world and approaching social problems. The assumption that Gandhi was an environmentalist tends to go hand-in-hand with the assumption that contemporary environmentalism is Gandhian. Undoubtedly the most significant instance of this type of 'myth' making surrounds the interpretation of the Chipko movement in India. What began as an isolated and pragmatic response to tree-felling in a region of the Himalayas, has come to be seen as India's primary example of both environmental action and the implementation of Gandhian principles. Gandhian institutions see Chipko as a modern example of *satya graha*, the term used to describe Gandhi's non-violent direct action. However, as Guha argues, 'in so far as the personal commitment and personal lifestyle of activists like Bhatt and Bahuguna[3] exemplify the highest traditions of Gandhian constructive work, the characterization is not altogether incorrect' (1994, p. 176). Nevertheless, 'at the level of popular participation the Gandhian label is…less appropriate' (1994, p. 176). He argues that the role played by external ideologies is limited. Chipko was a fight for basic subsistence, 'its 'non-violent' method being an inspired and highly original response to forest felling rather than ideologically motivated' (1994, p. 176). Thus, it is important to distinguish between the 'private' and the 'public' face of Chipko.

*The Chipko Myth*

In March 1973, agents of a sports equipment company, the 'Simon Company', based in Allahabad, came to supervise the felling of trees in Chamoli district, Uttarakhand, in the Himalayas. Ash trees from a state controlled forest had been allocated to them, for making cricket bats, by the State Forest Department. This decision denied the local community its supply of Ash trees, which they used to make agricultural implements. On 27 March, local people decided to *chipko* (to hug) the trees to physically prevent them being cut down. This collective, non-violent action by a determined local community was successful, and the permit to axe the trees was reversed without any felling actually taking place. Thus, the 'Chipko Andolan' was born. This pattern of resistance was repeated throughout the region and prevented other damage to the forests. For example, in one of the most often repeated stories it was the women who came to the rescue. In January 1974, almost two and a half thousand trees in the Reni forest, overlooking the Alakhnanda River, were auctioned. On the day of the felling all the men of the villages had been called away. The contractor's labourers were seen by a small girl who informed the leader of the women's circle, Gaura Devi. She rallied together a group of 27 women and girls and together they halted the axemen until the men returned, thus saving their forest (Weber, 1989).

The Chipko story has been reinterpreted and retold, not only by key figures who were involved, such as Sunderlal Bahuguna and Chandi Prasad Bhatt (Guha 1994, pp. 182–3), but also by other writers and activists within India (eg. Guha, 1990; Gadgil and Guha, 1993; 1995; Shiva, 1988). As Sinha et al. point out the most

---

[3]   Two of the primary figures in the Chipko movement actively drew upon the ideas of Gandhi, although in different ways and with different effects. Chandi Prasad Bhatt stressed the need for local, small-scale forest based industry, whereas Sunderlal Bahuguna emphasised the moral quality of Gandhi's teaching, urging the individual to eschew consumerism and to live a simple life. These differences are often considered to represent a rift within the movement (Weber, 1989).

ardent romantic regarding Chipko is the India ecofeminist, Vandana Shiva, who, in particular, argues that Indian women are the natural conservators of ecological harmony, and the worst hit by its destruction (1988). However, they suggest that women's relationship to nature is dictated more by 'needs' and 'responsibilities' rather than care for nature *per se*, and that women do not necessarily perceive this relationship as natural or fulfilling as Shiva would suggest (1997, p. 79; Jackson, 1995). By contrast, Guha takes a more historical approach than Shiva, pointing out that 'it seems clear from the description of different Chipko agitations that the role played by external ideologies is a severely limited one. Villagers see Chipko as a fight for basic subsistence denied to them by the institutions and policies of the state' (1994, p. 176).

Sinha et al. argue that Chipko has come to be used as an example of a 'civilizational response' to India's contemporary ecological crisis and the Himalayas have provided a model that 'new traditionalists' employ as a basis for human-nature relations throughout Indian history. Chipko has become an icon of the Indian environmental movement, both at home and abroad, an exemplar of local people fighting to preserve their natural environment and cultural traditions. The local people are depicted as genuine environmentalists whose religious and cultural traditions have contributed towards maintaining a harmonious relationship with their natural environment. However, as Sinha et al. argue, 'Chipko's central theme was not that forests should be left alone because they are holy, but that they should be used for local needs' (1997, p. 85). In reality, Chipko had a mixed political agenda, it was not ideologically homogeneous, it was 'less an articulation of uncontaminated traditional ecological values than of contemporary concerns for social justice and political democracy' (1997, p. 84). The Chipko myth has tended to simplify the Indian ecological situation, the narratives that are employed 'cannot sufficiently account for the kind and scope of environmental transformations which have occurred in the subcontinent over the past few centuries, nor provide an acceptable alternative for the future' (1997, p. 68).

The narrative structure of the Chipko story is enhanced by locating it further back in history, in the retelling of the story of a Bishnoi woman, Amrita Devi, who in 1731 laid down her life to protect a grove of Khejadi trees, which were sacred to her community as well as of great practical value to the local people. The Bishnoi sect was founded in 1485 in the Rajasthan desert and there are many stories of members sacrificing their lives to protect trees that were an essential resource to a desert community. Amrita Devi is said to have hugged the first tree marked for felling and came to her death as she was cut through with an axe. Her bravery stimulated widespread response from surrounding villages and hundreds of people resisted, many losing their lives. The Maharaja of Jodhpur, who had ordered the felling, heard that 363 villagers had been murdered and retracted his mission. Similarly, the non-violent nature of direct action in the Chipko movement is traced to Mahatma Gandhi and even further back to the Harappan age.[4] As Pereira and Seabrook write, 'the doctrine of *ahimsa*,[5] though first propounded by the Jains, is thought to have origins in Harappan civilisation. This appears to be confirmed by the fact that no weapons have been found in Harappan excavations' (1990, p. 143). This alone is hardly evidence to conclude that the Indus Valley civilisations were peaceful.

This simplified account of both ancient and more recent Indian history has provided the content of the Chipko myth, where the movement has become disembedded from the boundaries of geography and history. As Barthes writes

> myth acts economically, it abolishes the complexity of human acts, it gives them the simplicity of essences, it does away with all dialectics, with any going back beyond what is immediately visible, it organises a world which is without contradictions because it is without depth, a world wide open and wallowing in the evident, it establishes a blissful clarity: things appear to mean something in themselves (1972, p. 143).

Sinha et al. define this as the 'new traditionalist discourse', whereby traditional or precolonial Indian society is portrayed as 'marked by harmonious social relationships, ecologically sensitive resource use practices' and as 'generally far less burdened by the gender, economic and environmental exploitation which concern contemporary observers' (1997, p. 67; see also Mawdsley 1998). New traditionalists blame the colonial government for having imposed an alien set of economic, social and ecological relationships upon India which subsequent Indian governments have done little to rectify (Banuri and Marglin, 1993; Pereria and Seabrook, 1990). Sinha et al. argue that, 'social movements, specifically the Chipko movement, are represented in this discourse as popular initiatives to repudiate modernity and recover tradition' (1997, p. 67).

## Conclusion

This chapter has argued that environmentalism is a product of social or cultural factors as well as a response to environmental change. While the types of environmentalism found within the West tend to be global in focus (but not necessarily in relevance), they rely upon a particular socially constructed idea of nature, of an environment *out there* that ought to be protected for its own sake. In India, by contrast, the fact that for the majority of the population the natural environment is something upon which they are dependent for their basic survival, this influences the priority given to environmental concerns

---

[4]   Harappa is one of the sites in North India which has revealed archaeological remains of the Indus Valley Civilisation, dating from around 2300 BC until 1700 BC.

[5]   *Ahimsa* is the Sanskrit term for non-violence or non-harm.

and the types of problems that are identified as significant. In many cases, the identification and articulation of environmental problems is more likely to be local and related to survival issues than global and related to the fact that the Earth ought to be protected. Whilst this distinction is important it is not absolute. On the one hand, what has been called 'western' environmentalism is also found in non-western contexts (it is globalised). On the other hand, 'western' religious environmentalism routinely draws upon non-western religiocultural traditions. The boundaries between western and non-western become blurred, and it would seem to be inappropriate, therefore, to rely too heavily upon such a distinction, particularly under conditions of globalisation. However, while globalisation certainly can create less distinct cultural identities, it can also mask cultural distinctiveness and the socially constructed nature of much human social action.

The following chapters of this book move on to look at case studies of religious environmentalism and have two main aims. The first aim is to show how the narratives used by religious environmentalists are typically based upon two assumptions: that ancient traditions of nature religion are intrinsically environmentalist and that an 'ecogolden age' existed at some time in the past, or still exists, within preindustrial communities. The second aim of the fieldwork-based chapters is to establish whether or not religious environmentalist narratives have a limited relevance within an Indian context. These two religious environmentalist assumptions are closely related but are different. The first makes an assumption about the nature of religious traditions, as being environmentally friendly, whereas the second makes an assumption about the nature of preindustrial communities, as living in harmony with nature because of their religious traditions. It is implied that communities practicing nature religion hold deep environmental wisdom and this conclusion appears to be reinforced by the fact that many such communities are preindustrial and exhibit lifestyles that have a minimum impact upon the natural environment.

*The Religious Environmentalist Assumptions and their Relevance for India*

*The first assumption*   Religious environmentalists find support for the first assumption (that religious traditions are intrinsically environmentally friendly) by searching for environmental teachings within religiocultural traditions. For example, in India, tree worship, and hence environmental protection, is frequently traced back to the Indus valley Civilisation. Archaeologists in the first half of the twentieth century found remains of a complex and sophisticated civilisation which had flourished in north west India from about 2500–1700 B.C., before the dawning of the Vedic period. Steatite, soapstone seals were excavated which have been interpreted as depicting tree worship (Chandrakanth and Romm, 1991). For example, in one seal from Mohenjo-daro we can see what is probably a kneeling man offering a goat to a figure in a tree; possibly a tree deity or spirit. A similar scene is found on another seal where this time the offering could be a ram or, as Fairservis suggests, a painted bull (1971). However, the use of this to argue for the environmentalist credentials of the Indus Valley culture may well say more about the agenda of the environmentalist than the nature of the tradition. Pederson argues that claims about the environmental nature of religion are 'anachronistic projections of modern phenomena onto the screen of tradition' (1995, p. 264), that they are subjective interpretations of the particular tradition, of its written texts or folk practices. Similarly, Freeman argues, in response to the idea that the protection of the biodiversity within sacred groves in India is evidence of environmentalism, that 'cultural values are being imputed to populations not on the evidence of their actually espousing and expressing those values, but on the basis of inferring that they must hold some such values and beliefs from the requirements of the analyst's own ecological model' (1994, pp. 7–8).

There is an assumption that religious beliefs and practices, which result in the protection of elements of the natural world, originated in and reflect a broader ecological worldview that is shared by all preindustrial cultures. However, I suggest three reasons why members of traditional cultures, who sacralise or personify elements of the natural world, are not religious environmentalists. Firstly, it can be argued that the protection of certain patches of forest in India as sacred groves, for example, was out of respect for the resident deity rather than a reflection of an ecological consciousness (Freeman, 1997). They were preserved for religious rather than environmental reasons. Although the preservation of sacred groves in India has retained large areas of biodiversity, such groves were protected because of the presence of the deity rather than because of a concern to conserve the natural environment (I return to this in Chapter 7). At the risk of sounding overly broad, however, in important ways, this reflects a difference in emphasis where *it is sacred therefore it should be protected* rather than the contemporary religious environmentalist position which is *it should be protected therefore it is sacred*.

Secondly, traditional and environmentalist cultures can also have very different ideas of what respect for the environment means. For example, the Cree hunters of Quebec consider that all natural phenomena are 'enspirited', possessing a 'consciousness, reason, and volition, no less intense and complete than a human being's' (Callicott, 1982, p. 305). Whereas for the contemporary religious environmentalist this might call for a moratorium on hunting, the Cree recognise the moral integrity of their prey by presenting it with gifts, but consider it to give its life in return. As Milton writes 'the Cree and the animals they hunt belong to a single moral community whose members recognize and fulfil obligations towards each other' (1996, p. 127). This brings us to the third point, that it is only a contemporary religious environmentalist worldview that casts a sacred and protective canopy over *nature as a whole*. Thus, a religious worldview that involves practices associated with nature does not necessarily reflect an environmentalist worldview. Whilst in India, for example, it is common to protect particular species of plants and trees which are sacred and associated with particular deities, there is little indication that this worship and protection of sacred species is automatically extended to all of nature. Sinha et al. question the fact that 'within this pristine consciousness, the worship of specific trees is understood as leading to a general reverence for forests, in turn leading to an even broader reverence for nature' (1997, p. 71).

*The second assumption*    The second assumption that tends to be made by religious environmentalists involves the belief in an 'ecogolden age'. It maintains that preindustrial people lived in harmony with their natural surroundings, that they lived a simple and natural life whereby an ecological balance was maintained. Milton explores the legitimacy of what she calls this 'myth of primitive ecological wisdom' (1996, p. 31), 'the environmentalist myth that non-industrial cultures are ecologically benign' (1996, p. 107). She concludes that

> non-industrial peoples do not think like environmentalists. Some of them may live their lives in ways that are environmentally sound, but ecological balance, where it exists, is an incidental consequence of human activities and other factors, rather than being an ideal or a goal that is actively pursued. In other words, the practices in which some non-industrial peoples engage may be environmentally benign, but their cultures, their ways of understanding the world, are not (1996, pp. 113–14).

Many religious environmentalists tend to idealise the lifestyle and values of non-industrial communities. There is an assumption that religiocultural values sustained the idea that nature was more than a resource and that this put limits upon the extent to which nature could be abused. However, as Pederson argues, 'if some people did not harm the environment, this need not imply they were motivated by a strong conservationist commitment. They could be – environmentally speaking – harmless creatures for quite other reasons that had nothing to do with values, but which related to demography and technology' (1995, p. 265).

Although environmental values can be derived from religious traditions this does not imply that the original intention of the tradition was consciously environmentalist or that people's behaviour was environmentally friendly. The relationship between values and behaviour is more complex. Firstly, expressed values are not necessarily an accurate guide to people's behaviour. This is because people 'lie' or because values can express the ideal of what ought to be rather than what is. Secondly, it cannot be assumed that if people's behaviour does at times result in the protection of nature that this is necessarily a result of environmental values. Thirdly, it is not easy to distinguish values from descriptive beliefs. A statement such as 'that particular tree is sacred' could be a descriptive belief rather than an expression of values; it is what is believed to be the case and has no implications for behaviour. There is, however, overwhelming evidence to suggest that in many cases the environmentalist interpretation of religious traditions is more a reflection of the contemporary environmentalist agenda than evidence of the preexistence of an ecological awareness (Freeman, 1994; Kalam, 1996; Pederson, 1995).

*Religious Environmentalist Discourse and Narrative*

Religious environmentalist discourse relies heavily upon a narrative style of communication where 'the very authority with which narrative presents its vision of reality is achieved by obscuring large parts of that reality, for example by "suppressing" or ignoring dissident voices' (Harre et al., 1999, p. 73). As Cronon argues, humans 'inhabit an endlessly storied world' (1992, p. 1368), in that the use of narrative is a fundamental way in which humans make sense of and articulate their experiences: 'we narrate the triumphs and failures of our pasts. We tell stories to explore the alternative choices that might lead to feared or hoped-for futures' (1992, p. 1368). Human beings tend to organise their experience into beginning, middle and end, and this is reflected within religious environmentalism. The beginning of the religious environmentalist narrative is the ecogolden age, the middle corresponds to the contemporary environmental crisis and the end is the future, which will only be secure once humanity transforms its relationship with the natural world. However, as Harre et al. point out this 'narrative aspect is usually taken for granted...therefore, the "taken-for-granted" existence of narrative can be easily seen as a "natural existence" [and] has attracted little critical attention until recently' (1999, p. 72).

This book considers that religious environmentalism is largely unaware of and uncritical towards its use of narrative and discourse. I am not suggesting that there exists some sort of 'screen of tradition' (Pederson, 1995, p. 264) upon which contemporary environmentalists are imposing their modern concerns. Whereas religious believers themselves are often reluctant to admit to innovation for reasons other than divine intervention or a desire to return to the 'original' message, in many ways the study of both historical and contemporary religion is the study of religious change. The period since the Industrial Revolution has seen immense changes in religiosity. From the lessening of the hold of the established church on the moral life of the West, to the emergence of new, eclectic styles of spirituality and the impact that globalisation has had upon the popularity of non-Christian traditions in the West. However, scholars of religion ought to be concerned not only with the influence of the social, economic or political context upon religious change but also the impact of such change upon global society.

Narratives are more than words that are constructed in order to entertain or inform. On the one hand, they reveal something about the worldview or attitudes of the narrator. On the other hand, they may create and legitimate ways of seeing the world which, when translated into action, have an effect upon the social and material conditions of people's lives. As Cronon writes

> Narrative succeeds to the extent that it hides the discontinuities, ellipses and contradictory experiences that would undermine the intended meaning of the story. Whatever its overt purpose, it cannot avoid a covert exercise of power: it inevitably sanctions some voices while silencing others. A powerful narrative

reconstructs common sense to make the contingent seem determined and the
artificial seem natural (1992, pp. 1349–50).

Thus, inherent within the construction and use of narrative is the risk of such stories
contributing towards the oppression of less powerful groups, either intentionally
or unintentionally.

However, the opposite can also be true: narrative both reflects and provides a
framework of explanation and meaning which may act as a source of liberation.
Chapter 5 describes how the religious environmentalist narratives are used within
the context of the environmental direct action movement in Britain. Whilst
the narratives used can be shown to 'misrepresent' religious attitudes towards
the natural world and to idealise and romanticise the lifestyles and values of
preindustrial communities, with the effect of suggesting that such people have
a desire to and ought to remain close to nature, they are also profound sources
of motivation and meaning to the individuals involved. They are the basis of the
religious environmentalist teleology.[6]

My primary reason for concentrating upon environmental direct action (EDA),
as a means for exemplifying the issues raised in Chapters 2–4, is because it has
arguably been the most visible form of environmental activity within Britain.
Unlike Germany, for instance, Britain has no strong party political support for
environmental issues and since the beginning of the 1990s various incidents of
environmental direct action have rarely been out of the news media for long. From
the 'roads protests' of the early part of the decade to the more recent assaults upon
genetically modified crops, environmental direct action has simultaneously aroused
the interest, support and suspicion of the British public. Furthermore, the direct
action movement has strong links with the new social movements of the 1960s
counterculture, which, as I suggested in this chapter, was largely responsible for
raising the profile of environmental issues to a popular, national level. Furthermore,
the style of religious environmentalism found within EDA in Britain closely
corresponds to the 'western' understandings of religion and the environment, which
I have discussed in Chapters 2–4. Activists tend to hold a *Romantic* view of the
natural world and consider that the role of religion is to support and facilitate a
transformation of the relationship between humanity and nature.

---

[6] There are other examples of religious environmentalism in Britain, which are not
discussed at any great length within this book: for example, the contribution of the Christian
Church to environmental discourse. However, whilst there are differences between the
approach of environmental direct activists and the response of traditional religious systems,
my research has indicated that they often make the same religious environmentalist
assumptions (Oelschlaeger (1994) deals at length with the responses of different branches
of the Christian Church).

# Chapter 5
# Religious Environmentalism and Environmental Direct Action in Britain

*[handwritten margin note: bureaucratic emotional regime]*

## Introduction: Radical Environmentalism in Britain

The previous two chapters have discussed the emergence of environmentalism as a form of public discourse and action. However, while concern about the human impact upon the natural world is the focus of different expressions of environmentalism, as we have seen, different approaches have emerged to this dilemma which can be classified into two types: the *managerial* (anthropocentric) and, what I am calling, the *Romantic* (ecocentric). Whereas the *managerial* approach is defined by its anthropocentrism and considers that the capitalistic use of natural resources can be effectively 'managed' to avoid ecological decline, the *Romantic* approach is more likely to demand a reorientation of human-nature relations in the form of environmentally sustainable lifestyles.

This chapter is concerned with the emergence of environmental direct action (EDA) in the UK during the 1990s as a radical form of environmental politics that calls for precisely this. Frustrated with the apathy of the political parties, regarding environmental issues, and the perception that the 'mainstream' environmental groups, such as Friends of the Earth or Greenpeace, did not fundamentally support the need for radical change (Doherty, 1999), groups of people across the country began to engage in direct action against perceived environmental risks such as road building, quarrying and housing projects (Anderson, 2002; 2004a; 2004b; Doherty, 1999; Doherty et al., 2003; Seel et al., 2000; Wall, 1999). While concern for environmental issues grew in the 1990s – as Harris wrote, 'everyone from the Pope to the Prime Minister would have us believe that we are all environmentalists now' (1996, p. 149) – many felt that this concern was 'shallow' in not calling for a fundamental transformation in human-nature relations. Inspired by Social Ecology (Bookchin, 1986; 2005), Deep Ecology (Devall and Sessions, 1985; Tobias, 1985) and the example of Earth First! in the USA (Lee, 1995; Taylor, 1996; 2001a; 2001b), Earth First! UK had emerged by 1991 and initiated a new protest movement concerned to radicalise environmental issues (Wall, 2000).[1] The politics involved in this style of environmentalism is primarily anarchistic, with participants shunning formal political structures and the hierarchical institutions

---

[1]    Useful discussions of these and other terms/groups, such as radical environmentalism and the Earth Liberation Front, can be found at http://www.religionandnature.com/ern/sample.htm (last accessed 18/07/08).

of mainstream society (Merchant, 1992; Purkis, 2000; Smith, 2002). However, as Seel and Plows write, while there is a 'mass of literature on "ecophilosophy", "biocentrism" and "environmental ethics"', and these schools of thought have had an influence upon sections of Earth First!, 'it is rare for activists to espouse specific academic ideas on these topics' (2000, p. 114). For activists, there is a strong emphasis upon a radical 'do-it-yourself' (DIY) politics (McKay, 1996; 1998) and many emphasise an anarchic 'neo-primitivism' which looks back to (assumed) ecological affinities of preindustrial communities and forwards in terms of attempting to model contemporary ecolifestyles on the past (Smith, 2002). Not all activists are 'primitivists' in the strict sense of advocating a return to 'hunter gatherer' style economies and a literal 'return to the past'. Nevertheless, most do articulate the view that communities in the past lived more harmoniously with their environment and the societies that they envisage are more basic, less wasteful and are 'primitive' as regards valuing a closer connection of humans with the natural world.

Considering the anarchistic backdrop to this form of environmental politics, one might expect that this is the last place we would find religion, since any form of religious or spiritual belief and practice might be 'considered as a surrendering of personal autonomy, an enslavement to irrationality' (Szerszynski and Tomalin, 2004, p. 198). In an important sense this is true, and activists actively disengage from any association with the hierarchies and formalism of traditional religious systems, which they consider to have been part of the cultural matrix responsible for ecological decline. However, despite this avoidance of mainstream religion, many activists do embrace of style of 'deregulated' religiosity which more properly corresponds to the category 'spirituality', 'a term increasingly used by individuals in Western society to denote a belief in "something more" than the empirical, material world while at the same time avoiding what are seen as the stultifying features of traditional "religion"' (Szerszynski and Tomalin, 2004, p. 202; King, 1996; Taylor, 2001a). This feature of environmental direct action, however, has not received much scholarly attention. The work of Bron Taylor on radical environmentalism in the USA is one notable exception (1996; 2001b), but within the UK this site of cultural production has received little more than passing comment (Butler, 1996; Letcher, 2001; Szerszynski and Tomalin, 2004).

One likely reason for this is that the work on EDA has, to date, been predominantly carried out in politics, sociology or geography, disciplines which have been traditionally wary of engaging with religious themes or identifying 'religion' as a category of analysis. While these studies are of value in providing an understanding of the political or sociological aspects of this form of direct action, there is a lack of emphasis upon the cultural, specifically religious or spiritual, dimensions of activism and the ways in which this provides participants with meaning and motivation. As Doherty et al. write, 'while the media has tended to focus upon protesters' lifestyle at the expense of political issues, studies of social movements often treat culture and identity as secondary to overtly political goals' (2000, p. 13). By contrast, my study adopts a religious studies methodology[2] which seeks 'the attentive and detailed *description* of the phenomena packaged as "religion"...paying close attention to the "believer's own account" as part of the explanatory process' (Sutcliffe 2004, p. xxiii). However, I also argue that the subjective accounts of believers 'require social, cultural and historical contextualization if adequate analysis is to be achieved' (2004, p. xxvi) and that in drawing on various methodologies (historical, textual, ethnographic etc...) 'qualitative approaches construct religion not as an ahistorical essence...but as a "social formation"...embedded in and generated by particular cultural and political contexts and essences' (2004, p. xxvii).

This chapter is concerned with the ways in which activists routinely draw upon cultural resources to give meaning to their values, identities and actions. Not only this, but also that these cultural resources are politically significant in shaping and maintaining commitment to a shared cause. However, what is of particular interest here is that often these resources are explicitly religious or spiritual in nature. Moreover, this case study has relevance for this book more broadly in that some activists adopt a *Romantic* ecologised religiosity that draws upon environmental struggles and religiocultural traditions from across the globe.

**Research Methods**

Whilst there have been many instances of direct action in Britain, this chapter is based upon research within a direct action community which existed from May until October 1996 in Wandsworth, South London. It also draws upon my experiences of festivals and gatherings in which I participated during the Summer of 1996: the 'Big Green Gathering',[3] the 'Buddha Field Festival'[4] and an Earth First! gathering.[5] In addition to these, I refer to literature produced within the movement, including leaflets and magazines.

The research undertaken for this book has involved a combination of methods. Chapters 2–4 rely upon an historical and sociological analysis of how a particular religious form *and* a particular understanding of nature have provided the foundation for contemporary religious environmentalism. The sources for this have been secondary, and I have engaged with a broad range of thinkers, mainly since the 1960s, to describe and explain the genesis and form of religious environmentalism, which reflects upon *biodivinity* as a means of approaching modern environmental problems. Chapters 5–7, by contrast, are based upon the outcome of periods of fieldwork in both Britain and India, spanning four years. Chapters 5 and 6 involved ethnographic methods: participant observation;

---

[2]   See Appendix for a discussion of religious studies as a discipline.
[3]   24–28 July 1996, Longbridge Deverill, Wiltshire.
[4]   17–20 July 1996, near Shepton Mallet, Somerset.
[5]   12–15 June 1996, North Wales.

unstructured/informal interviews; and documentary analysis of 'grey' literature. In both contexts I joined the communities/gatherings as a participant, but at the earliest opportunity informed people on a one-to-one basis the 'dual' purpose of my interest. In the context of EDA in Britain, I soon found that I was not the only person interested in researching the movement from an academic perspective and, moreover, found that there was a risk of suspicion from activists that I was not really 'on their side' since the academic epistemological framework I carried with me reflected the values of the system against which EDA activists positioned themselves. Anderson notes this with respect to his own research with EDA groups in Britian: 'they positioned me as part of the wider societal system their actions resisted and I became stereotyped as a potential colonizer, at one with the academic system they routinely vilified' (2002, p. 307). He quotes from the EDA newspaper SchNEWS:

> Well, [academia] sums up everything that is wrong with the printed word. How it is easy to change, distort, revamp, omit, edit and corrupt…SchNEWS is written by activists – not academics…[it is] our words – words of people actually out there doing it – in black and white and cyberspace for the academics, historians and analysts to pick over the bones with and come up with amazing theories about our 'glorious movement' (SchNEWSround, 1997: 5) (cited in Anderson 2002, p. 307).

While this seemed to be a dominant discourse adopted by the activist community, my presence at the camps and gatherings on an ongoing basis and my participation in the day-to-day life of the community (cooking, building, gardening, making leaflets etc.) soon meant that any potential distance created by my academic status more-or-less evaporated. This is also noted by Anderson, that the 'assumed distance between academics and activists did not hold when face-to-face relations had been established. There can be little doubt that I benefited from being in age and outlook "one of them"' (2002, p. 307). Moreover, he writes that:

> It became clear that each individual had multiple motives for being involved in EDA, and only some of these motives could be construed as being directly related to the specific environment under threat. Many were influenced by their politics, their chosen lifestyle, the bonhomie of site-life, or by other personal problems they were encountering. Thus my academic interest in EDA came to be perceived as just happening to be one of my motivations contributing to involvement and, as with (the majority of) other people's multiple influences, did not adversely affect my 'right' to be there (2002, p. 311).

Becoming an actual participant, however, is much more than a strategy to gain acceptance but is also crucial to gaining insight and understanding into what motivates and sustains involvement. In addition, my own interest in this research was motivated by the academic questions that I pose throughout this book, but also reflects a sympathetic personal engagement with many EDA values and activities. So the process of participation that I undertook in order to carry out the research for Chapters 5 and 6, placed me in an environment in which I felt comfortable and at home, and able to engage (albeit critically at times) with the underlying values of the movement both intellectually and personally/emotionally. There is a potential danger with participant observation, nonetheless, that emersion within a particular movement or community can then make it difficult to 'step outside' to provide academic commentary and analysis. However, training as an academic researcher should aim to prepare the individual to shift between different spaces of engagement and to make it quite possible to be more-or-less sympathetic to a particular set of issues on a political level, yet to also provide a rigorous academic analysis. With respect to my research, my engagement and background was sufficient that I could genuinely participate, yet not so fundamental that my purpose was to provide an unconditional apology for movement aims and activities.

## The British 'Environmental Direct Action' Movement

Since the early 1990s a radical style of environmentalism employing direct action as an ecopolitical tool has emerged in Britain (Anderson, 2004a; 2004b; 2002; Barry, 1999; Doherty, 1999; Doherty et al., 2003; McKay, 1996; 1998; Rootes, 1999; 2007; Routledge, 1997; Seel et al., 2000; Wall, 1999). Hundreds of thousands of individuals have taken part in non-violent direct action against perceived environmental risks such as road building, mining, the 'car-culture', urban sprawl, genetically modified crops and anti-globalisation/capitalism (Bircham and Charlton, 2001).[6] This style of radical environmentalism is not confined to Britain, but the character of the movement in Britain is coloured by social, cultural, economic and political factors specific to that place. Plows suggests, for instance, that one major difference between Earth First! in the UK and the USA is that the latter has been more strongly influenced by Deep Ecology whereas the former 'identifies the interdependence of social/human rights, and accords them equal value' (1998, p. 154; for a discussion of spirituality and direct action in the North American Earth First! movement see Taylor 1996; 2001a, 2001b). Doherty et al. also consider whether the British experience of direct action has a comparative, cross-cultural dimension. However, they confine their discussion to comparisons with Europe

---

[6]    Whilst, on the whole, protesters have a commitment to pursuing their aims non-violently, there have been many instances of violence at protests, either as a deliberate policy by a minority or as an unintended outcome of clashes between protesters and the police. The Hindu concept of *ahimsa*, non-violence or non-harm, and its association with the political strategy of Mahatma Gandhi, is frequently cited by activists in support of their non-violent stance. However, as Doherty et al. suggest, for Gandhi, *ahimsa* was an end in itself, whereas within EDA it is a strategic means and protestors may use violence if they deem it to be necessary (2003, p. 683).

and North America (2000, p. 15). In looking at sites of cultural production in both Britain and India, however, my investigation necessitates reflection upon a broader concept of cross-cultural since the cultural products of EDA explicitly draw upon non-western ethics and traditions. The next chapter of this book extends the cross-cultural theme to a non-western context – India – where I discuss a case study of radical and countercultural environmentalism that shares much in common with EDA in Britain.

Direct action in itself is nothing new: Britain has a rich history of sociopolitical protest. However, 'until the 1990s direct action was a tactic used by movements, not the defining feature of a movement' (Doherty et al., 2003, p. 671) and it was not until the road protests of the early 1990s, beginning with the protests at the M3 site of Twyford Down, Hampshire (Bryant, 1996), that an actual 'environmental direct action movement' emerged in Britain (Anderson, 2004b; Wall, 2000). Whilst prior to the 1990s, groups such as Friends of the Earth and Greenpeace, as well as the anti-nuclear movement, had taken part in direct action, such protest was not as continuous or high profile. Greenpeace, in particular, has a reputation for risky and visible protest activity, but activists are not drawn from within the general fee-paying membership, and instead are handpicked and their actions tightly controlled (Doherty, 1999, p. 278; Jordon and Maloney, 1997). A new band of enthusiastic environmentalists, reflecting the increase in concern about environmental issues since the late 1980s, felt that existing environmental organisations had little chance of fundamentally changing anything since they were 'neither very democratic nor participatory in practice so they offered no opportunity for radicals to express alternative ideologies through protest' (Doherty, 1999, p. 278).

Studies on the direct action movement in the UK agree that it mostly, although not exclusively, attracts individuals with higher education and who are keen to pursue life-styles and careers that express 'postmaterialist' values (Doherty, 1999; Wall, 2000). Additionally, activists are more likely to be under 35 and to have no dependents. This profile has tended to be contrasted with that of the locals who become involved at protest sites. The conventional wisdom, and certainly that promoted by the media, is that 'local' activists did not match the profile of those committed to the movement more broadly. They were depicted as 'affluent, often Conservative-voting, "Not in my back yards" (NIMBYs)' (Wall, 2000, p. 3). Nevertheless, a study by McNeish (2000), concerning local anti-roads campaigners, suggests instead that most activists he interviewed were members of environmental groups already (particularly Friends of the Earth), were middle class and shared a leftist politics. Moreover, the majority of those involved in the environmental direct action movement in Britain are from ethnically white backgrounds. This is because of social/cultural factors rather than a deliberate exclusion policy. As a British Asian photographer working at direct action sites suggested, countercultural values and lifestyles are less appealing to immigrant ethnic groups who have different experiences of and aspirations within British society. Such groups have other historically and culturally defined interests that may not coincide with the prioritisation of environmental issues:

You find there's very little involvement from Asian/Black people because Asians
I think generally have lived this kind of lifestyle for such a long time [feeling
oppressed and underprivileged] and they're trying to climb the ladder of success
in many ways and it's kind of growing in the opposite direction.[7]

By contrast, individuals involved in EDA tend to exhibit certain traits including
anti-authoritarianism, a tendency to challenge and question dominant institutions,
for example the conventional family or educational system, a desire to be different
or 'alternative', a lack of interest in pursuing a 'career' and a lack of concern for
material comforts and possessions. The reasons why people matching this profile
chose at this time to engage in environmental direct action, is clearly to linked to
the rising concern about environmental issues since the late 1980s and the lack
of faith in established environmental groups and political parties. Research also
suggests that by the early 1990s, linked to rising unemployment and a growth
in higher education, the values of the young in general were changing, and they
increasingly expressed a 'greater rejection of party politics, politicians and the
effectiveness of the parliamentary system and stronger support for protest that
might include violence to property' (Doherty, 1999, p. 280).

However, two other significant factors, which encouraged the effective
mobilisation of segments of a 'countercultural' youth, was the explosion of the
*rave culture* in the late 1980s and the introduction of the Criminal Justice Act in
1994. McKay singles out in particular a 'rave' held at Castle Morton Common in
1992, during which, for eight days 'anything from twenty to forty thousand people
camped to enjoy free music and entertainment in the single biggest countercultural
gathering since what became the last Stonehenge Free Festival in 1984' (1996,
p. 120; Earle et al., 1994; Hemment, 1998; Wright, 1998). Although these 'illegal'
gatherings spread like wildfire across the UK during the 1990s, fuelled particularly
by the increasing popularity of the drug 'ecstasy', the introduction of the Criminal
Justice and Public Order Act (1994) included 'specific anti-rave clauses' (Wright,
1998) which led to a clampdown. The Act would also have implications for protest
activity, and both ravers and direct activists protested against this proposed legislation.
Ironically, according to the protesters themselves, the Criminal Justice and Public
Order Act, which was intended to criminalise many of their activities, actually united
diverse anti-establishment and countercultural groups, during and following the
massive Criminal Justice Bill march held in London that Summer, which culminated
in a party in Trafalgar Square. This protest had a profound effect on many individuals
who attest to having become involved, or more effectively involved, in direct action
following this event. As McKay argues 'the irony is of course that, while the Act
has aimed to snuff out many of the events and groups that constitute the culture
of resistance in Britain, its effect to date has been quite the opposite: to encourage
new and to revitalise older campaigns and actions' (1996, p. 160). The Criminal
Justice and Public Order Act entailed legislation, which effectively outlawed the

---

[7]     Wandsworth Eco-village, 2/7/96.

lifestyle and activities of certain groups of people: travellers, ravers and direct activists. In fact many involved in the direct action movement considered that there has been a resurgence of interest in countercultural lifestyles and politics. The direct action movement shares many features of a broader 'counterculturalism', having its genesis in the 1960s, which saw a burgeoning subculture rooted in alternative values and ways of life, including styles of dress, music and spirituality which expressed opposition to mainstream culture. As one older 'activist' expressed 'the 90s are like the 60s. The energy and internationalism has returned'.[8]

During the 1990s this style of ecopolitics was highly visible, particularly the anti-roads protests (at Twyford Down, the M11 at Wanstead and the Newbury bypass) which emerged in response to the road building agenda of the then Conservative Government. At the time, these activities received a high level of media attention and it became common for the 'front pages' to carry pictures of dreadlocked protesters being dragged from trees by security guards or police. However, the shift in road building policy by the time that Labour came to power in 1997 saw a decline in anti-roads actions, and energies have been channelled into campaigns against genetically modified crops and, more recently, the anti-capitalist and anti-globalisation movement, which has grown in size and impact since the protests in Seattle against the 1999 World Trade Organisation meeting (Anderson, 2004b, p. 110; Clark and Rose, 1999; Dodson, 2003; Taylor, 2002). Doherty et al. view the British direct action movement as a NSM, which encapsulates broader concerns than environmental: it is 'intended to directly change perceived political, social or environmental injustices' (2003, p. 670). While the authors locate the genesis of the movement in the activities of Earth First! in the early 1990s, the movement has always been concerned to look beyond 'single' issue politics and to embrace the interconnectedness of facets of modern capitalist ethics and institutions as problematic on a broader scale. Despite this shift towards protests that are less obviously about the environment, this broader conception of direct action is congruent with a key facet of the movement's thinking, which is to transcend 'single issue' politics. As an article in the news-sheet *Do or Die* tells us

> To tackle one issue is an easier (and within reason necessary) option, but to ignore the realities of the whole struggle is dangerous and leaves us no closer to a sustainable future...If we don't fight against the totality of the system by understanding a campaign in the context of the wider struggle, capitalism will just rear its ugly head elsewhere (Anon and Anon, 1996, p. 93).

For example, one issue taken up by direct activists has been against genetically modified crops, and a number of actions have taken place within Britain where fields of trial crops have been destroyed. Whilst this is an issue relating to the environment, as there are intense concerns about the environmental consequences of the effects of the cross fertilisation of genetically modified crops with standard

---

[8]   Big Green Gathering, 24/7/96.

crops, it has also raised issues relating to the ethics of multinational corporations that promote GM technology, such as Monsanto.

Although today the anti-roads issue, in particular, is not of the scale witnessed during the 1990s, there are still instances of environmental direct action across the country. This radical environmental network is physically maintained largely by word of mouth, freely distributed printed literature, the Internet and a circuit of festivals and gatherings that individuals attend throughout the year. Moreover, the actual protest sites help facilitate the maintenance of the network that exists between different campaigns. Activists move between different sites, perhaps to attend an open-day, to visit friends or to add to numbers if an eviction is imminent. People swap details on different campaigns, hand out leaflets or hold workshops. Thus, activists, previously having no direct contact with the area, set up camp with the aim of physically preventing activities that are seen as environmentally damaging, for instance, in constructing tree houses and tunnels where activists take up residence (Wall, 2000). While the decision to set up protest sites in particular locations is always instrumental, the actual sites themselves become 'communities of resistance' where activists might live for weeks or months on end. There is a perception of the movement not only as a protest movement but also as evidence of an alternative social sphere, based upon environmental values, with its own style of social organisation, politics, economics, and culture. The political significance of direct action in this context goes beyond securing a desired outcome, such as preventing a road from being built, and is seen as a concrete expression of an alternative ecological value system. It has a wider symbolic significance which points beyond particular issues; it is an end in itself.[9] As Melucci argues, it is not the content of action alone that is significant but that the action itself presents a symbolic challenge to institutional powers (1996, p. 183). What is envisioned is not a reformed more ecological capitalist society but an entirely new social, political and economic order.

### The Wandsworth Eco-Village

One example of such a community existed from May to October 1996 in Wandsworth, South London, on the banks of the River Thames. A group had set up the 'Wandsworth Eco-village' on land owned by the brewing giant *Guinness* in objection to plans to develop the site for high-end housing and a supermarket.

---

[9]   Doherty et al. outline seven key themes that they consider to be particularly relevant to a discussion of British environmental direct action: the novelty of EDA: whether EDA is legitimately a New Social Movement; whether EDA should be considered in terms of its instrumentality or its 'identity-oriented logic'; the social basis of EDA; the tactics and strategies of EDA; the extent to which this movement is peculiar to the UK; and, finally, the impact of this style of environmental politics (2000, p. 4). This study is concerned primarily with the third dimension: should EDA be considered in terms of their instrumentality or their 'identity-oriented logic' (Rucht, 1990).

Following an initial protest in May 1996, led by the Oxford based group 'The Land is Ours', thirty or so people decided to stay and to develop an 'eco-village'. As a pamphlet produced for distribution at one of the many open days explained:

> Since the first week the site was handed over to the local community, and to any homeless people who wish to live on it to be used as a public amenity and to demonstrate an environmentally friendly lifestyle...this involves creating homes from reclaimed materials, planting gardens, using renewable energy (wind and sun) and enjoying life without consumerism.. This land was occupied as a protest. It has now become a home for people living here...The proposed developments on this site will provide little benefit to the local community. We are offering a better solution.[10]

Unlike many of the anti-roads protest sites, which were in the countryside, the 'eco-village' was located just off a major intersection of the busy South Circular road in London on the River Thames by Wandsworth Bridge. Nestled between the River Thames and the trappings of modern industrial suburbia, the entrance to the site bore a big metal gate, the fences and walls painted in bright colours with the slogan 'Pure Genius', the name of the site as well as the slogan used by the Guinness brewery to advertise their product. When I first arrived the site had been occupied for a few weeks and there were about thirty people living there, including many who had been involved in other direct action campaigns around the country. The site had been empty and unused for at least seven years and in a relatively short time its new occupants had achieved a remarkable transformation. Dozens of vegetable beds had been planted, windmills for generating electricity stood high above the site and many small houses and 'benders' had been erected from recycled materials collected by site members or donated by supporters. However, the central feature was a large octagonal building, with an adjoining kitchen area, nicknamed the 'round house' or 'Octavia'. This was the communal space, built by the protesters, where people congregated for meetings, to share meals and to socialise. It also operated as an information centre with its walls plastered in newspaper articles and pamphlets about the site and other campaigns around the country, as well as leaflets on permaculture and vegetarianism/veganism. One leaflet bore a slogan, summing up the aims of EDA: 'if you want to bring pressure to bear on a government, don't wait for the legislation you need. Do it yourself!'

The communal roundhouse at the 'eco-village' became a space where people pinned up book chapters and stylised pictures of Native American and Hindu deities. For example, the walls were decorated with a diverse range of religious symbols, pictures and prayers. These were mainly from eastern and Native American traditions, including drawings of *aums* and *yin yangs*, and postcards and posters of the Indian religious figures *Radha*, *Krishna* and *Buddha*. There was also a section from a book entitled the 'The Sacred Tree' called 'Code of Ethics' which was concerned

---

[10]    Wandsworth Eco-village.

with "'...teachings universal to all tribes...'", including giving thanks to the creator, respect for others, the Earth and all religions and cultures: "treat the Earth and all of her aspects as your mother'" (Bopp, 1985). Similar aspects of the material culture of EDA have been discussed by Butler, with respect to the protest site at 'No. 68 Claremont Road' against the extension of the M11 in Wanstead (1994–95) where 'protestors...chose to describe and to commemorate their experiences as a "festival of resistance"' (1996, p. 341; Szerszynski, 2002). She writes that:

> this ordinary row of Victorian terraced houses had been transformed with paint, creativity, humour and vision into an urban shrine to the culture of protest. Homes, pavements, abandoned cars, trees, all suddenly blocked with murals of flowers, New Age symbols and icons, with dragons and dancers and theatre and play (1996, p. 338).

The 'eco-village' was a protest against the proposed development on the site as well as an attempt to create a community based upon ecological principles, with many activists valuing the ideal of 'returning' to a more 'natural economy' as necessary for environmental sustainability. Although there was a tendency to eschew modern technology, in particular the industrial machinery of global capitalism, many activists do appreciate modern inventions such as the 'sound system' and the computer. Increasingly, the Internet is becoming a primary mode of communication amongst the disparate groups involved in environmental direct action. The food production at the site aimed to incorporate organic and permacultural principles and whilst it was not possible to produce all the food required by the community, very little was actually bought in, coming instead from donations or 'skip-runs' (collecting out of date or damaged food that shops throw into refuse skips). However, it was not just the food production or recycling of materials to build dwellings that reflected 'ecological' guidelines. The idea of following 'natural principles' also underpinned the rationale given to the style of non-hierarchical social organisation favoured within the community. This reflected a view of nature as an 'organic' system of interconnections where each element has its own integrity but at the same time is dependent upon and linked to the entire biotic community (Everden, 1992). Echoing the 'social ecology' of the eco-anarchist Murray Bookchin (1986; 2005), activists linked the domination of the Earth to the domination of human beings by rules and authority structures. Bookchin, and others, attempt an historical analysis of the evolution of social hierarchies that accompanied the shift from 'organic' to 'resourcist' societies.

Thus, in addition to adopting environmentally friendly lifestyles, activists also sought to subvert the authoritarian tendencies of mainstream society in fostering an ethos where everyone felt valued, was encouraged to express their own ideas and had the opportunity to develop emotionally and psychologically. Alongside this, at the level of the community, there was a strong emphasis upon common goals, mutual trust and participation. This ecological frame of reference was taken to be anarchistic in its essence: it marked a sharp opposition to the 'exploitative institutions' of mainstream society and is the basis of the 'spontaneous order' which would underpin alternative systems of material, moral and social organisation. The assumption is that there is nothing coercive about communities modelled along ecological principles: this is the way things would evolve when left to their own devices, in the absence of force. Where there were 'rules' they were seen as an attempt to protect the community and to foster these common goals rather than to restrict the freedom of the individual. For instance, new members were supposed to attend weekly site meetings and after a week's trial period to become a 'project carer', involving responsibility for the project and the requirement to build a 'house'. There was also an agreed policy that anyone who was violent or using hard drugs should be asked to leave, and a general feeling amongst many people living there that the amount of tobacco and alcohol consumed on site compromised the ideals of sustainability. However, the project carer system was rarely enforced, many people appeared unmotivated or lacked the skills to build permanent accommodation and little was done to remove disruptive and violent drug users and alcoholics. By the time the site was evicted (16 October 1996) it was a far cry from the original vision of a cooperative, self-sustainable community. The open-door policy had attracted some violent and mentally ill individuals and the unwillingness to violate anyone's self-expression or freedom left many very disgruntled but limited in their capacity to improve the situation. However, the tension between the autonomy of the individual and the stability of the community was eventually as much a cause of the demise of the 'eco-village' as the eviction of protesters by police.

Anderson (2004b) notes that 'EDA camps become a "homeplace" (after hooks 1990), a safe haven where the languages, customs and behaviour through simply existing reinforced and refueled an individual and collective sense of empowerment' (2004b, p. 110). Activists are bound together by a common mistrust of conventional political structures and a belief that the Earth is in need of protection. For activists, the Earth is of 'ultimate concern' (Tillich, 1957) and their protest activities reflect this foundational 'belief'. While for many activists this 'ultimacy' of the Earth is expressed in terms of clearly defined political stances against capitalism (e.g. green anarchy or socialism), for others the Earth as a focus of 'ultimate concern' is expressed in spiritual terms. However, whether or not activists choose to express their values about the Earth in religious language, most, if not all, feel a connection to the natural world which is deeply personal and which sustains their involvement in the movement. As Anderson writes: 'living outside, often in temporary dwellings ("benders") of canvas and wooden poles, individuals become sensitive to the vagaries of weather, temperature and the availability of fruits of the Earth. This proximity of engagement with place often generates feelings of identification with the non-human environment' (Anderson, 2004a, p. 50).

## The Role of Religion in the British EDA Movement

*Modern Millenarians*

In the reminder of this chapter I want to look more closely at the role of religion in the British EDA movement. As with members of other anarchist inspired movements, environmental direct activists have dissociated themselves from and are deeply critical of the norms, values and institutions of mainstream society, including religion. However, as Cohn (1970) and Bookchin (1982) have argued, the emergence of anarchist movements throughout history has been closely connected to religious movements such as millenarianism (Purkis, 2000). In its most specific sense, millenarianism relates to the second coming of Christ and the establishment of his 'Kingdom on Earth', as predicted in the Book of Revelations in the New Testament of the Bible. Purkis argues that behind the religious rhetoric of millenarian movements has been a political message, which stresses 'deep anti-authoritarianism and self-organisation' (2000, p. 97). He suggests that EDA activists exhibit a number of similarities with millenarians in the past and that these are worthy of consideration. Firstly, these 'modern millenarians' have adopted a 'rhetoric of disaster and collapse' and look forward to the creation of 'a profoundly ethical-moral-just society (a 'Heaven on Earth' if you like) through individual lifestyle practices untied with self-organised radical political campaigning' (2000, p. 107). They submit modern consumerist tendencies to a radical critique and articulate the desire for a more 'fulfilling state of being – whether defined in religious or secular terms' (2000, p. 107). Moreover, the practices and values of activists enable them to challenge dominant dualistic codes of mainstream society, 'between how things are and how things could be, between private and public actions, between leaders and led' (Szerszynski and Tomalin, 2004, p. 202; Purkis 2000, p. 107). This echoes the earlier millenarian strategies to overcome the dualism between earthly humanity and a transcendent God, and the sociopoltical elites and the masses, in heralding the more egalitarian social conditions which would accompany the second coming of Christ to Earth. Finally, just as with earlier forms of anti-ritualism and iconoclasm in religious history, this 'modern millenarianism' has developed its own rituals, symbols and myths as key features of its movement (we shall return to these below) (Szerszynski, 2002).

*Religion, Spirituality and Radical Environmentalism in Britain*

The extent to which activists understand these features of the movement as 'religious' is, however, contested. Firstly, for many involved in EDA this millenarianism appears to be 'secularised', it is articulated without recourse to religious and spiritual values, myths and notions of the 'sacred'. According to Cohn, millenarianism became secularised around the time of the French Revolution and was influenced by the utopian ideals of Enlightenment thinking (1970). There are many within the movement who believe that the spiritual ritual and symbolism detract from engagement with more pressing political issues.[11] Secondly, for those who do articulate their millenarian vision with reference to the sacred, the view that their politics are in any way 'religious' is normally vigorously rejected. Religion tends to be sharply differentiated from spirituality within the direct action movement. This term is increasingly used in western societies by both academics and 'believers' to reflect a belief in something lying beyond everyday experience, yet is not defined in terms of the so-called 'world religions' (King, 1996; Taylor, 2001a; Zinnbauer, 1997). As one female protester expressed her doubts about 'religion', 'I could see the same mistakes being made again and again…I worship wherever I am even if it is concrete.'[12] She saw 'mistakes' being made in different religious traditions, in terms of their having lost the idea of sacred nature, and considered that religion relied upon hierarchy, exclusion and dishonesty.

Activists tend to raise most objections towards Christianity, which they associate with a conservative British establishment. They consider that it is rigidly hierarchical and patriarchal, the very antithesis of the kind of future they anticipate. Furthermore, it is seen as supporting the humanity-nature dualism and to justify the exploitation of nature, as discussed by Lynn White Jr. in his seminal article (1967). Other 'religious' systems, by contrast, are more popular, particularly those lying outside the Abrahamic traditions (e.g. eastern and Native American traditions). However, there is a tendency to overlook the fact that such traditions are rarely as egalitarian or individualistic as contemporary spirituality. Neither are such traditions always as compassionate towards animals or the natural world as modern environmentalists believe they are. Moreover, aspects of these traditions are typically taken and then adapted in a piecemeal fashion to create a 'bricolage'. As Bron Taylor writes, 'with sufficient creativity, almost anything is ripe for appropriation into the amalgamated and fluid religion of radical environmentalism' (2002, p. 37).

Woodhead and Heelas (2000) suggest that the most successful styles of religiosity in the West today are those which 'resource the individual', 'that are concerned more with the here and now than with the afterlife, and that nurture the unique individual, lived life rather than simply promoting life in a particular prescribed role' (Szerszynski and Tomalin, 2004, p. 202). Although affiliation to the Christian tradition is in decline in the UK, evidence suggests that many individuals opt for a style of 'spirituality', which allows them to choose their beliefs, practices and way of life. While this 'DIY' spirituality has been described as 'New Age' (Heelas, 1997), there is reluctance within EDA to adopt this term. As Plows stresses, this is

---

[11]   At one Earth First! gathering a disagreement broke out during a group meeting. About fifty people were present, sitting in a circle discussing the pros and cons of non-violent direct action. At the summation of the meeting one man suggested that we all praise the 'Mother' and began a song to the 'Earth Goddess'. This was met by ridicule and the departure of a number of participants. The singers, however, were not deterred and continued their worship.

[12]   Buddha Field Festival, 18/7/96.

not New Age spirituality, 'you won't find many New Agers on protest camps for the simple reason that the New Age perspective is one of "social change through individual change"' (1998, p. 169). What she means here is not that personal transformation is unimportant (see below) but that New Age spirituality tends to focus on the individual in a 'selfish' way, neglecting the broader interconnections with the social and ecological. Nevertheless, the spirituality expressed by activists does share certain features with New Age. They both reject traditional hierarchical and authoritative religious systems, in particular Christianity, are attracted to non-Abrahamic traditions, including paganism, and engage in a process of 'bricolage', where individuals select, borrow and interpret diverse religious symbols for novel purposes (Beckford, 1990; Campbell, 2002; Roof, 1999; Taylor, 2002). However, even though many activists draw upon paganism to inform their ecological values and participation in direct action, most are not members of any specific pagan groups. While paganism emphasises a spiritual relationship between the individual and nature, and the worship of the Goddess as the feminine and creative principle, or 'Mother Earth', activists shun formal participation in 'religious' groups and tend to be critical of any tradition which focuses upon the 'self' at the expense of direct action to change society. Thus, while many consider that there is a place for paganism in EDA, it must be 'practical paganism; first and foremost as an approach which has solid foundations in informing our attempts at radical change. Belief in 'Earth energy' does not prohibit political realism. On the contrary it is an added incentive' (Plows, 1998, p. 168).

Thus, in contrast to traditional religious systems, which are maintained *via* the authority of an historical tradition, authoritative texts and religious leaders, this style of contemporary or 'DIY' spirituality is highly eclectic and not bound to any particular tradition. Many EDA activists articulate their commitment to environmentalism in terms of a belief in the sacredness of the Earth and it is common for them to refer to the Earth as the 'Goddess' or the 'Mother Earth'. However, as Plows notes:

> For many direct activists the value of nature and self can be described as a spirituality, literally an awareness of spirit, of life force. I need to stress that this is a very personal thing. Many in the movement will identify this sense of connectedness as something that motivates their actions, but would not describe it as spirituality, simply as a socially committed and environmentally aware attitude (1998, p. 168).

Conversely, just as with Zinnbauer et al.'s (1997) study, the understanding of spirituality held by other EDA activists means that it is often used to describe their entire way or life without any explicit reference to usual indicators of religiosity such as the divine, the supernatural or the afterlife. Religion is identified with the discrete, established, traditional religious systems, whereas spirituality is frequently used by protesters to describe their entire way of life and social vision (Bloch, 1998, p. 59). This account suggests that, with reference to activists' use of the word spirituality, the line between the secular and the sacred is difficult to discern. As Plows indicates it is a 'very personal thing' and activists do not feel constrained to label their experiences and motivations in a particular way, as spiritual, religious or secular.

The flexibility of the use of spiritual/religious language has also been noted by Bron Taylor in his work on the Earth First! movement in the USA. He indicates that even those who do not consider themselves as religious often use spiritual/ religious language to express their feelings and concerns (1996, pp. 547–8). However, he also notes that the Earth First! movement shares many features in common with religious traditions, such as an 'emerging corpus of myth, symbol, and rite' (1996, p. 547). Moreover, as with British EDA, many Earth First!ers in the US explicitly trace their 'ecocentric sentiments to such diverse religious traditions as Taoism, Buddhism, Hinduism, Christian nature mysticism, witchcraft and pagan Earth-worship' (1996, p. 548). He is struck by the pervasiveness of religious forms within Earth First!, including the use of spiritual language, and concludes that this seems to reveal 'the emergence of a dynamic, new religious movement' (1996, p. 547).

*Is Radical Environmentalism a New Religious Movement?*

For Taylor, the suggestion that Earth First! is like a new religious movement has a heuristic value:

> My perspective on 'religion'…has an affinity with the simple statement about the value of the term religion once made by Benson Saler: 'The power of religion as an analytical category…depends on its instrumental value in facilitating the formulation of interesting statements about human beings' (Saler 1993: 68). Like Saler, I am not attached to the term religion per se, except where its construction and deployment, or an analysis of the controversies over it, can illuminate our world (2007, pp. 13–14).

In assessing whether or not radical environmentalism is a new religious movement we first need to ask whether it is 'like' things that we normally call religion. As Taylor writes: 'is religion a useful term for analysis? If it can be, what are the ways it should be understood? Where does religion end, and where do social phenomena that are not religious begin?' (2007, p. 11). Thus, in calling something 'religious' we must somehow enhance our understanding of the phenomenon that is being described: the term must do some useful 'work'. There are many important resemblances between radical environmentalism and religions, as Taylor notes, but he is also aware that radical environmentalists do not use the term 'religion' to describe their activities, even when they appear to exhibit features of what we might normally call religion. Instead, they would be much more likely to use the term 'spirituality':

In contemporary parlance people increasingly speak of 'spirituality' rather tha 'religion' when trying to express what moves them most deeply; and many consider the two to be distinctly different. Most of the characteristics scholars associate with religion, however, are found whether people consider themselves 'spiritual' or 'religious.' From a 'family resemblances' approach, therefore, there is little *analytical* reason to assume these are different kinds of social phenomena. It is important, however, to understand what most people understand the distinction to entail, especially because the term spirituality is more often than religion associated with nature and nature religions (2009, forthcoming).

For me, this distinction is crucial. And an understanding of what people mean by it, in the context of radical environmentalism, makes it difficult to retain the descriptive label 'religion' despite family resemblances. The meaning of a term, for those who are described by it, is as important as its analytical value for academic commentators. In particular, the flexibility of the use of the term 'spirituality' captures an important feature of EDA that evades categorisation in terms of the conventional distinction between the religious and the secular. Like earlier millenarian movements, I have suggested that EDA is a style of politics that aims to overcome the 'dualistic codings of a dominant social order' (Szerszynski and Tomalin, 2004, p. 202). This applies no less to the dualism between the religious and the secular than between the signifiers of other dualisms that maintain power and exclusion. As King writes, the word 'spirituality' 'seems to include both the sacred and the secular, and to enable a fundamental rethinking of religious boundaries' (King, 1996, p. 345).

For EDA activists the focus of 'ultimate concern' is the Earth and underpinning this concern is an ecocentric philosophy. While some activists choose to articulate their politics in terms of what we might normally think of as 'religion' or 'spirituality' and others might use the language of spirituality even though they would not consider themselves to be 'spiritual', there are those who avoid such language and who do not feel comfortable with overtly spiritualised rituals and activities. What attracts my attention here is not those activists who are 'spiritual/religious' or those who appear to be secular: we are familiar with both these views since they correspond to the religious-secular dualism. Instead, the existence of those who use spiritual language but do not consider themselves to be spiritual/religious poses a challenge to the taken-for-granted distinction between the religious and the secular. Why do people use the word spiritual when they do not believe in what it normally stands for? In shifting to the language of spirituality there is an attempt to express the idea that what is of 'ultimate significance' to the individual can be articulated *outside* the dualism of the religious and the secular. It is difficult to find an appropriate description for certain experiences or convictions when they are of 'ultimate significance', yet to do not correspond to what we would normally call religious. It is this 'in between' position that can attract the label spirituality. The word spirituality can, thus, be used to 'reclaim' a realm of human experience from the rigidity of the distinction between the religious and the secular. It is a concept that can have meaning for those who embrace what we might normally think of as 'religious' (belief in the supernatural etc.), as well as those who reject all aspects and features of 'religion'.

Thus, in embracing the term spirituality activists are not only rejecting the idea of religion but also of the secular. Many do not feel that their experience and vision falls into either (whether defined 'religiously' or not). As discussed in Chapter 2, the distinction between the secular and the sacred is a product of the Protestant Reformation and the Enlightenment, whereby secular was marked as a realm of rationality and materiality. By contrast, the religious was the domain of the emotions and the divine: of 'ultimate significance'. For direct activists, whether 'religious' or not, it is the emergence of such dualisms which are to blame for the current environmental crisis and which their social vision would seek to reunite. It is useful here to return to the earlier discussion, concerning the idea that the dualism between the religious and the secular reflects western Christian understandings of religion and is problematic when we attempt to apply it as a cross-cultural tool of analysis. It only *seems* to work because we have already decided that there are certain world religions which correspond to our category 'religion', but when we look more closely there is much about non-western/non-Abrahamic 'religious' traditions and their relationship to other aspects of human life that do not fit this model (Fitzgerald, 2000). The suggestion here is that the secular-religious dualism is not only problematic for the interpretation of non-western, non-Abrahmic religious traditions, but it also means that the dominance of this tool of analysis makes it difficult to understand other domains of human experience which we might not ordinarily think of as 'religious' (since they do not fit into the secular or the religious). It is my suggestion that aspects of environmentalism would provide one example, particularly, but not exclusively, where people employ the term spirituality to describe their experiences, motivations and lifestyles. As Bron Taylor writes, many environmentalists 'use rhetoric of the sacred to express awe and reverence towards the 'miracle' of life or wider universe, while disavowing supernaturalism of any kind' (2004, p. 1001). The line between the sacred and the secular becomes difficult to draw, since activists frequently choose to use a similar language and to value particular symbols whether they consider themselves an explicitly spiritual person (Deudney, 1995; Taylor, 1996). However, the boundary between the sacred and the secular becomes blurred only because of where the boundary was drawn in the first place: between Christian understandings of 'ultimate concern' as religious and all else as secular (Deudney, 1995).

The remainder of this chapter will show the ways in which EDA does reveal an 'emerging corpus of myth, symbol, and rite' (Taylor, 1996, p. 547) and as such shares resemblances with new religious movements. However, for me, the attempt to transcend the dichotomy between the religious and the secular, through the use of the word spirituality, suggests that without qualification the label 'new religious movement' is inappropriate. I would also hesitate in using the word spiritual to describe the movement as a whole. Even this word has connotations with which many activists would not wish to be associated (such as belief in the supernatural, although as we have seen this is not how it is always used). I will describe how certain forms normally associated with religion, such as myth and ritual, also have an important role to play in EDA. However, the role of these 'religious forms' of action and thought are a resource for sustaining the involvement of the individual and the group within the movement, and for orienting them towards the focus of ultimate concern which underpins EDA. While some activists use explicitly religious/spiritual resources to express their concern and maintain their commitment, others do not.

### 'Religiospiritual Themes' and EDA

Many activists experience an 'enchantment' with the Earth, whether or not they express this in terms of spiritual language. Although not all activists adopt the language of spirituality to express their values and motivations, 'a critique of western religions of transcendence frequently accompanies a strongly felt identification with cultures considered to exemplify holistic and environmentally friendly lifestyles' (Szerszynski and Tomalin, 2004, p. 203). The following section will discuss different 'religiospiritual themes' that are typically found within EDA – both explicitly and implicitly: beliefs, myths and values; identity, conversion and personal transformation; healing, ceremony and action; and worship and celebration.

*Beliefs, Values and Myths*

Melucci (1989; 1996) suggests that social movements act like social laboratories: they are places where individuals can 'experiment' with different ways of life that challenge and subvert society's dominant codes. Such movements present their own 'figured worlds', where participants can come to share particular experiences of the world (Holland et al., 1998). Despite the sharing of these values, there are many types of politics held by protestors (e.g. socialist ecology, social ecology, deep ecology, ecofeminist, anarcho-primitivism etc.). However, they do share a critique of society as ecologically malign and damaging to the individual. Thus, although diverse, there is distinctiveness to the culture of EDA communities, which is both reactionary and reconstructive. Activists contrast their values with those of western consumerist societies which 'embody or evoke the worst aspects of capitalism and an alienation – economic, political of psychological – from individual and collective fulfillment' (Purkis 2000, p. 107). Activists frequently refer to society as 'Babylon', the term for the spiritually bereft exile of the ancient Hebrews and more recently the Rastafarian term of derision for western society. Babylon is used not only in a substantive sense but also adjectivally: for example, 'Babylon drugs' (western medicine) or 'Babylon press' (mainstream media). In line with previous uses of the term, this suggests that something is felt to be lacking in 'normal' society, which is to be found instead in the exiled group: at the most basic level this missing element can be seen as a lack of awareness of the ultimate significance (or even sacredness) of the Earth. However, there is also a very strong feeling amongst activists that 'Babylon' is oppressive and that mainstream society with its hierarchies and consumerist culture subdues and traps the individual (including 'religions of transcendence').

Within EDA, shared values about the ultimate significance of the Earth are the starting point from which activists envisage alternative ways of life that are less ecologically harmful and more socially egalitarian. For those who express this with respect to religion/spirituality, the most basic belief is that the Earth is sacred, that it is imbued with divinity. In particular, the divine is often understood as feminine (as the 'Goddess' or 'Mother Earth') and the Earth itself is considered as a living organism with which humanity is interconnected. This also reflects the ideas behind the popular Gaia theory of James Lovelock. He rejects the idea that the Earth is an inanimate collection of separate parts and instead argues that it is a living organism made up from interconnected and mutually dependent parts. However, he also uses this theory to suggest that if any element of the Earth's ecosystem is destroyed or reduced that the Earth will eventually achieve a new balance (Lovelock, 1979; 1995). Nature is often personified by EDA activists and is assigned human attributes, such as feelings and intention. Some may consider the environmental crisis to be the Earth's revenge upon the human race for treating it so badly.

Another 'implicitly religious' theme is the tendency for activists to articulate the status of the movement in mythic form. Particularly popular are myths concerning the dawning of a 'new age'. This is often described in terms of a battle between the forces of good (the protesters) and the forces of evil (the government or Babylon). For example, one male activist explained how the movement had been called by the Earth to fight in a cosmic battle to save the planet from the forces of greed and evil that dominates society. He saw the fight to save the planet as more than a material struggle, but also as a spiritual quest. This tendency to interpret EDA as having mystical and soteriological qualities is similarly expressed by other activists. In particular, certain Native American myths that prophesy the dawning of a new age are recounted within the movement. One popular myth prophesises that a time will arrive when children of the white people will come and seek the wisdom of the 'Elders' and they will be wearing long hair and beads (see the discussion below about activists' dress and identity); this will signal a time of purification.[13] Another Native American myth, which is popular, involves a prophesy surrounding the birth of a female white buffalo that will signal the beginnings of an era of world peace and ecological harmony. EDA is considered to be an aspect of this rejuvenation and the tendency to talk about the movement in prophetic terms, as if its emergence

---

[13]    This particular story has its origins in the Rainbow Family, an alternative social movement that originated in the USA in the early 1970s. In the next chapter I will discuss how versions of this myth/prophecy have come to underlie the history and identity of the Rainbow Family.

and existence were inevitable, was shared by many activists. Some activists told me that they had heard that the white buffalo had been born. Such an event had in fact occurred on 20 August 1994 in Janesville, Wisconsin, on Heider Farm. It was the first time since 1959 that a female white buffalo – nicknamed 'Miracle' – had been born and survived. As the Houston Cronicle reported on 24 September 1994: 'The white buffalo is an important symbol for a lot of Plains Indians because they are messengers of creation. It is an important sign of well being on the verge of an awakening.'[14] There is an identification of activists with other oppressed groups, such as Native Americans, which serves to reinforce their identity as a revolutionary and emancipatory force. They see themselves as part of a wider resurgence of oppressed groups who are considered to be reasserting their values and way of life in the face of the homogenising forces of global capitalism.

*Identity, Conversion and Personal Transformation*

This process of the disembedding and reinvention of religious and cultural symbols and ideas is fundamental to the creation of activists' identity. The identification with particular cultural groups, namely small-scale, preindustrial communities which are not only perceived to be most subject to political oppression and environmental change, but also to hold spiritual values which reflect respect for the Earth. Whilst it has already been suggested that this represents an idealised, abstracted notion of such communities, it aims to serve the function of distinguishing the aims of the protesters and groups 'like us' from mainstream capitalist society. This cultural affinity is also reflected in the movement by the adoption of diverse elements of 'tribal-like' culture. For example, after the 1996 'Reclaim the Streets' protest in London (the name given to the illegal street parties held around the country in objection to the car culture) the *Observer* newspaper reported that there were 'hundreds in fancy dress' (Vidal and Nowicka, 1996). However, the groups of people, drumming and dancing, mingling with the crowd to join the spontaneous outbursts of singing and chanting, adorning painted faces and bodies, with plaited hair, tattoos and dreadlocks, were dressed little differently from usual. Surrounded by rather uneasy looking police officers, complete with riot gear, the protesters drummed, chanted and danced all afternoon and well into the evening. Thus, not only do protesters differentiate themselves from mainstream society through their ideology and way of life but also by adopting different styles of physical appearance and social activities, which borrow elements from prominent features of tribal-like societies.

Beyond the borrowing of such features, protest communities are neo-tribal in terms of their marginalisation from mainstream society. This isolation is deliberate and further illustrated in the adoption of an alternative way of life. A good example of this 'neo-tribalism' is the 'Dongas Tribe'. As 'Spirit' magazine reports with reference to the Twyford Down protest, 'what started as a spontaneous gathering

---

[14]    http://www.powersource.com/gallery/whiteb.html (last accessed 27/1/09).

of people in 1992 was to crystallise over the next few years into the formation of a modern day nomadic "tribe"...part of this encampment became known as the Dongas' (1997, p. 27). Both the Twyford Down protest and the Dongas Tribe are seen by many to mark the beginnings of the contemporary environmental direct action movement. They provide a kind of model upon which to build and develop nomadic lifestyles based upon ecological principles:

> Whilst she was protesting, Ingrid, along with the other Dongas, was learning to live in harmony with what she had around her. During their stay at Twyford, the tribe relearned old traditions; how to weave hazel branches, spin their own fleece and wool; make natural dyes from leaves and flowers. They started to make jewellery, hats, jumpers and wicker baskets to sell at markets and gatherings...In coming together and living in community each individual discovered their own talent and made a part of the whole. Some discovered musical talents on penny whistles and mandolins, singing or Earth chanting...It was a new and extremely natural way of life (1997, pp. 26–7).

Dongas is originally a Matabele word, meaning gully in the land, the tracks made by people and their carts going back and forth to market. It was used to refer to the ancient pathways on the proposed site of the Twyford Down road. The adoption of this as the name of the tribe thus indicated the specific area that was being protected but goes beyond this in suggesting an affinity with preindustrial lifestyles based upon the land. The aim of the Dongas is to wean 'itself off what it sees as a destructive society ruled by commercial images and shopping. They are rediscovering their roots and heritage' (1997, p. 27). Indeed, Becky of the Dongas tribe refers back to the 'peasants':

> [They] had the right to make a living off the land, growing vegetables and coppicing but over the centuries they were evicted by landowners. The land was fenced off in the Enclosures Act and the peasants were forced into the cities. They lost the land which was their means of living and they had to start relying on money and jobs. I don't want their jobs or their money, I want land but I don't have any right according to the property laws of this country (1997, p. 27).

This neo-tribal identity allows individuals to step outside the confines of western culture and to forge an alliance with communities across the globe which they consider to be 'like them' and are most under threat from the forces of capitalism and industrialisation. There is an atmosphere of immediacy amongst protesters, a sense that their political stance, both in terms of lifestyle and forms of action, is necessary in order to save the planet from environmental destruction. According to one male protester:

> The situation on this planet is so intense, we are on the edge of an abyss. There
> is no second chance, if it doesn't go in the right direction we've had it. [We must
> be] as frugal and basic and as green as we can.[15]

The sense of urgency portrayed by the British environmental direct action movement results in an almost missionary and 'millenial' fervour (Purkis, 2004). Activists believe so strongly in what they are doing and maintain that people would listen and make the right choices if they had all the facts: 'there is nothing more powerful than the idea that the time has come'.[16] Thus, no matter how pervasive and powerful the mechanisms of environmental destruction are perceived to be there is an imperative to continue the struggle. As a female protester admitted:

> If I really thought that people still wouldn't care even if they knew the facts then
> I would drop out of society and become more Buddhist or meditative. The social
> protest movement really believes people will change. People who are involved
> are transformed.[17]

Protesters revel in stories about 'locals' who remain involved and interested in direct action even when the protest in their locality is over. A female activist who had been involved in the M11 anti-road protest in East London excitedly explained to me that there had been some suburban housewives in Wanstead who were affected by the proposed road plans and joined the protesters in objection:

> They are still wandering around dressed like hippies a year after everyone has
> gone and they are still political, like fighting the CJA.[18] People wake up, the
> most unlikely people, suburban housewives![19]

Personal accounts of transformation are invariably spoken about in highly emotional terms. Many activists I spoke to attested to the fact that taking part in direct action had changed their lives. I first met Joe, 22 years old, at an Earth First! gathering and later in many other situations. He explained to me that it was through the protests against the Criminal Justice Act in 1994 that he had first become involved in direct action and had lived at many protest sites including Newbury and Wandsworth. However, he said that now he cannot imagine living any other way; direct action has become a way of life, his way of life. Similarly, as another activist claimed: 'I've never been happier or healthier' since adopting this lifestyle.[20] Protesters attest not only to a sense of satisfaction from feeling that

---

[15]   Wandsworth Eco-village, 16/7/96.
[16]   Wandsworth Eco-village, 16/7/96.
[17]   Buddha Field Festival, 18/7/96.
[18]   Criminal Justice Act (1994).
[19]   Buddha Field Festival, 18/7/96.
[20]   Wandsworth Eco-village, 16/7/96.

they are contributing to positive social change but also claim that they benefit from the personal challenge.

However, direct action pushes individuals to their physical and psychological limits. They tread a precarious path between positive personal transformation and achievement, and serious risk to mental and physical health, or 'burn out'. For example, there were widely covered stories in the press about individuals involved in tunnel digging at road protest sites. Their aim was to make it as difficult for the contractors to clear the sites in preparation for development. With activists buried deep under the ground, often 'locked on' to concrete blocks, any disturbance to the land above would potentially lead to the collapse of the tunnels. This begs the question whether it is bravery or insanity that drives activists. An article, headlined 'Buried 50ft down in sodden red clay, Swampy[21] plots Britain's biggest fight yet with the car!', reports that he plans to 'live almost permanently underground…in readiness for when the bulldozers move in' (Jury, 1996). This issue of personal transformation and challenge is emphasised by a female activist, Alex Donga, who writes,

> DA (direct action) is the result of empowerment of the individual. It implies self-control, self-belief and a person's self-determination. It is a way of life in itself. The other results of DA – publicity, empowering capabilities and results of the action itself are by-products of the act – albeit something useful (1996).

Thus, direct action is seen as much as a source of personal transformation as social. The motivation to remain involved is more than a rational, intellectual response to deteriorating environments and the social injustices this generates but is deeply emotional and often spiritual. Whilst there are many direct activists who are not particularly sympathetic to an explicitly spiritual perspective, Deudney argues that appeals to self-interest alone are likely to be insufficient to maintain commitment to a particular cause, particularly once the initial goal has been achieved or abandoned. He suggests that 'Earth religion' helps maintain a commitment to environmentalism (1995, p. 290) and argues that 'Earth religions and radical ecologism are passionate political agendas. Unlike more mainstream or reformist environmentalism, they evoke emotion, passion, and intense personal commitment' (Deudney, 1995, pp. 285–6). Whilst some direct activists articulate their aims in terms of the need for political transformation others consider that the spiritual transformation of humanity is necessary not only to remedy environmental destruction but to bring about a more egalitarian global society. The Earth itself is recognised as a sacred entity, as divine, with which the individual is fundamentally interconnected; human and environmental justice can only be

---

[21]   Swampy became a media 'hero' with both his protest activities and personal life the subject of newspaper articles and TV chat shows. It ought to be pointed out that many other activists resented his media status and were sharply critical of the way in which he came to be seen as a spokesperson for the movement.

achieved through recognition of this sacred principle. Thus, Earth religion, or religious environmentalism, provides individuals with a rationale for pursing such activities, as well as a vehicle for expressing their concerns. It is a means of justifying and facilitating personal transformation.

*DIY Healing, Ceremony and Action*

The direct action movement is frequently referred to as 'DIY culture'. This not only reflects the idea that if you want to change something you have to do it yourself, but also the idea that it is flexible and responsive to situations, that its form of articulation is not bound to any pre-existing rules or institutions. The attitude towards spirituality within the movement reflects this idea of 'DIY'. Individuals tend to reject the authority of established traditions and instead draw upon a range of religious and cultural traditions that are interpreted ecologically. For example, most gatherings include what is known as a 'healing area' where a wide range of therapies including homeopathy, reiki, acupuncture and crystal healing, as well as spiritual disciplines from Paganism, to Buddhism and the Hare Krishna are offered. As the programme for the 1996 Big Green Gathering explains:

> In this 1996 Big Green Gathering we in the healing area will be coming together to celebrate and enhance the joy of life, but also to recognise ourselves as witness to the deterioration of our environment which threatens the quality and even the very fabric of life itself. As consciousness and self-awareness increases we will be able to learn and grow together in an atmosphere of loving support.

Despite the great variety of spiritual techniques and ideas that are used by activists, it is possible to identify central core beliefs and values underlying this eclectic expression of spirituality. These beliefs and values, on the one hand, reflect the understandings of religion and the environment discussed in earlier chapters and, on the other hand, are expressed in terms of the two religious environmentalist assumptions; that religious traditions are inherently environmentally friendly and that at some time before the modern era an 'ecogolden age' existed to which it is desirable to return.

*Healing*    One of the functions of gatherings is to contribute towards healing. For example, an Earth First! gathering offered a number of workshops on health issues including 'Camp Living and its Attendant Diseases' (which involved the sharing of experiences on how to live on a camp and stay healthy), first aid, self defence sessions, discussions on how to avoid 'burn out' and information on diet and the effects of toxic pollutants. Additionally, the gathering had a formal healing area, a space at the centre of the field within which a large bender had been erected and where individuals ran sessions on Earth healing and meditation, as well as offering massage and other therapies. People make their homes at protest sites, often for months on end, but live with the constant anxiety that at any moment their tree houses, benders or whole communities could be demolished. Coupled with the personal investment in the cause itself, the stress of this lifestyle often brings immense pressure to bear upon individuals. It is not uncommon for people to become depressed, with alcoholism and drug abuse emerging as serious problems within the movement. This highlights the importance of attending gatherings and festivals as an opportunity to 'chill out' away from the pressures of the ecobattlefield and is also a reason given for the existence of healing areas or sacred spaces at such events as well as within protest communities. The protest movement cannot survive if individuals are unbalanced or out of touch with themselves and lose sight of their goals. The 'return' to traditional or holistic healing can be seen as a broader reaction within this alternative community against contemporary medicine, which is considered to concentrate on the physical at the expense of the other aspects of human nature; healing cannot be successful unless it considers the whole person (Cant, 1996; Easthope, 1986; Graham, 1999). Healing, in this broad sense, is considered to be fundamental to the underlying ethos and ultimate success of the movement.

In addition to confirming and expressing individual and shared values, there are rituals that are considered to have a direct power to heal the Earth. 'Ecomagic' or Earth healing aims to access the divine powers inherent in nature and the individual, and to direct them towards healing the Earth.

*Worship and celebration*   It is common to find rituals at gatherings and protest sites which seek to reaffirm common values. At the 1996 Big Green Gathering a group called 'Tree Spirit' (an organisation based in Wales, which is concerned with the protection of trees and woodlands. It is not 'religiously based', considering that it cuts across such 'artificial' divides), organised a tree planting ceremony where 13 trees associated with the eight seasonal festivals[22] were blessed in preparation for planting as a sacred grove. Celebration of the eight seasonal festivals and the 13 annual full moons are popular amongst activists and individuals may travel to sacred sites or conduct their own rituals at protest camps. However, there is often no set formula for celebration during these periods, which may involve anything from a big party to carefully planned rituals and prayers. The ceremony included praise to the Goddess and to the spirits of each tree as an expression of the re-sacralisation of nature. As Glennie Kindred, a founder member of Tree Spirit, writes,

> Throughout the world, trees have been revered as divine sources of wisdom and worshipped as deities. The ancient people believed that trees were sacred and contained a spirit who could be talked to. There are many documentations of

[22]   The Winter Solstice (20–23 December) – Birch and Rowan, Imbolc (beginning of February) – Willow, Spring Equinox (20–23 March) – Alder and Ash, Beltane (early April/ Beginning May) – Hawthorn, Summer Solstice (20–23 June) – Oak and Holly, Lammas (beginning of August) – Apple and Hazel, Autumn Equinox (20–23 September) – Blackthorn and Samhain (end October/beginning November) – Yew and Elder (Kindred 1995).

ceremonies for felling trees, warning the tree spirit, or asking for its forgiveness. Trees were honoured and thanked for their gifts and treated with respect and awe (1995, p. 3).

Shortly after the tree planting ritual there was a Druid ritual at a nearby set of standing stones, erected during the previous gathering, and in a far corner of the healing area the Hare Krishnas were chanting. Many individuals attended all the above rituals as general expressions of Earth spirituality, of re-affirming the sacredness of the Earth.

*Activism and non-violence*    Activism itself is also considered by some individuals to be a ritual activity. As an expression of environmental values, it is seen as a ritual expressing love and respect for the Earth. Furthermore, protest activity is largely non-violent and in general protesters will not deliberately use physically violent strategies in the course of actions. However, non-violence does not generally extend to violence against property. Criminal damage is common in the course of actions as are forms of 'psychological violence', such as the use of loud music in trees at protests, verbal abuse used against police on the front-line and even harassment in the form of letter writing or phone calls to directors of construction companies.

There are strong ideological reasons for the avoidance of physical violence, which are based upon the concept of Babylon, which, as mentioned previously, is considered to use aggressive means to control nature and humanity. If physical violence is used then the protesters are playing by Babylon's rules; if Babylon is to be fundamentally challenged then alternative non-violent strategies must be employed. As one activist argues, 'social transformation requires personal transformation. We need to become the type of person we would like to live in our communities'.[23] However, activists also refer to the example of Mahatma Gandhi and the Indian idea of *ahimsa*, non-violence or non-harm. Gandhi extended this traditional Indian teaching to the domain of political protest where he emphasised that fighting the 'aggressors', the British, with their own tactics, violence, was not as effective as approaching them non-violently. It could be argued that Gandhi resorted to this traditional idea as a strategic measure because his followers did not have the resources to wage a violent battle against the colonial army and indeed this is suggested by some activists as a good reason to adopt a non-violent approach. However, Gandhi's freedom movement drew great support and was eventually successful in bringing about an independent India. Despite the suggestion of this as a tactical move, it is generally believed that the movement was at least partially successful because of its adherence to the spiritual teaching of *ahimsa* (Chapple, 1995; Gupta, 1995).

---

[23]    Workshop on non-violence at Earth First! gathering, 14/6/96.

## Conclusion

This chapter has illustrated how some radical environmentalists in Britain utilise spirituality to express their concern for the natural world. Spirituality, rather than religion *per se*, provides a source of legitimation for their commitment and is seen as a means of facilitating personal transformation. The type of religious environmentalism found within the environmental direct action movement is not bound to any one religious tradition; there are no religious specialists and no particular places of worship. At the most basic level the Earth is considered as sacred and individuals chose from a range of traditions that can be interpreted as supporting an ecological ethic. The sacredness of the Earth is not considered to be a new revelation but instead to be found within most religious traditions, particularly those of preindustrial societies.

There is a tendency, nonetheless, for activists to idealise the lifestyle and values of small scale, non-industrial societies. This is juxtaposed against the belief that it is the humanity-nature dualism of Christianity and the growth of capitalism and modern technology, which has thrust the planet into environmental crisis. I have also suggested that this celebration of certain non-western and preindustrial lifestyles is selective in that it overlooks the hardships or gender inequalities often found within such communities and is anachronistic in that it is unlikely that such societies were/are as consciously environmentally aware as we are often lead to believe. Many radical environmentalists abstract and interpret certain religious concepts and practices to match their own ideology asserting that these traditions are concerned with the natural environment and that their beliefs and practices have traditionally helped maintain harmony with the natural world. Religious environmentalism within the environmental direct action movement tends to make two fundamental assumptions: that non-Christian religion/spirituality is environmentally friendly and that an 'ecogolden age' existed at some point in history to which it is possible to return. Smith argues, however, that 'many primitivists go wrong in thinking that innocence is a state of being, a life that can be lived; that the state of nature is something that we can actually inhabit, a future possibility" (Smith 2002, p. 421). While this 'state of nature' may well be a mythic place, it is also important to reflect upon the role that narratives about it play in capturing something important that people feel they have 'lost' within modern society. Various styles of cultural borrowing and anachronistic re-readings of the past are important ways of defining and maintaining social action with respect to the environment as well as other concerns (and, as such, have their own inherent value). Grand narratives and myths can serve to be affective and motivational, but they can also marginalise and essentialise other groups in ways that can undermine their self-determination.

Thus, the critique of 'neo-primitivism' here is not just concerned with the factual accuracy of its meta-narratives, but also with the postcolonial critique of the idealisation, romanticisation and 'mis'-representation of certain non-western and preindustrial peoples as essentially 'close to nature'. Globalisation has exacerbated environmental risk and problems but has also meant that people have increased access to knowledge about other cultures. This in turn, however, has meant that cultures can be represented in ways that might be damaging to their members' self-determination. People involved in EDA clearly care very much about what is happening to people in other parts of the globe, but scholars who emphasise the unequal power relations underlying dominant representations of environmental concern (e.g. Guha, Baviskar, Nanda), may well suggest that the efficacy of EDA activists is diminished when their vision of the situation is skewed by romanticism and a tendency to interpret the needs of others in terms of their own experience and priorities. Others have drawn attention to the borrowing of religiocultural resources to suit modern and novel causes as tantamount to 'cultural theft' or even 'ethnocide' (Niman, 1997).

However, I would argue that these critiques can become over-extended and hyperbolic. Charges of 'cultural theft' often do not take adequate account of the fluidity of the boundaries between traditions and cultures. There is often an implicit assumption in such critiques that there is something sacrosanct about 'tradition' or 'culture'. The homogenising forces of globalisation have also given birth to their opposite: a virtual sacralisation of cultures and traditions where it is argued that these must be preserved intact. The idea that 'traditions' should be preserved is as much a *Romantic* response as the idea that people ought to remain close to nature. Moreover, the issue about cultural theft is not just a concern about preserving tradition, but also about who has the right to interpret and transform tradition. This again brings our attention to the unequal power relations underlying dominant representations of environmental concern. But this consideration too can become over-stated and over-inflated, for example, when it fails to account for the instances when the poor appropriate environmental stereotypes about themselves to serve strategic ends (Brosius, 1999). Thus, I would argue that there is a danger that the hyperbolic over-use of charges of 'cultural theft' or the 'myth of primitive ecological wisdom' can lessen the efficacy of these important critical tools: to 'essentialise the essentialisers' is potentially undermining. My aim in the following two chapters is to explore the use of religion in the Indian environmental movement. While I am sympathetic to the arguments of scholars, such as Baviskar and Guha, that the discourses presented by the global environmental movement do often idealise and romanticise poor people, I am also interested in how these discourses are actually played out in an Indian context.

# Chapter 6
# Hinduism and the Environment: Radical to World Religions Approach

## Introduction

In the following chapters my aim is to look more closely at religion and environmentalism in India. Firstly, however, I would like to outline the reasons why I consider India to be a relevant focus for a study on religious environmentalism. Carrying over the discussion from the previous chapters, one of my central research questions in this study is to consider the extent to which religious environmentalism is a narrowly conceived, romantic western agenda or has a broader relevance and appeal. India has a large and prominent environmental movement and also a strong and vibrant religious culture. I am interested in whether the two intersect in a way that is genuinely useful to the concerns of people in India or is the union of religion and environmentalism a postmaterialist phenomenon of little relevance to the majority of the population, predominantly an ideology of Baviskar's 'well meaning middle class activists' or 'bourgeois environmentalists' (1997; 2004)? Moreover, my primary focus will be upon the Hindu tradition for a number of reasons. Firstly, Hinduism is the oldest and largest religion in India (in the region of 85% of a population of over 1 billion); secondly, it is the tradition that has received most attention with respect to environmentalism in India and has also been written about widely outside India; finally, a focus upon Hinduism will allow me to engage with recent critiques of the union of religion and environmentalism in India that draw attention to the links between religious environmentalism and the Hindu Right.

## Hinduism and Environmentalism

Having visited India more than a dozen times, spending close to two years there in total, I am acutely aware that it is both one of the most religious places upon the Earth as well as one of the most ecologically compromised. Traffic and industrial pollution, poor sanitation and filthy waterways, devastating annual floods, and rapid and widespread deforestation all threaten the health and wellbeing of a mostly poor, rural population. At the same time, India is heading for status as one of the world's fastest growing economies, with the emergence of a new middle class that is educated, urban and affluent. It is a country frequently beset with communal religious tension, most heightened between Hindu and Muslim communities, and continues to be socially stratified according to caste and gender.

There are literally thousands of environmental NGOs in India, but relatively few are faith-based. In the course of researching this book, my interviews with ecologists, members of NGOs and faith traditions did reveal that religion is a component of the environmental movement in India but not to the extent that one might imagine considering the high level of religiosity. A number of hypotheses can be suggested to account for this. Firstly, perhaps Hinduism is not 'environmentally friendly'. This is an important point and one to which I will turn shortly: as argued in previous chapters I consider religious environmentalism to be a contemporary phenomenon – an *interpretation of tradition rather than a traditional interpretation*. Secondly, is it the case that religious environmentalism is postmaterialist and as such not really relevant to environmentalist thought and action where people cannot afford to put the Earth first?

Finally, it is likely that issues around secularism in India mean that public organisations desist from identifying themselves as religious. When India gained independence from Britain in 1947, the first government, under the Congress Party of Nehru, adopted a secular form of politics: one where there would be a distinction between religion and the state. This position has had its supporters and critics. Anti-secularist thinkers, such as Nandy (1997) and Madan (1992), have argued that this is a model that has been imported from the West and is not appropriate for a country such as India where secularisation has not really taken hold. As Varshney points out, although secularism has become an accepted feature of western culture, 'there is no similar civilizational niche for secularism in India. Religion was, and remains today, the ultimate source of morality and meaning for most Indians' (1993, p. 243). Such thinkers argue that secular politics in India has in fact allowed the rise of aggressive forms of religious nationalism, where the Indian version of secularism (which emphasises that the state should be equidistant from different religions rather than reject religion) has resulted in a situation where the government is seen by rival religious factions as favouring one religion over another. Thus, the state has been unable to deal with religions on an equal basis (and at times has clearly shown favour to one over another), which has allowed religious unrest to multiply (Varshney, 1993). Others, such as Nanda (2002), are avowedly secularist and whilst they draw attention to the shortcomings of current understandings of Indian state secularism, are against any call for a greater involvement of religion formally in political matters. These concerns and debates in India have a clear relevance for thinking about the role of religion in environmentalism in India. For instance, with respect to Hindu groups there seems to be suspicion that they are typically affiliated to various 'Hindu Right' groups, or that they can be easily co-opted. As I will discuss in more detail in the next chapter (where I discuss the links between religious environmentalism in India and the Hindu Right) this history of 'secularism' has led to a great deal of suspicion about public expressions of religiosity in India. In particular, the ascendancy of the Hindu Right and its attempts to 'capture' civil society mean that it can be difficult for groups to identify themselves as religious for fear of being aligned with malign religiopolitical forces.

However, before we look at the case studies, I will first review the types of publications that exist around the theme of Hinduism and environmentalism. Much of the work here has been done already, in a useful review article by Van Horn (2006), and below I outline the main themes in his study.

*The Literature on Hinduism and the Environment*

Is Hinduism 'environmentally friendly'? My particular approach to this question relates to a concern that much of the literature on Hinduism and the environment presents a somewhat abstract exegesis of the tradition rather than a reflection of what people actual do and believe in. So in answer to this question, my response would be: 'yes and no'. While there is much in the tradition that would seem to support care for nature ('yes'), Hindus do not practice an ecological religion ('no'). What interests me is the extent to which and the ways in which ecological interpretations of Hinduism can be translated into actual practice or changes in behaviour. This will be the focus of the case studies presented below. To foreground this discussion, however, I will now turn to Van Horn's review of literature on Hindu traditions and nature, which provides a careful survey of the fairly substantial body of work in this area (2006). He divides the literature into five sections: 'green' themes in Hindu traditions; sacred topography (this will also be the focus of Chapter 7 of this book); the legacy of Gandhi; globalisation; feminism and resistance; and animals (I will not review the section on animals as it is not directly relevant to this study).

With respect to '"green" themes in Hindu traditions', Van Horn writes that 'some scholars have sought to bring to the fore whether particular religious traditions can be interpreted (or revised) in ways that promote or reinforce environmentally-beneficial behaviours' (2006, p. 8; e.g. Chapple, 1998; Gosling, 2001; Kinsley, 1995; Prime, 1992). While he considers that this is based upon the assumption that systems of beliefs can influence behaviour, and points out that some have been critical of this approach for its 'turn to the East' in search of alternative paradigms (e.g. Larson, 1991; Nelson, 1998b), he considers that this literature is a useful starting point for those 'interested in the broader debates of whether or not Hinduism, or select Hindu traditions, are "green" or potentially so' (2006, p. 8). Turning to 'sacred topography: rivers, forests, and land', we find that 'the topography of India has often been associated with gods and goddesses, which provided Hindu practitioners with ritual referents that are rooted in the physical landscape' (2006, p. 16). The worship of the Ganges River as the goddess Ganga Ma is discussed by Eck (1996) and the work of Alley (1998; 2000), which is discussed in Chapter 7 of this book, draw attention to the apparent paradox between the veneration of the Ganges as a goddess and its pollution with material waste. Other works on rivers include Feldhaus' (1995) study of 'powerful riparian metaphor of fecundity and motherhood' (Van Horn, 2006, p. 17), with respect to rivers in Maharashtra, and Haberman's (2000) study of the 'textual ideals related to the Yamuna river and their impact on religious culture' (Van Horn, 2006, p. 17). There is also a substantial literature on forest protection and sacred groves (discussed in Chapter 7 of this book), with a focus upon the Chipko movement in particular. Whereas James (2000) considers Chipko to be rooted in 'a religious perception of nature, the sacred nature of the trees' (2000, p. 508), Van Horn indicates that 'the religious significance of Chipko is an area of considerable debate' (2006, p. 18). Lee in his article on the Ramayana, including its extensive stories of sacred forests, argues that these can be 'effectively used to encourage respect and teach natural history' (2006, p. 19). As we will see in Chapter 7, there is also much debate about whether or not the existence of sacred groves in India, which are still found throughout the country, is evidence of an attitude of environmental conservation inspired by religious belief. On the one hand, Appfel-Marglin and Parajuli consider that such groves indicate a 'moral ecology' amongst tribal peoples that has emerged from their direct engagement with the forests (2000). On the other hand, Freeman is critical that this is anachronistic and that it tells us more about the contemporary ecologist than it does about Indian society (1999).

The next section of Van Horn's review article considers the legacy of Gandhi, 'a prophetic figure and a source of inspiration to those who participate in ongoing environmental struggles' (2006, p. 23). In particular, Gandhi's legacy is felt in 'some of the more effective resistance movements against destructive development in India' (2006, p. 23) and Gruzalski discusses this influence with respect to the leaders of the Chipko movement, Sunderlal Bahuguna and Chandi Prasad Bhatt (1993, pp. 101–2). In opposing development projects that promote the idea that 'bigger, faster and more is better' (1993, p. 111), the Chipko movement is 'also expressing the ideas of economic equality, sustainable village economies, respect for ecosystems, and liberation from economic colonization' (1993, p. 118). However, what is the link here with religion and spirituality? Shinn (2000) points out that while Gandhi was neither an environmentalist nor theologian/philosopher, his thought and practice have become resources for the environmental movement. He integrated Hindu religiophilosophical concepts such as non-violence (*ahimsa*), self-rule (*svaraj*) and truth (*satya*) into a set of practical teachings about the integrity of the small-scale village economy in India and the view that independence from British rule should be sought through non-violent means. To extend Van Horn's review, it is worth mentioning here the work of Gadgil and Guha (1995) which considers that there are three strands of environmentalism in India: the 'crusading Gandhians'; the 'ecological Marxists' and the 'appropriate technologists'.[1] For our purposes, the 'crusading Gandhian' is most relevant, in that it:

---

[1]  I will not outline the second two styles here. See Gadgil and Guha (1995, pp. 108–10) and the discussion in Chapter 4 of this book. In addition to these three styles found within the public environmental movement, they identify two further strands that do not have a following amongst the public although they do influence government policy: the 'wilderness enthusiast' and the 'scientific conservationist'.

Relies heavily on a moral/religious viewpoint in its rejection of the modern way of life. Here, environmental degradation is viewed above all as a moral problem, its origins lying in the wider acceptance of the ideology of materialism and consumerism, which draws humans away from nature even as it encourages wasteful lifestyles....These environmentalists call, therefore, for a return to pre-colonial (and pre-capitalist) village society, which they uphold as the exemplar of social and ecological harmony. Gandhi's own invocation of Ram Rajya (the mythical but benign rule of King Rama) is here being taken literally, rather than metaphorically. In this regard, crusading Gandhians frequently cite Hindu scriptures as exemplifying a 'traditional' reverence for nature and lifeforms (1995, p. 107).

Apart from the influences upon the Indian environmental movement, Gandhi's thought has also impacted upon western ecological philosophies. Van Horn discusses the influence of Gandhi upon the deep ecological thinking of Arne Naess (Aitken, 1985; Jacobsen, 2000). Naess had been particularly inspired by Gandhi's interpretation of the *bhagavad gita*, which he 'sees as commensurate with certain deep ecological principles: an understanding of the organic unity of life, self-realization, and non-injury' (Van Horn, 2006, p. 25; Jacobsen, 2000, p. 242).

In the section of the review article entitled 'globalization, feminism and resistance', Van Horn explores literature that draws attention to the ways in which globalisation and colonialisation have created India's environmental problems and that adopt a 'Hindu civilisational' response as social resistance. The ecofeminist work of Shiva (1988) and Gnanadason (1996), both of whom draw upon the Hindu feminine principles of *prakriti* and *shakti*, assert that 'nature has been symbolized as the embodiment of the feminine principle, from the time of the pre-Aryan thought in India, and this must form the core of an Indian feminist eco-theology' (1996, p. 76). Others such as Pintchman (1993) and DasGupta Sherma (1998) are critical of this tendency to romanticise and essentialise women as close to nature, particularly since the veneration of the feminine divine in India is at odds with the low status of women in society. Similarly, Guha's article (discussed in Chapter 4 of this book) critiques deep ecology for its romanticisation of eastern cultures and for its cultural bias towards wilderness preservation as counterproductive in a country like India, where people are directly dependant upon natural resources (1989).

Critiques of the 'Hindu civilisational' response to environmental problems are increasingly showing a marked shift from a sole emphasis upon its romanticism and idealism, to focus upon the ways in which Hindu religious environmentalism in India is interlinked with the Hindu nationalist movement. On the one hand, the styles of rhetoric used (i.e. about a pure Hindu culture having been manipulated and devalued by outside influences) show marked similarities. On the other hand, actual organisations that make up the Hindu nationalist movement in India seem to be taking up environmental causes and forming alliances with environmentalists. This is discussed in an article by Mawdsley (2005) where the involvement of the

Vishva Hindu Parishad (VHP) in protests over the building of the Tehri Dam on the River Ganges is analysed. As Van Horn writes, 'Mawdsley's article serves as a reminder that "resistance" comes in many varieties, and environmental issues are not impervious to bids for fundamentalist religious and political power' (2006, p. 31). This is an important feature of religious environmentalism in India and will be taken up in Chapter 7 where I discuss issues and concerns around the pollution of the Ganges River.

The above discussion has sought to answer the question 'is Hinduism environmentally friendly?' However, rather than providing a 'yes' or 'no' answer it has instead given rise to a series of issues that will be explored in the following case studies. What is the relevance of the interpretation of religious texts to support contemporary environmentalist thought? Are these exegeses of any value if they do not reflect what people actually believe and do? What is the vision of these religious environmentalist narratives? The apparent emphasis upon the 'return' to small-scale traditional economies lends itself to critique for being over-romantic and postmaterialist. Concerns over who is providing these interpretations (e.g. 'bourgeois environmentalists'?) and for what end (e.g. to bolster the agenda of the Hindu Right?) have emerged as crucial considerations in assessing the relevance of religious environmentalism for India. Therefore, it is also important to consider the fears of those who argue that religious environmentalism in India is actually 'harmful'.

In the remainder of this chapter I will present two 'contrasting' case studies of examples of religious environmentalism in India. The first of these is an example that closely resembles the style of environmentalism and religiosity discussed in the previous chapter: radical environmentalism and deregulated spirituality. In July–August 1997 I attended a 'Rainbow Gathering' in India at Almora, in Kumaon region in the state of Uttarakhand. During this gathering both Indian and non-Indians assembled to discuss environmental issues facing India and to 'celebrate the sacredness of the Earth'. In common with the environmental direct action movement in Britain, the 'Rainbow Family' tends to be ideologically opposed to mainstream society and is committed to pursuing the creation of an alternative social sphere. In fact many individuals involved in British environmental direct action movement also consider themselves to be 'Rainbows'. Conversely, whilst the Rainbow Family is not explicitly an environmental direct action movement, if individual members become involved in environmental action then it is more likely to be radical. In terms of Gadgil and Guha's styles of Indian environmentalism (1995), the 'Rainbow Family' in India involves the influence of both 'crusading Gandhians' and 'wilderness enthusiasts'. While, as I will illustrate, the sort of radicalism and counterculturalism found in the Rainbow Family does have limited appeal in India, it is nonetheless a suitable place to start our exploration of religious environmentalism in India. On the one hand, there are clear synergies and overlaps with the material presented in the previous chapter on EDA in Britain, indicating a fluidity of cultural boundaries with respect to the flow and influence of ideologies and practices associated with concern for nature. On the other hand, it is an interesting place to begin a discussion of the broader relevance of religious environmentalism for India, since it is markedly postmaterialist and *Romantic*.

This second case study presented in this chapter is concerned with a different approach to religious environmentalism that is not radical or countercultural in outlook and that stresses the contribution that particular religious traditions or world religions can make towards environmentalist thought and action. This 'world religions' approach is clearly articulated by a UK based organisation called the Alliance of Religions and Conservation.[2]

TWO CASE STUDIES FROM INDIA: FROM 'RADICAL ENVIRONMENTALISM' TO THE 'WORLD RELIGIONS APPROACH'[3]

## 1. Rainbow in the Himalayas: The Radical Environmentalism Approach

*Introduction*

The gathering was held in a small hamlet, *Papar Saili*, a few miles from the town of Almora, in the Himalayan foothills. Participants assembled at 'Tara's Tea Shop', a popular roadside cafe owned by the Tewari brothers, which for twenty years had attracted a mixture of expats, travellers and locals making their way down the mountain road back to Almora. This was one of the heartlands of the hippy counterculture, and the so-named 'Rainbow House' (a large colonial-style building whose veranda afforded stunning views of the Himalayas and which formed the focus for the gathering) was rumoured to have been a favourite haunt of counterculturalists such as Timothy Leary and Herman Hesse. The veranda of the building provided the communal focus and was decorated with pictures of Hindu deities and posters about the gathering:

> We will gather together in a beautiful forest area near Almora. We will live together and share from our hearts, celebrate the full moon with music, *bajan* chanting and art programs. We have no fees and no membership cards. We live and provide everything through our own effort and contribution. We have no leaders. As activists we put our talents and skills together and devote our time with spiritual awareness. We see ourselves as one family on one earth, interconnected. We work to overcome hostility and separation. We go beyond the limitations of nationalism by seeing ourselves as brothers and sisters.

---

[2]  The research undertaken at the Rainbow Gathering employed similar research methods to those used for the case study on radical environmentalism (Chapter 4). The research for the remaining India-focused research presented in this chapter and the next involved tape-recorded in-depth unstructured interviews and the documentary analysis of 'grey' literature.

[3]  See also Bron Taylor's distinction between 'green' and 'dark green' religion (2009).

We come together with the acceptance of our differences, religious, social, political and cultural and by celebrating our unity beyond as one global family. Each of us are splashes of colour creating the rainbow in which all colours exist. We seek to live as one family on this mother planet, learning from each other how to live in peace, dignity and friendship.

We plan an environmental gathering in Almora. Its aim is to reinforce the Indian Rainbow Movement and the global protectors. We will have workshops, teaching and exchange of knowledge about environmental protection. It will be a meeting from activists all over the globe. We pray that the Indian people awake and begin to live an environmentally friendly lifestyle. First of all we are one creation and one planet, we all have one and the same mother and only one. We open our heart to her and she feeds us and enables us to live. She is the divine mother. What I give to her she will give me back a hundred times. If I plant one corn she gives a hundred. We could live in an endless park in harmony with each other and the earth, but we are unable to! We create dump places, pollution of the elements, wars, hostility. We destroy the earth! Wake up! Change your life! The heart of the mother is wounded! If you destroy her she will destroy you. If you love her and you give to her, treat her well she will give you her love!

Many local people are already involved and with our help are interested in forming an environmental co-operative. The main activity of the co-op being the creation of environmental awareness programs for both children and adults through theatre, discussion and practical workshops as well as planting and maintaining organic-permaculture gardens and providing a voice for the people on environmental issues. We have organised for local school children to come to the gathering to talk about the environment, to draw, paint and be involved in small plays about the environment. We also plan after clear discussion to invite local farmers, forestry officials, business people etc. to talk about their situation, to learn and participate…This is a unique opportunity in India, help make it real. (All workshops, information in India will be in Hindi and English wherever possible.)[4]

So who are these 'Indian Rainbows'? Who participated in the gathering? And how does this radical, countercultural, alternative spirituality style of environmentalism fit into the broader landscape of the Indian environmental movement?

The above 'posters' suggest a number of themes central to the identity of the Rainbow movement. Firstly, we can see the idea of the Rainbow family as a vanguard to herald a new era, which resonates with the millennial fervour of the environmental direct activists in Britain. Secondly, there is an emphasis upon transformation – 'Wake up! Change your life!' – and, finally, it is globally orientated. This global dimension is reinforced by the theological orientation expressed on the poster: there is one Earth and one 'mother' upon which we are all dependent and with which we are all connected. The stress here lies not only

---

[4]    Rainbow Gathering posters, Almora, 1997.

upon the global scope of Rainbow's activities in that it expects and aims for global change but suggests the importance of global membership and participation: it is a 'global family'. The first Rainbow Gathering was held in Colorado, North America, in 1972, and this event heralded the inception of a now global 'Rainbow Family', 'Rainbow Tribe' or 'Rainbow Nation'. The Rainbow movement grew from two previously distinct separate social groups: the 1960s peace campaigners and Vietnam War veterans; 'the peace activists promoted peace, while the veterans were sick of violence. It was a natural union' (Niman, 1997, p. 34). More generally, the Rainbow Family is comprised of individuals belonging to a range of pacifist, anarchistic, alternative lifestyle and spiritual groups with the aim of creating an alternative society based upon 'peace and harmony'. However, as with the environmental direct action movement in Britain, there is no official membership and members of the Rainbow Family share similar traits to the direct activists discussed in the previous chapter. They hold postmaterialist values, are strongly countercultural and tend to be attracted to alternative spirituality.

Owing to the North American origins of the movement, the cultural and religious resources appropriated by family members were drawn from Native American traditions, in addition to the typical affiliation of such 'alternative' seekers with eastern spiritual and cultural traditions. However, as Rainbow has moved beyond North America it has absorbed and reflected the spiritual traditions of other regions. The gathering that forms the focus of this case study was held in India and hence exhibited a greater reliance upon Indian religiocultural beliefs, symbols and practices (e.g. the main Indian organisers described themselves as followers of Bhagwan Sri Rajneesh). Furthermore, the narratives used by members of the Rainbow Family reflect the two religious environmentalist assumptions/ narratives: that religious traditions are environmentally friendly and the belief in an 'ecogolden age'. However, as with the environmental direct activists, 'Rainbows' are likely to be highly critical of the dualisms of Christianity. Whilst the Rainbow Family has always extended 'peace and harmony' to include that between humanity and the Earth, the pursuit of environmental sustainability has become increasingly central to the aims of the movement over time.

The 'Rainbow Family' considers itself to be the fulfilment of a Hopi Indian myth, which prophesied the emergence of a tribe that will bring liberation to all oppressed and downtrodden communities across the globe. In fact one of the primary characteristics of the Rainbow Family is that members consider they are part of a libratory social movement; the vanguard of a new era based upon social and ecological justice and harmony. However, as Niman argues, in his book on the Rainbow Family in North America,

> Rainbows have written themselves into Hopi prophecies. One supposed 'Hopi prophecy' in particular seems ubiquitous on the Rainbow scene…'there will come a tribe of people of all cultures, *who believe in deeds*, not words, and who will restore the earth to its former beauty. This tribe will be called Warriors of the Rainbow' (1997, p. 134).

According to Niman, 'the prophecy is the Rainbow Family's ultimate romantic vision. It is *not*, however, Hopi' (1997, p. 134). He explains that a book written in 1962 by William Willoya and Vinson Brown, *Warriors of Rainbow*, elaborated upon information given to them by Thomas Banyaca, 'the sole survivor of a group of four young Hopis selected by Hopi elders in the 1950s to interpret their message and prophecies to the outside world' (1997, p. 134). Banyaca himself suggested to Niman that Willoya and Brown had come up with the idea of Rainbow Warriors, albeit based upon an interview with him. Niman considers this process is tantamount to 'ethnocide' (1997, p. 146) and at times insulting and arrogant as 'many Rainbows are not satisfied to align themselves with Native Americans, or to try to learn from them. They want to *be* Indians. A few even claim to out-Indian the Indians, claiming that they are here to teach Indians how to be Indians' (1997, p. 133).

This critique is also reminiscent of the broader rejection by some Native American groups and individuals of the appropriation of Native American spirituality by environmentalists, for the way in which it takes away their voice and misrepresents their culture. In previous chapters I also discussed this as part of the 'myth of primitive ecological wisdom' and put forward the view that this ecological essentialism can compromise a community's right to self-determination. However, as Bron Taylor argues, 'some cross-cultural borrowing reciprocal influencing, and blending is an inevitable aspect of religious life – thus at least *some* of the hand-wringing over appropriation and syncretic processes is misplaced and over broad' (1997, p. 206). On the one hand, traditional cultural and religious systems often develop *via* a process of borrowing elements from other systems. New systems emerge from old ones taking with them revised versions of traditional myths or prophecies, the development of Christianity from Judaism being but one example. Traditions absorb elements from other indigenous or nearby systems sometimes by accident and sometimes deliberately. This type of change may also be necessary if a tradition is to keep up with the times and to retain its followers. On the other hand, however, we also need to be attuned to the ways in which this process of cultural borrowing and representation is not a level playing field and may hide power differentials that silence marginalised voices. Nevertheless, the work of Broisius is worth drawing attention to here again. He is interested to highlight the strategic appropriation of 'the myth of primitive ecological wisdom' by certain communities as part of their struggle for ecological rights and is concerned that scholarly critique may undermine crucial strategies or resistance employed by the poor (1999).

This issue of 'cultural borrowing' and representation will be returned to in the concluding chapter of the book. For now, I intend to return to the case study of the Rainbow gathering in India and to assess its place within the broader context of Indian environmentalism.

*The Gathering: People and Activities*

There were a range of participants at the gathering, including non-Indian 'back-packers' who had heard about it through word of mouth or posters in cafes and hostels as far afield as New Delhi, expat locals and several local young men. While it is clear from the above posters that the participation of the local community was anticipated this was not successfully achieved and the numbers did not rise much above ten at the most. There was a degree of local curiosity and some interest, but the group remained isolated from the wider community. Quite a few local men came up to the Rainbow House to smoke *chilums* and to chat at sunset, relaxing and enjoying the peaceful atmosphere, and throughout the day women wandered by from the forest collecting branches and leaves for fuel and fodder, carrying huge bundles on their heads. Moreover, there was little participation from other members of the 'Rainbow Family' in India. Various reasons were given for this, including the suggestion that many Rainbows in India were not sufficiently dedicated to become involved in such environmental activities. It was suggested that they were used to the sort of 'lifestyle' gathering, resembling something more like the 'rave culture' discussed in the previous chapter.

The organisation of the day-to-day activities at the gathering closely resembled the typical Rainbow model. All meals were communal and people took it in turns to cook food in the old kitchen at the 'Rainbow House'. It was usual to invite passers by to join the meal and money for food was collected in the 'magic hat' earlier in the day. Before each meal there was a 'circle' where everyone joined hands and chanted the Sanskrit *aum* to give praise for the food and to strengthen the identity of the group. A circle was also formed prior to any meetings during which the 'talking stick' was passed to anyone speaking. The 'talking stick' was a long piece of carved wood with an animal horn tied to the end, which indicated to the rest of the group that someone was speaking and was felt to provide the speaker with the 'strength' to express their point of view. This was particularly important during a 'vision circle' where each person gives his or her vision or ideas about a particular issue whilst holding the 'talking stick'. A 'vision circle' aims to draw upon the collective energy of the group and to inspire individuals to participate effectively in the discussion.

Following the evening meal, local men would entertain us with religious or folk songs and others sang from the Rainbow songbook accompanied by a range of instruments: drums, guitars and sitars. There were popular Rainbow songs praising the Mother Earth Goddess, celebrating interconnectedness and the idea that we are all 'one', as well as many religious chants and songs of worship in Sanskrit and Hindi to Rama, Krishna and Shiva, and songs from Sufism, Judaism and Christianity. This ecumenical and unifying emphasis reflects the spiritual orientation of 'Rainbow': taking elements from a range of religious traditions whilst rejecting the traditional systems in themselves as inhibiting and limiting (this is also an important feature of the spirituality of Bhagwan Shri Rajneesh, discussed below).

One of the key topics of conversation during the gathering was a forthcoming trip that two of the organisers (one Indian and one European) were planning to take down the River Ganges by raft: following a route from its source, through the major industrial centres of India which have a strong religious culture surrounding the goddess Ganga and ending in Calcutta (Chapter 7 will discuss the enviro-religious culture of the Ganges). They planned to set up 'seed camps' along the way and to 'collect' new people. They planned to start in Gomukh, just north of Gangotri the source of the Ganges, and to walk to Haridwar at which point they intended to build a raft and travel down the Ganges to Calcutta to arrive in time for a festival called the *Ganga Mela* which marks the time when an island in the Ganges (*Ganga*) appears above the surface of the river. A myth associated with the origins of the Ganges tells of a powerful *sadhu* who lived there. A local king had a magical horse that could fly, which was stolen and was tied up on the spot where the island now stands. He thought that the *sadhu* was responsible so he sent hundreds of his warriors but they were turned to ashes. The king went to the god Shiva who took one of his dreadlocks (*jatas*) and transformed it into the Ganges. When the Ganges arrived in Calcutta it washed over the ashes and the warriors were revived (Eck 1985). They had produced a leaflet explaining the journey and also planned to write a booklet of stories about *Ganga* for other Rainbows as they did not understand its significance:

> The message spread after the vision council in Sept 96. It is the beginning of the Age of Aquarius. The bowl held by Aquarius is filled with the blood of the wise and is a sign of spiritual and mental purity and clarity. The bowl will be filled in Gangotri and will be brought all the way to Calcutta. The vision is deep and has many aspects belonging to the tribe.
>
> The *Ganga* is about 2500km long. It is the river which is a symbol of India and for mystical reasons it has been holy since Vedic times. Many spiritual devotees have gone to the *Ganga* throughout ages worshipping the holy places along the river. Such pilgrimages are common in India. Through ritual activity one relates to an inner process of psychic development and this is known as a powerful spiritual method to increase insight and realisation.[5]

The three local young men who took an active role in the gathering all described themselves as environmentalists and as followers of the Indian guru Bhagwan Sri Rajneesh (Osho). They were all in their twenties and educated to degree level. They were passionate about working to alleviate the environmental problems facing their region (e.g. deforestation, out-migration) but had found that other local people did not share their interest and concern: they put this down to a lack of education and spare time. Besides their participation in the gathering, they had a threefold agenda which they hoped would overcome these obstacles: firstly, to increase local awareness about the environment through education; secondly, to establish

---

[5]    Almora, July 1997.

an ecological farm as an example of how more environmentally friendly practices could be incorporated into already existing agricultural activities; and, thirdly, to raise the profile of the significance of a spiritual perspective to the above aims.

They had prepared a letter of introduction to send to potential funders:

Dear friends,

This is a call from the land of saints and spiritual devotion. We believe that we are all one creation on one planet and this earth being the eternal mother, so we need to live as a cosmic family in harmony with each other and with nature. Friends we are seeking for help to start a perma-culture project in Himalayan region where we have plenty of land to work on with the idea of restoration of nature. At present we wish to work on a land area of 15 acres which is barren but ideally located. This will be the first experiment of its kind in northern Himalayas. We wish to bring the active participation of local villagers in this agro-forestry which will be a great inspiration to all the people of northern Himalaya. We are a group of young and experienced people coming from various parts of Kumaon hills who have knowledge about the ecology of the Himalayan region. Friends our projects need a big finance and technical assistance but your little support could be a Big start. Hope you will share our vision of 'Global Family of love and light'. Any kind of help and support is always welcome.

Blended with this very practical initiative, however, is the influence of a style of spirituality reminiscent of that found within radical environmentalism more broadly. Whilst this letter indicates a desire to implement sustainable farming in their own region, statements such as, 'we are all one creation on one planet' and 'we need to live as a cosmic family in harmony with each other and with nature', resemble the rhetoric of EDA and the Rainbow Family. However, these young men very much saw these beliefs as part of their religiocultural traditions and considered that environmental protection and spiritual development went hand-in-hand. More specifically, their point of contact between traditional Indian religiosity and the more eclectic and deregulated spirituality of Rainbow and of EDA was the guru Bhagwan Sri Rajneesh, a controversial and radical Indian Guru who died, or 'left his body', in 1990 but not before he had accumulated a massive following across the globe. He was controversial as the famous 'sex guru'; his methods for spiritual enlightenment included tantric and other sexual techniques and he was seen to encourage and draw upon the permissive and hedonistic tendencies of the posthippie western counterculture. He challenged and rejected 'organized religions, worldly politics, and traditional notions to do with relationships, sex, marriage, and children...The crucial point is that all these activities are seen as being damned by virtue of their being dominated by externally imposed rules, stereotypes and expectations' (Thompson and Heelas, 1996, p. 48). For Rajneesh the mind and its attachments are a fundamental impediment to freeing oneself from the ego: therefore, the intellectual search for truth and order through politics or organised religion is doomed to failure. Neither religious creeds nor political ideologies can free humanity from mental slavery because they are not predicated upon the surrender of the ego (Rajneesh, 1976, p. 221).

*Rajneesh: Ecochange is Inner Change*

Rajneesh held an image of 'the new man' [*sic*], a fundamentally transformed individual who had surrendered the ego and no longer resorted to externally imposed rules and ideologies: the 'new man' has given up trying to change. This was the lesson accredited to Rajneesh following his own 'enlightenment', which is believed to have occurred on 21 March 1953. Born in Kuchwada, Madhya Pradesh, in 1931, with the gift of being able to recall his previous lives, Bhagwan is credited with having been a particularly gifted and inquisitive student, prone to ruminating upon the 'big questions'. As a young man he became interested in politics and soon began intensive periods of meditation, fasting and other austerities. However, he became aware that his extreme efforts were getting him nowhere and he stopped trying. Shortly afterwards he became enlightened. Following this revelation he returned to the world of work as a professor of philosophy until 1966 and in 1970 established the 'Neo-Sannyas International Movement' which at first attracted many Indians but by 1971 had begun to establish a solid base of western support. In 1974 a site was chosen in one of Pune's (in Maharashtra) most prestigious neighbourhoods and a permanent Ashram was founded. As Mullen tells us, 'from 1974 over 30,000 persons – predominantly middle-class, well-educated and young, but not completely so – travelled to Poona each year from all parts of the globe. At any one time there were about 6,000 rajneeshees in Poona' (1983, p. 23). These individuals underwent an initiation process where they acquired a new name and, at least whilst they were attending classes at the Ashram, wore 'sunset' coloured robes. During the following two decades communities were established across the globe, predominantly in western nations, and in 1981 Rajneesh moved his base to Oregon in the USA, and formed a community called Rajneeshpuram. However, by 1985 Rajneeshpuram had collapsed amid legal scandal and internal schisms and now the headquarters can be found back in Pune (Mullen, 1983).

From the very beginning, the Pune Ashram had an emphasis upon vegetarianism, growing food and physical health. Today, the cleanliness of the environment in which Osho Commune International in Pune is located contrasts with much of the rest of the city: there are paths and curbs running alongside well maintained roads, trees and plants flank the roadside and there are no open sewers or piles of garbage. For Osho the root of the problem underlying environmental degradation is the individual consciousness. As Swami Satya Vedant, the director of the Ashram's 'Multiversity', explains:

> Unless your inner ecology is taken care of, outer ecology will never work. Because what we do outside is a manifestation of the inner world. Because we feel so clean, so quiet, so together inside that we would like to see the same thing happening outside ...You know it's like a messy child and the mother keeps coming and cleaning his room and the next morning she comes and the room is messy. It has nothing to do with the room it has to do with the child. The child is messy. So if we are messy inside, this mess is going to appear obviously outside.[6]

So the key is meditation in order to cut through the socialisation and conditioning we all experience from birth. The approach of Osho parallels the more radical ideology of the British direct activists and the Rainbow family who are suspicious of environmentalism when it does not deal with the fundamental core problem of the human/nature relationship. As Joshi writes,

> The resolution of the issue of ecological sustainability, therefore, is not in putting band aids on environmental problems, but in addressing now, immediately, the state of humanity, the state of ourselves. And any honest investigation will show that the missing link, the one magic formula that will allow us to be at ease with ourselves – consequently allowing us to be at one with our neighbours and the trees – is meditation (1996, p. 6).

Unlike Osho, however, direct activists aim to directly transform society, being sharply critical of capitalism, and this is reflected in the emphasis upon direct action to effect environmental change. By contrast, for Osho the starting point is the individual. As Joshi writes, 'the reason we find ourselves in the mess we are in is because that is how we are – messy. Until we change, until the individual changes, the earth will be a mess' (Joshi, 1996, p. 6). However, both examples emphasise the need for personal transformation, although Osho is less likely to advocate environmental direct action as a valid means of social and personal transformation.

Whilst he drew upon and wrote voluminous commentaries about traditional religious systems, he respected what he saw as their core wisdom but rejected what he considered to be their rigid organisational and dogmatic superstructure. In particular, with the notion of 'Neo-Sannyas' we can see a borrowing of the Hindu concept of renunciation. However, for the traditional Hindu, *sannyas* is a concept that means to renounce the world in order to overcome attachments and reach enlightenment. By contrast, as Mullen points out, the teaching of Rajneesh fits Wallis's[7] category of a 'world affirming' new religious movement (1983, p. 16). Osho presents a critique of science and technology that differs from that of radical environmentalists and which fits his 'world affirming' orientation: it is not science

---

[6]   Pune, 24/2/97.

[7]   Roy Wallis (1984) makes a distinction between world rejecting, world affirming and world accommodating religious movements.

and technology itself which is environmentally damaging but rather that it is in the hands of individuals who do not know how to use it for the benefit of humanity and the Earth. However, for Osho, science and technology result in a level of wealth which means that people do not have to struggle for their survival; it furnishes them with their basic needs and more besides in order that they may devote themselves to spiritual progression. Not surprisingly, from the very beginning of his mission, Rajneesh attracted followers from predominantly western backgrounds rather than Indian ones.

Carter suggests that one reason for the relative absence of Indian followers is that 'Bhagwan Shree Rajneesh is only one of thousands of "godmen" practicing in that country' (1990, p. 111). However, unlike many of these other 'godmen' the message of Bhagwan is more likely to appeal to a 'western psyche', with its emphasis upon individualism, radicalism and the rejection of external authority. Belfrage describes followers of Rajneesh as

> inevitably well-off, if only in the post-hippy flower-child sense of caring little for cash but always able to summon up enough to fly halfway round the world...It's also the kind of money that seems to breed in its owners dissatisfactions requiring extreme measures to put right. Through with radical politics, drugs, communal living, feminism, psychoanalysis, encounter groups, they're seeking still more exotic solutions for problems that are luxuries in the first place (1981, p. 7).

The young male followers of Osho who organised the Rainbow Gathering would seem, to a degree, to fit this 'postmaterialist' profile. While only one of them had attended courses at the main Ashram in Pune, the others attended the 'Osho Camps', which periodically occurred in the area; these cost a few hundred rupees, a fraction of the price of joining a course in Pune.

Participation in radical environmentalism and alternative spiritual movements is relatively uncommon in India. The style of religious environmentalism reflected in both Osho's movement and the Rainbow Family is postmaterialist and *Romantic*, stressing inner or personal transformation. How does this radical, countercultural, alternative spirituality style of environmentalism fit into the broader landscape of the Indian environmental movement? In the next section of this chapter I will be interested to look at the 'world religions approach' in India. A good place to begin a discussion of this is with respect to the work of the Alliance of Religions and Conservation. This is a UK-based organisation that works across the globe to support and encourage conservation work linked to religious traditions and faith-based organisations. I will particularly focus upon an initiative that they supported in India from 1992–98 called the 'Vrindavan Forest Revival Project'.

## 2. The World Religions Approach: The Alliance of Religions and Conservation and the Vrindavan Conservation Project

*Introduction*

The scope of the activities of *The Alliance of Religions and Conservation* (ARC) extends across the globe. ARC grew from the ideas and interest generated by a meeting held in September 1986 when representatives of five of the world's major religions (Christianity, Buddhism, Islam, Hinduism and Judaism) met in Assisi to present declarations concerning the environmental nature of their religious traditions. This meeting was jointly organised by the World Wide Fund for Nature (WWF) and a Manchester based organisation, the International Consultancy on Religion, Education and Culture (ICOREC), and, as the patron of WWF, Prince Philip, the Duke of Edinburgh, attended this event. These statements became known as the 'Assisi Declarations' and they reflect the two religious environmentalist narratives outlined above: the belief that religion is environmentally friendly and the recourse to ideas of an ecogolden age. For example, according to the Buddhist declaration:

> Buddhism is a religion of love, understanding and compassion, and committed towards the ideal of non-violence. As such, it also attaches great importance to wild life and the protection of the environment on which every being in this world depends for survival.
>
> From existing sources there is evidence to suggest that for all their limitations, people in the past were aware of this need for harmony between human beings and nature. They loved the environment. They revered it as a source of life and wellbeing in the world (WWF, 1986, p. 6).[8]

And the Hindu declaration:

> In the ancient spiritual traditions, man was looked upon as a part of nature, linked by indissoluble spiritual and psychological bonds with the elements around him. This is very much marked in the Hindu tradition, probably the oldest living religious tradition in the world...[T]he natural environment also received the close attention of the ancient Hindu scriptures. Forests and groves were considered as sacred, and flowering trees received special reverence...The Hindu tradition of reverence for nature and all forms of life, vegetable or animal, represents a powerful tradition which needs to be re-nurtured and re-applied in our contemporary context (WWF, 1986, pp. 17–19).

---

[8]  Given by the Venerable Lunrig Namgyal Rinpoche, Abbot, Gyuto Tantric University.

While this style of religious environmentalist discourse has been criticised for being anachronistic, for romanticising the link between interpretations of tradition and what people actually do (in the past and today) and for essentialising poor, 'religious' people as inherently close to nature (therefore making a range of assumptions about what is ultimately in their best interests), my aim in this chapter is to look more closely at the ways in which the two religious environmentalist narratives are operationalised. I do think that this critique ought to be taken seriously, but that it can also be over-laboured thus missing important work being done with respect to the environment that draws upon religious belief and the local networks and legitimacy of faith-based organisations. I am less concerned with this critique when the religious environmentalist narratives have a clear instrumental effect, and are strategically adopted by local environmental groups, than when they represent the edenic longings of postmaterialist environmentalists.

## *ARC and its Impact in India*

Following the meeting in Assisi, the 'Network on Conservation and Religion', of which WWF were the primary sponsors, was formed and a magazine called the 'New Road' (this was later replaced by another publication, 'News from ARC') was launched to publicise its activities and to present articles upon different aspects of religion and environmental conservation across the globe. This publication contained articles about people inspired by their religious traditions to undertake environmental projects, as well as about the ecological content of religious traditions and stories about environmental disasters or the destruction of 'ecologically benign cultures'. By 1995 Baha'is, Jains, Sikhs and Taoists had joined the alliance and representatives of a total of nine faiths were invited to meetings in Japan and Windsor Castle for the 'Summit of Religions and Conservation'. At these meetings, the 'Alliance For Religion and Conservation' was launched and a nine-year plan agreed for each tradition. While ARC focuses upon the so-called world religions, and avoids affiliation to alternative spiritual groups, it is more sympathetic towards indigenous or tribal religiosity. ARC has five main aims:

1. To assist and encourage the evolution of practical educational projects which increase the involvement of religions in caring for the natural environment.
2. To assist and encourage the development of religious and ethical programmes within conservation bodies.
3. To assist and encourage events which bring together religion and conservation groups to promote ties and develop practical conservation projects.
4. To raise and grant funds for the above aims.

5. To publish and promote materials which explore the links between religions and conservation and broaden the aims of ARC.[9]

Underpinning this list are two broad but interconnected aims: to encourage religious communities to increase their involvement in caring for nature and to introduce a religious and ethical component into conservation projects. The first can be seen as an attempt to heighten the awareness of environmental issues within religious communities as social groupings. Religion is used as a means of encouraging the involvement of religious communities, of making environmental issues more relevant. This aim is based upon a belief that recourse to the authority of religious traditions can motivate people to change attitudes and behaviour towards the environment.

The scope of ARC's activities extend across the globe, with funded projects and networks in countries including India, China, Indonesia, Thailand, Egypt, Tanzania, Lebanon and the UK.[10] In India there are currently six projects: 'Hindus restore sacred forests in Orissa'; 'Jains rebuild earthquake village'; 'Parsis recycle fire temple flower offerings'; 'Sikh Gurdwaras use alternative energy'; 'training and aid for rural women'; and 'Zoroastrian sacred Baval groves'. ARC has incorporated these projects as part of its 'Sacred Gifts' initiative:

> Every religion believes that the gift of life itself is sacred: we do not own it, but we have responsibility to care for it. It was this shared understanding that led WWF and ARC to create a special term of praise and recognition for major significant new projects launched by the World's religions in 2000.[11]

In addition to the support of such projects and networks, since 1996 ARC has met with representatives of the World Bank to encourage it to incorporate faith considerations into development and environment work. A number of joint publications have emerged between ARC and the World Bank (2003; 2006) and there are several jointly run projects.[12] Thus, in addition to working at the grassroots level, ARC has also been successful in courting the support of major influential development bodies, such as the World Bank.

The remainder of this chapter will look more closely at a project that was funded by ARC and WWF from 1992–98, in Vrindavan, a popular pilgrimage town in North India that is believed to be the birthplace of the god Krishna. In July 1991:

---

[9]  Taken from a document produced by ARC which outlines the guidelines for applicants for funded projects.

[10]  http://www.arcworld.org/projects_by_region.asp (last accessed 18/07/08).

[11]  http://www.arcworld.org/projects.asp?projectId=49 (last accessed 18/07/08).

[12]  See, http://www.arcworld.org/projects.asp?projectID=50. These are outlined in the 2006 publication available at http://www.arcworld.org/downloads/FaithsandEnvironment%20adobe.pdf (last accessed 18/07/08).

WWF India started to work with Vrindavan's people, to *learn how their specific faith and spiritual beliefs could be mobilised to save their environment*. The focus was on greening the 11-km sacred pilgrimage route, and on highlighting the original conservation traditions of cleanliness and respect for nature.[13]

The project 'aimed at educating the local people and pilgrims and motivating them to protect their spiritual homeland. It began with tree-planting as a focus, but has since extended to embrace a much wider range of environmental activities'.[14]

## *The Vrindavan Conservation Project*[15]

Vrindavan, and the surrounding area of Braj/Vraj, is the most important pilgrimage place in India for worshippers of Krishna. As Alan W. Entwistle writes,

> Braj can be seen as the Hindu equivalent of a 'theme park', the most extensive of its kind in India, a 'Krishnaland' for devotees seeking tangible stimulus for the imagination. This was so even in the sixteenth century when devotees came to Braj and mapped everything out, 'inventing' a location for every canonical and apocryphal incident in the life of Krishna...Braj is, *par excellence*, a centre for a devotional type of pilgrimage (1987, pp. 103–4).

It is associated with mythological accounts of the birth and life of Krishna. These usually include rich and evocative descriptions of the natural environment, of forests, lakes and animals that provide the backdrop to much Krishna mythology. By contrast, the Vrindavan area today is heavily polluted and deforested/ urbanised. The sacred river Yamuna, or Jamuna, has become a dumping ground for local waste as well as a carrier for toxic effluent from nearby New Delhi. In addition, the tourism industry, which has been built up to accommodate the hundred of thousands of pilgrims who visit the region each year, creates further environmental hazards. However, as Ajit suggests (2004) the role of religious institutions in environmental management in pilgrimage towns in India has been marginalised in favour of other stakeholders typically at the forefront of processes of 'participatory governance' (involving the management of natural resources). He writes that the 'traditional focus of research in participatory governance seems to revolve around inclusion and interaction of prominent stakeholders such as private sector, industry, NGOs, and Voluntary and Non-Profit Organizations. Religious institutions, though an important part of society have received little

---

[13]    WWF India Publication, 'Vrindavan Conservation Project'.

[14]    ARC document, 'Current Arc Funded Projects, Reforesting the Sacred Forest of Krishna, Vrindavan, India'.

[15]    It was originally called the Vrindavan Forest Revival Project, but was re-named to reflect a broader remit beyond tree planting: 'greening, cleaning and education' (http:// www.fov.org.uk/history/history.html, last accessed 18/07/08).

attention, if any, in such discussions' (2004, p. 1). Vrindavan has more than 5,000 temples devoted to Krishna and attracts more that 25,000 pilgrims every day, rising to 200,000 on religious holidays (MVDA, 2001). It has a population of 56,000 and in 2000 around 2 million pilgrims visited (MVDA, 2001). Thus, its sanctification as the 'play area' of Lord Krishna contributes towards local environmental pollution, but considering that the 'strengths of religious institutions include moral authority; capacity to shape worldviews; a large base of adherents; significant material resources; and community building capacity' (2004, p. 1), the role of religious institutions in mitigating ecological problems is worthy of consideration. The Vrindavan Conservation project is amongst the few initiatives discussed by Ajit (2004).[16]

The Vrindavan Conservation Project began its life under the auspices of two men – one local, Sevak Sharan, and another from the UK, Krishna devotee Ranchor Prime, who had been visiting the area since the mid-1970s and had watched its environmental problems develop. Together they sought funding from WWF International and 'in November 1991 the Vrindavan Forest Revival Project was launched, boldly funded in its first year [1992] with £25,000 from WWF in Geneva'.[17] It was established as part of WWF's 'Network for Conservation and Religion' and became one of the first projects to be supported by the 'Alliance of Religions and Conservation', when it was formed in 1995. When I first visited Vrindavan in 1993 the emphasis lay upon 'greening' the *parikrama* path (a path which runs around sacred places in India, in Vrindavan, the *parikrama* path runs around much of the ancient town) and the upkeep of a tree nursery which had been established along the path on land belonging to ISKCON[18] with the aim of distributing a tree to all the residents of Vrindavan. However, at that time the project was poorly managed and many of the trees planted along the *parikrama* path were carelessly destroyed. From 1992–98, the project was funded by WWF and since 1998 by a UK-based charity called Friends of Vrindavan (FOV). FOV was started by Ranchor Prime in 1996 to work alongside and eventually take over the work started by WWF, and after some years managing the work from a distance they went into partnership with a local charity called 'Food for Life Vrindavan' (FFLV). FFLV, whose wide-ranging humanitarian work in Vrindavan includes environmental activities, partially supports itself with funds raised by FOV.[19]

---

[16]   The project is also discussed by David Haberman in his recent book about the River Yamuna (which flows through Vrindavan) and environmentalism (2006, ch. 5).

[17]   http://www.fov.org.uk/history/history.html (last accessed 18/07/08); the project received six years' funding from WWF: WWF International in Geneva funded the first three years and WWF India the second three years. This original work has now led to the development of several government-funded initiatives, backed by both the U.P. State and the Government of India, to protect the Braj environment.

[18]   International Society for Krishna Consciousness.

[19]   Overtime, a number of different organisations have emerged. The original UK-based FOV (http://www.fov.org.uk) is winding down and its work is being continued by

In 2005 Vrindavan was chosen as one of four Eco-cities (along with Puri, Tirupati and Ujjain) by the government of India for basic sanitation and waste management funded by UNDP. FFLV works as a principle partner in this project.

FOV was established in Leicester, one of several specially designated 'Environment Cities' in the UK. However, there was some concern about how to involve the large Asian community in environmental activities. FOV is concerned with encouraging the local Asian population, mainly Hindus in this case, to become involved in preserving Vrindavan's environment because of their religious and cultural ties to India. For instance, several sponsored cycle rides, from the source of the river Yamuna to Vrindavan, have been held:

> Friends of Vrindavan is a unique project linking the community of Leicester, UK with the regeneration of sacred rain forests in Vrindavan. At the 1992 UN Conference on Environment and Development, great emphasis was placed on North-South links, encouraging communities from our Western societies to form partnerships with communities in the developing world to tackle environmental problems...Leicester and other cities in the UK owe much of their relative affluence, directly or indirectly, to Britain's historic link with the sub-continent of India. In the case of Leicester, with its thriving Asian community, this relationship is inescapable. Friends of Vrindavan is therefore an important symbol of commitment to a shared approach to the problems of our planet.[20]

FOV aimed:

1. To preserve and enhance the sacred forests and ecology of Vrindavan in order to protect its culture and traditional way of life for the general good of the community.
2. To advance the education of the general public, both in the UK and India, particularly in the region of Vrindavan, by and through improving the environment and ecology of the sacred forests of Krishna, as a focus for understanding sacred values and cultural traditions.
3. To advance the education of the public, particularly the children, by encouraging them to undertake practical environmental projects, such as planting, preserving and protecting trees.
4. To conduct research into ecological practices appropriate to Vrindavan and to publish and disseminate that research for the benefit of the general public both in UK and India.[21]

---

Food For Life Vrindavan (http://www.fflvrindavan.org). There is also a locally-based Friends of Vrindavan that now runs its own projects (http://www.friendsofvrindavan.com) and a newer NGO in the region called the Braj Foundation, carrying out similar work (http://www.brajfoundation.org) (last accessed 18/07/08).

[20]   www.btinternet.com/~jeff.cank (last accessed 3/07/07).

[21]   Friends of Vrindavan Newsletter 1997.

As Ranchor Prime explained:

> Everyone in Vrindavan doesn't so much see Krishna as being some religion out
> there, it's so much part of their daily lives, they kind of take it for granted. It's
> almost like football for kids here or something. It's part of their daily lives and
> they don't see it as something special or separate. Krishna could just be one of
> the blokes! What it's really aiming to do is make connections: 'okay you are
> worshipping Krishna or whoever, but what about the fact that Krishna loves
> nature and the environment?[22]

It is believed that this depth of familiarity with and commitment to a religious
tradition may be used to persuade people to become more environmentally
conscious in their daily activities. In Vrindavan, for example, I came across the
following myth again and again in a new environmentalist context. According
to this myth a huge poisonous serpent named Kaliya decided to live in the river
Yamuna and the whole river and surrounding area subsequently became polluted.
Krishna found out about this after his cowherd friends became unconscious having
drunk from the river. Krishna fought with and eventually overcame Kaliya and the
water returned to its pure state. Ranchor Prime explained to me:

> A good example of that is the story of Kaliya and the poisonous snake. Now at
> no point in history up until now has the Yamuna been poisonous. Now it is the
> most polluted river in India. So all of a sudden that story has a new significance
> that it just didn't have before. So I think it is perfectly right to say to people
> 'Look again! And in the light of what you see now do you see a message there?'
> I think it is okay to do that.[23]

*Krishna in Vrindavan*

The idea of the environmental idyll of Krishna's mythic time in Vrindavan is the
central religious theme that FOV utilises. As Entwistle writes,

> The devotional poets of Braj, in their descriptions of this sylvian setting, often talk
> of lanes leading through the tangled thickets to secluded seasonal bowers, and
> sometimes include such formal elements as pavilions and summer houses. Such
> forests are places where natural passions are given free rein, contrasting both
> with the town, where life governed by social norms, and the older conception of
> the forest as a place where ascetics retire to practise austerities (1987, p. 301).

This forms the dominant expression of the 'ecogolden age' that is used in
Vrindavan today in the context of concern for the environment. This image

---

[22]   Interview London, 24/9/96.
[23]   Interview London, 24/6/96.

of how Vrindavan used to be in Krishna's time is juxtaposed against the open sewers and deforestation, which are so familiar today. However, this narrative in itself is by no means a modern creation, as Entwistle points out: 'from the medieval period onwards, under the influence of devotional Hinduism, more emphasis was given to the idea that the wooded areas are reminders or relics of the *environment of a golden age*' (1987, p. 301). Thus, the recollection of a Vrindavan, surrounded by a serene and beautiful environment, has for several hundred years been linked to a yearning for the time when Krishna was present in Vrindavan, an era when people were constantly graced with his divine presence and blessings, a time when people were more connected with the *dharma* (truth, law or duty). This symbolic image of Vrindavan is a strong element of local culture. Therefore, the idea of regenerating the sacred forests of Krishna has a potent local resonance. However, Entwistle's 'environment of a golden age' is not an environmental golden age. Whilst the natural environment features in the myths of Krishna and has a strong place in the collective local memory it serves as a symbol of better times in general rather than a symbol of environmental harmony. Thus, a traditional symbol of Vrindavan is being given new environmentalist significance.

*Renovating the Sacred Places of Krishna: Mansarovar*

In the traditional literature about Krishna's life and exploits, there are twelve forests mentioned around Mathura and Vrindavan and, as Entwistle writes, they 'have always been an essential element in the setting for Krishna's bucolic adventures. The oldest name for the wooded area is 'Vrindavana', which, in the earliest sources, refers to an extensive forest rather than to the specific place known as Vrindaban' (1987, p. 299). However, whilst these forests no longer exist, the entire Vraj region is littered with the memory of natural features associated with the mythology of Krishna. These include Govardhan Hill, which Krishna lifted up to protect the shepherds and their cattle from a terrible storm sent by Indra. Witnessing this feat the shepherds came to recognise him, rather than Indra, as their god (Winternitz, 1990, p. 429). There is a *kadamba* tree beside the river Yamuna where Krishna is said to have hidden the *gopis*' ('cow girls') clothes whilst they were bathing. There are actually two places in Vrindavan with a *kadamba* tree by the Yamuna, both called Chir Ghat, where this incident is said to have taken place. As Entwistle points out, people are unperturbed by such duplication; 'no problem', he said, 'we can make a third if we want' (1987, p. 276). Also popular in Krishna mythology are the bathing places where Krishna would retire to cool off and to play with Radha (one of Krishna's consorts) and the other *gopis*. One such place is called Mansarovar and FOV have been involved in its restoration. Mansarovar is about three kilometres from Vrindavan and beside the lake there is a temple to Radha and two bathing 'ghats', one for the women and one for the men. FOV intended to develop Mansarovar as a picnic spot.

Mansarovar (also the name of a lake high in the Himalayas, one of the two lakes on either side of mount Kailash which is the abode of Lord Shiva) is a place which local people are familiar with through mythological stories about the life of Krishna. As Jagannath, the 'operations manager' of FOV explained: one day when Krishna didn't come to play with Radha she went to Mansarovar to sulk. Eventually he found her there and they were reconciled. There is also a myth about how Shiva came to visit Mansarovar. A sage called Asun lived on a mountain and practised austerities, meditating on Krishna and Radha. One night he desparately wanted to find Krishna and went searching everywhere. He found Shiva on mount Kailash and asked him for help. Shiva praised Asun for his diligence and told him that he could find Krishna with the *gopis* in Vrindavan. Shiva and Asun went together to the bank of the Yamuna and found their path was blocked by the *gopis* who said that Krishna was the only male who could participate in the *rasa* dance and that they would first have to become *gopis* by bathing at Mansarovar. They did this and went off to join Krishna. They praised Krishna and he was impressed by their asceticism and offered them a boon. They asked to stay in Vrindavan and this was granted (Entwistle, 1987, p. 59).

Whilst bathing in the waters of Mansarovar is traditionally believed to be auspicious, the area had largely fallen into disuse. The lake was clogged by water hyacinths, which 'poison' the lake with carbon as they decay to make way for new growth. In the summer they suck up a tremendous amount of water, which is then lost as it evaporates into the atmosphere. FOV employed a team of men to clear the lake of water hyacinth and to remove some trees and bushes to plant fruit trees and religious trees. Whilst water hyacinths were still clogging up large sections of the lake, wildlife was slowly returning to the area; a large variety of birds were now feeding and nesting by the banks of the lake. The men who were clearing the lake were considered to be 'very brave' as most local people were scared of the water because of water snakes and other creatures. I asked Jagannath whether they see it as a privilege to clean up Krishna's place. He replied that it is just a job like any other for which they were grateful. FOV have been successful in creating further employment for the local community. Michael Duffy, an Englishman living in Vrindavan and one of the directors of FOV there, explained that whilst they started off with the aim of protecting and regenerating the sacred forests of Krishna also took on board a project to collect refuse in Vrindavan. The 'municipality' had not managed to organise this successfully and most of the town's refuse was dumped on the banks of the river Yamuna. At the time, they had employed thirty *harijans*[24] and had used funds raised to purchase a tractor to help shift the refuse[25] (see also Haberman, 2006, pp. 153ff).

---

[24]    *Harijan* means 'children of God' and was the name used by Mahatma Gandhi for members of the untouchable or outcaste community.

[25]    Interview, Vrindavan 29/4/08.

**Conclusion**

Many of the studies reviewed in Van Horn's article (2006), discussed at the beginning of this chapter, would seem to indicate that a consequence of ecological interpretations of Hinduism is that they are likely to leave one with an inflated image of the significance of religious and cultural values to conservation of the environment in both past and present India. For instance, this 'over inflation' is found in the writing of the Indian ecofeminist Vandana Shiva, who writes that 'all religions and cultures of the South Asian region have been rooted in the forests not through fear and ignorance but through ecological insight' (1988, p. 57). She argues that the culture of the forest 'was not a condition of primitiveness but one of conscious choice' (1988, p. 56). Whilst it is true that the environmental impact of such societies was low, it is unlikely that this was deliberate or from a sense of environmental consciousness or that it was inspired by religious values. Moreover, a further critique that has been sidelined in this chapter, is concerned with the distinct unease that many (secular) commentators in India feel about the overt *Hinduisation* of many sociopolitical agendas; environmental or otherwise. The project in Vrindavan, for instance, has been criticised for employing similar symbols and discourses to the Hindu Right in India, a chauvinistic religiopolitical force in the country that has as its priority the establishment of a Hindu *rashtra* (nation). This critique will be returned to in the following chapter, where I discuss the blurring of the boundaries between genuine concern for ecological issues and an aggressive religionationalistic agenda that also employs religious environmentalist language.

However, putting this critique to one side for now, the above case studies would suggest that religion does play a role in the contemporary Indian environmental movement. While we must be critically attuned to the problems associated with such discourse, the presence and significance of religious environmentalism should not be ignored in India. We have to look carefully at the context to know whether and what sort of criticism is appropriate; otherwise charges of romanticism and misrepresentation can become overextended and hyperbolic. My research has indicated that we can find examples of environmental initiatives that employ seemingly romantic religious environmentalist language and symbols to encourage people to maintain certain types of behaviour with respect to the environment and to transform others.

The first case study of the Rainbow gathering in Almora indicates a style and use of religious environmentalism that closely resembles radical environmentalism and deregulated spirituality found within EDA in Britain. In common with the environmental direct action movement in Britain, the 'Rainbow Family' tends to be ideologically opposed to mainstream society and is committed to pursuing the creation of an alternative social sphere. In fact some individuals involved in British environmental direct action movement also consider themselves to be 'Rainbows'. While the sort of radicalism and counterculturalism found in the Rainbow Family does have limited appeal in India (we should not overestimate its appeal in Britain or the USA either, it is a marginal or sub-culture) there are clear synergies and overlaps with the material presented in the previous chapter on EDA in Britain, indicating a fluidity of cultural boundaries with respect to the flow and influence of ideologies and practices associated with concern for nature. The second case study, by contrast, is concerned with a different approach to religious environmentalism that is not radical or countercultural in outlook and which stresses the contribution that particular religious traditions or world religions can make towards environmentalist thought and action (see also Taylor's distinction between 'green' and 'dark green' religion (2009)). The symbol of Krishna is particularly useful in drawing attention to environmental issues in Vrindavan, to raise funds and secure public support for environmental work in the region. The traditional religious worldview is typically strong in India and religious projects can attract support from even the poorest sectors of society. So the contrast that I wish to draw here is between postmaterialist, *Romantic* religious environmentalism (such as the Rainbow gathering in Almora) where people are responding to expressive ethics about protecting nature for its own sake, and the way in which motivational language is used in Vrindavan, not because of an ethical call to protect nature for its own sake, but rather because of the association of the natural world with stories about the god Krishna. If we return to the discussion in Chapter 2 about the different 'ethical styles' suggested by Charles Taylor – theism, disengaged reason and *Romantic* expressivism (1989, p. 495) – the Vrindavan example would seem to correspond to the 'theistic model' (reflecting the way in which traditional religion exerts authority over the individual) and the Rainbow example would seem to match the expressive style (typically concerned with the creative imagination, intuition and individuality as a source of morality and authority).

Whilst many people in Vrindavan do seem to have a strong connection with their natural environment, this is not necessarily an indicator of environmental awareness. Instead the local natural environment is tied up with the mythology of Krishna and a yearning for the time when Krishna was visibly and perpetually present in Vrindavan. This is locally understood more as a symbol of a golden age in general rather than an 'ecogolden age' in particular. However, groups, such as Friends of Vrindavan, are attempting to transform this local religious sentiment into environmental concern. Thus, we can suggest that the motivation to become involved with the forest conservation project may not be for the sake of the environment *in itself*. As Oliver Yih-Ren Lin points out, with respect to some ecological Buddhist organisations in Taiwan, people are taking on board environmental concerns as an additional way of generating merit rather than for the sake of the environment.[26] People are changing their behaviour for religious rather than environmental reasons. I would argue that we can see a similar process in Vrindavan, where environmentalists are using the power that religion has in people's lives to encourage them to change their behaviour. It is a way of making

---

[26]   Personal communication, April 1999.

people concerned about issues beyond their immediate needs. Moreover, the Friends of Vrindavan have also created economic opportunities for local people to become involved in looking after the local environment (e.g. collecting refuse, clearing water hyacinths).

In Chapter 4 I suggested that in addition to the globally oriented *managerial* and *Romantic* styles of environmentalism there exists a third type, which I termed the *local pragmatic* (see also Friedmann and Rangan, 1993; Taylor, 1995). Firstly, in some contexts the local environment upon which people are dependent for their day-to-day needs is more likely to be the focus of concern rather than the global environment. Secondly, people are more likely to engage with environmental activities for pragmatic reasons rather than as an expression of ecocentric values. It is worth returning here to Hannigan's suggestion that claims about the environment make use of two main rhetorical tactics 'which vary according to the nature of the target audience' (1995, p. 35). The first of these is the 'rhetoric of rectitude', which 'justifies consideration of environmental problems on strictly moral grounds' (1995, p. 47) and the 'rhetoric of rationality', where 'ratifying a claim will earn the audience some type of concrete benefits' (1995, p. 36). *Local pragmatic* environmentalism appeals to a 'rhetoric of rationality' whereas the *Romantic* style appeals to a 'rhetoric of rectitude'.

How does this tripartite schema (*Romantic, managerial* and *local pragmatic*) map onto the case studies presented in this chapter? While, in practice, it is of course not possible to differentiate between these three styles clearly within particular examples of environmentalism (a mixture of these different types is likely to be demonstrated), one style will typically tend to dominate within different examples. I would argue that the gathering in Almora is a fairly straightforward case of the *Romantic* style. The second case study is more complex since it employs the *Romantic* narrative but within a context that more closely reflects *local pragmatic* environmentalism. We find a blending of *Romantic* discourse within the context of *local pragmatic* environmentalism.

In the next chapter of this book, I suggest that religion is often used 'strategically' by environmentalists and ecologists in India to encourage people to adopt environmentally friendly behaviour. This strategic approach differs from the *Romantic* in two main ways. First, religion is being used for pragmatic reasons. Whereas for the *Romantic* religious environmentalists, a spiritual/ religious approach is considered to be fundamental to changing the relationship between humanity and nature, I suggest that in India there is often no particular commitment to pursuing a religious approach in itself. I refer to this as 'weak religious environmentalism' in contrast to the 'strong religious environmentalism' that is typical of the postmaterialist, where recourse to religion and spirituality are felt to be *essential* elements of the total transformation that humanity needs to undergo in order to prevent ecological disaster (e.g. EDA in Chapter 5). The terms 'strong' and 'weak' are used here in the sense of capturing the degree to which those using the discourse 'buy into it'; the strong religious environmentalist strongly affiliates with the discourse and values it highly in itself, whereas the weak religious environmentalist is much less attached to it and employs it for practical or instrumental reasons. Moreover, for proponents of strong religious environmentalism, ecological concern is considered to be an authentic and critical element of religious belief and practice (rather than *just an* interpretation that can be put to strategic or practical use).

Secondly, rather than referring to ideas of how humanity 'ought' to act towards the natural world and notions of global responsibility, weak religious environmentalists in India are more likely to stress particular religious customs and symbols to motivate behaviour change more locally (the theistic ethical model). The aim is not to necessarily challenge and transform human-nature relations in totality, but instead to effect more immediate and practical improvements to the local environment. It is to do with improving material conditions rather than expressing postmaterialist values. So how does the Vrindavan project fit this distinction between strong and weak religious environmentalism? Instead of considering strong and weak to be two distinct alternatives, it is more appropriate to consider them as lying on a spectrum. The Vrindavan project, I would suggest, is not very strongly affiliated to the religious environmentalist discourse, since its primary aim does not so much seem to be to challenge and transform human-nature relations, but instead to effect more immediate and practical improvements to the local environment: their version is not postmaterialist nor does it invoke expressive ethics about protecting nature for its own sake (it should be protected because of its association with Krishna). However, in contrast to the examples that will be discussed in the next chapter (of ecologists 'weakly' employing the religious environmentalist narrative), the members of Friends of Vrindavan are devotees of Krishna, and as with the proponents of 'strong religious environmentalism', ecological concern is considered to be an authentic and critical element of religious belief and practice (rather than *just an* interpretation that can be put to strategic or practical use).

# Chapter 7
# Religious Environmentalism in India[1]

## Introduction

This chapter looks more closely at two main critiques of religious environmentalism in India and will assess the extent to which they undermine its role in addressing ecological concerns. First, we find the critique that religious environmentalism is anachronistic. Pederson, for instance, argues that claims about the environmental nature of religion are 'anachronistic projections of modern phenomena onto the screen of tradition' (1995, p. 264). The material presented in this chapter, to assess this critique, will focus upon case studies where the two religious environmentalist narratives are employed: the protection of sacred groves and the protection of sacred rivers (with particular reference to the River Ganges). It is still common in India to find worship of elements of the natural world (including plants and trees, mountains, rivers and certain animals, birds and reptiles) within the range of beliefs and practices that permeate the spiritual landscape of the subcontinent. These must, however, be distinguished from religious environmentalism, which is a conscious and reflexive application of 'nature religion' to contemporary concerns about the destruction of the natural environment. While features of the natural world emerge as a focus within Hindu religious belief and practice, any assessment of the extent to which such elements of the tradition can actually be translated into ethics and action that serve the interests of environmental conservation, needs to be carried out with careful reference to specific situations. As Baviskar writes 'all belief systems are embedded in social and political structures; simply appealing for a change of heart is not enough. If an ecologically sound way of life is to be brought about, the arrangements for extraction and exploitation need to be transformed' (1999, p. 27). While the existence of nature religion, therefore, does not necessarily imply environmental values and awareness, what potential is there for nature religion within Hinduism to be transformed into ecological religion? What would such an ecological religion look like in India, where, as I have already argued, *Romantic* and postmaterial environmentalism (which argues that humanity should put the Earth first because it is sacred) is less convincing? And what challenges faces such an ecologising of religion in the light of concerns of the 'Hinduisation of civil society'?

This brings us to the second critique of religious environmentalism in India, which relates to the particular history of secularism in Indian politics since

---

[1] Parts of this chapter have been published in earlier form in Tomalin, 'Bio-divinity and Biodiversity: Perspectives on Religion and Environmental Conservation in India', *Numen* 51/3 (2004). Permission to reuse this material has been granted by Koninklijke Brill NV.

independence in 1947 and the ensuing diversity of views about the proper role of religion in public, political and social life.[2] One of the defining features of contemporary India over the last two decades, has been the rise of the Hindu Right which engages in an aggressive style of religious politics promoting the ideology of *Hindutva* ('Hinduness') that calls for a *Hindu rashtra* (Hindu nation) (Bhatt, 2001; Hansen, 1999). In recent years, many have become wary of the so-called 'Hinduisation of civil society', which specifically refers to the endeavours of the Rashtriya Swayamsevak Sangh (one wing of the Sangh Parivar – 'family of organisations', also including the BJP – Bharatya Janata Party – and the VHP – Vishva Hindu Parishad) to infiltrate erstwhile Hindu organisations or to co-opt secular groups under their mandate (see Roy, 2002; Sarkar, 2002). A number of commentators are sharply critical of the 'Hindu civilizational' response to environmental problems in India for their close resemblance to the ideology of the Hindu Right (Bhaviskar, 2001; Nanda, 2005; Mawdsley, 2005; 2006).

## Sacred Trees

The association of trees and plants with particular deities or nature spirits is a traditional feature of Indian religious life (Banwari, 1992; Gandhi, 1994; Gupta, 1971). Gupta tells us that marriage ceremonies are sometimes performed between certain trees, most commonly between an *aswattha* or *peepal* tree, which are considered to be male, and a *neem*, which is considered to be female. In Rajasthan and Gujarat this gendering is reversed and women in *purda* cover their faces when they pass a *neem* tree. In Orissa the *banyan*, as male, is married to the *aswattha*, as female (Gupta, 1971, pp. 52–3). As the nineteenth-century French missionary Abbe Dubois observed, 'almost the same formalities are observed for this curious marriage as in the case of a Brahmin marriage' ([1905] 1993, p. 739). Trees also feature prominently in mythology where plant life is often attributed human qualities. In the Hindu epic the Ramayana, Rama and his brother Lakshmana are banished from their kingdom and begin a journey through the forest, accompanied by Sita, the wife of Rama. This section of the epic is filled with beautiful descriptions of the natural surroundings; it reflects a forest culture of sages and ascetics, forest spirits and wild animals. However, whilst the forest is described as a 'place of refuge for all creatures', it is also a place of danger due to evil spirits, demons and ferocious wild animals. This ambivalent attitude towards the forest contrasts with the *Romantic* desire to preserve a benign wilderness. These examples suggest that features of the natural world have a socio-religious significance, yet this does not indicate any necessary connection with people's concern about and interest in nature conservation. This chapter, however, is concerned with instances where individuals or groups attempt to transform traditional religious practices associated with nature into environmental awareness.

---

[2]   See Chapter 6.

*Modern 'Religious Forests'*

In Hindu temples throughout India, and most Hindu households, rituals, or *pujas*, are performed to the deities during which it is customary to offer a series of specific leaves and petals. Some will be carried out daily and others only on special festivals. As Dr Surynath Kamath, of the Mythic Society[3] in Bangalore explained:

> [When] we celebrate the Ganesha festival, [or] the Gauri festival we have to offer [the] God or Goddess certain flowers, certain leaves. Twenty four leaves need to be offered. Everyone will know by performing his religious duty this flora. It brings about a relationship between you and nature. *Neem* leaves, then *mallika jasmine* leaves...The list is given. Similarly flowers are to be given and we chant mantras.[4]

Whilst people still perform these pujas today, Kamath explained that it is less likely that the correct flower or leaf will be presented and they are often substituted with grains of rice: people have lost touch with this traditional knowledge about the ritual use of plants and can find it difficult to locate the correct species for each ritual. In response to this situation there is an initiative in the state of Karnataka, South India, to encourage temple authorities to create gardens in which these plants could be grown. In addition, the Karnataka forest department had also established a number of 'religious forests'. In 1984 the first 'religious forest' was opened in Sirsi, Uttara Kannada district. A second had been established by 1989 in Ramanagaram, Bangalore district, and then a third in 1991, the Kaivara reserve forest, in Chintamani, Kolar district. As Mr Yellapa Reddi, retired conservator of forests for the state, explained:

> In the olden days they used to earmark certain forest areas as the forest of God, *devarakadus*, sacred gardens. Those gardens have not been managed; they have been subjected to a lot of biotic interferences and also encroached and destroyed. So I thought of reviving this knowledge and creating these gardens like any other park. Instead of putting a park of ornamentals, something not from the locality, we can have a park of this. The intention is to educate and bring awareness. The people should start respecting the plants and they should develop some sort of a reverence for the plants.[5]

---

[3] The Mythic Society was founded in 1909 with the collaboration of Indian and European residents of Bangalore. Its aim was to gather and publish information about the history of Indian civilisation. In 1994 it organised a conference on 'Ancient Indians' Attitude towards Nature and Environment', 'with a view to finding out whether the ancients had any regard for nature, its conservation or had any ideas, beliefs or practices from the point of view of protection of the environment' (Kamath, 1994, p. i).

[4] Interview Bangalore, 29/1/97.

[5] Interview Bangalore, 5/5/97.

The Kaivara reserve forest was established in 1991 at the location where a popular nineteenth-century philosopher sage Narayanappa or Yogi Nareyana Yathindra, born in the 1830s, attained *jiva samadhi* (he became enlightened while he was still alive). The area is also famous in having been identified as the site of battles recounted in the Hindu epic the Mahabharata. Therefore, this region was already popular with pilgrims who visit such holy and historical sites, often for days out and picnics with their extended family (Entwistle, 1987, pp. 103–8). The popularity of the area was a prime factor in choosing this site as the location for a 'religious forest'. The forest consisted of a number of different areas where separate gardens had been created according to a religious theme and were linked by pathways named after different Sanskrit terms for the planets. The 'Ritual Forest' was comprised of rows of standing stone slabs bearing inscriptions of *pujas* to different deities that included details of the different plants and flowers to be offered. Alongside each stone slab the species mentioned in the *puja* had been planted. The 'Zodiac Forest' was a square garden bordered by small trees. In the centre there was a raised square platform around which were stone reliefs of the different zodiac signs. Each tree in the border lined up with the sign of the zodiac with which it was traditionally associated.

The *Shiva Panchayatana* garden was modelled upon a traditional form of Shiva worship where 'the lord is seated surrounded by Vishnu in the 'ishanya' (Northeast), Sun-god in the 'aagneya' (Southeast), Ganpati in 'nairutya' (Southwest) and goddess Ambika in 'vayavya' (Northwest) directions. Purana Chudamani makes mention of the importance of Shiva worship in this form' (Yellapa Reddi, 1988, p. 55). This garden consisted of such an arrangement of icons representing these deities beside which their associate plants had been grown. For example, Shiva is traditionally associated with the *bilva* tree and Vishnu with the *aswattha*. Similarly, there was a garden with plants associated with seven celebrated *rishis* (sages), as well as a garden of plants linked to the planets and their associated deities.

Whilst the association of plants with particular deities is traditional, and many people will refrain from damaging such sacred species, the arrangements of these plants in the Kaivara forest is a product of the imagination of Mr Yellapa Reddi. One of the ideas underlying the creation of these forests was the desire to encourage people to become more respectful towards nature. As Mr Swaminath, in the Karnataka state forest department, explains, 'the aim was to motivate people to develop a love, the interest about tree conservation. So through religious things it was very easy you know to tell people how important they are, part of environment, part of ecology, part of religion'.[6] Again, as Mr Yellapi Reddi argues:

> Even today, whatever may be the other influence of the West, or whatever, still there are a number of people still respect their religion. So the biggest motivating force is when you say this is a plant meant for the God, they will look at the

---

[6]   Interview Bangalore, 30/4/97.

plant in a different perspective, a different angle, with reverence. This is not an ordinary plant; this plant is offered to lord Shiva. So once they know that they don't cut it, they don't pluck it, they don't destroy it.[7]

However, only a selection of species are be protected and respected, suggesting that such plants are significant because of their association with particular deities rather than for their own intrinsic or ecological value. Within a contemporary religious environmentalist world view a sacred and protective canopy is cast over nature as a whole. Thus, a religious worldview, which involves practices associated with nature, does not necessarily reflect an environmentalist worldview. Whilst in India, for example, it is common to protect particular species of plants and trees which are sacred and associated with particular deities, there is little indication that this worship and protection of sacred species is automatically extended to all of nature. Sinha et al. question the fact that 'within this pristine consciousness, the worship of specific trees is understood as leading to a general reverence for forests, in turn leading to an even broader reverence for nature' (1997, p. 71).

In order to explore this further it will be useful to look at the preservation of traditional sacred groves, one of the most significant unions of religion and conservation in contemporary India. A number of surveys are in process in India to assess their extent and to document religious beliefs and practices associated with them. Within India the existence of such sacred groves is a central topic of environmental discourse and many environmentalists call for their preservation from encroachments. Whilst the rhetoric surrounding the significance of these groves reflects the religious environmentalist assumptions, calls for their protection are also couched in scientific language with environmentalists anxious to preserve them for their biodiversity. I am suggesting that religious environmentalist discourse is utilised as a 'strategy' to secure their protection for practical reasons. The utilitarian significance of this discourse is primary rather than as an expression of religious values.

*The Preservation of Sacred Groves*

Although environmental projects that are based upon religion are relatively few and far between, one area that has received attention concerns the preservation of sacred groves (Gadgil and Vartak, 1974a, 1974b, 1981; Gadgil, 1989; Gadgil and Chandran, 1992; Chandran and Hughes, 1997; Chandrakanth and Nagaraja, 1997; Ramakrishnan, 1996; Ramakrishnan et al., 1998; Apffel-Marglin and Mishra, 1993; Apffel-Marglin and Parajuli, 2000; Kalam, 1996; Khurana, 1998; Nirpunge et al., 1988). To this day one can find patches of forest all over India that have been protected due to religious custom, 'sometimes as much as twenty hectare in extent' (Gadgil and Vartak, 1974b, p. 152). In comparison to surrounding agricultural land, these *refugia* are described as 'hotspots of biodiversity', both in terms of the

---

[7]  Interview Bangalore, 5/5/97.

age and range of species, and are claimed to be of ecological significance to the locality in providing watershed functions or, in the case of larger groves, helping to regulate the climate (Ram Manohar, 1997). Thus, whilst communities farmed the surrounding land for their daily needs, the groves themselves are depicted as having remained more or less untouched, where 'the removal of even a small twig, is taboo' (Gadgil and Vartak, 1981, p. 273). As M.G. Nagaraja, a local campaigner for the preservation of sacred groves (*devarakadus*), explained with respect to sacred groves in Coorg (a region in Karnataka, South India):

> Every *devarakadu* will have a god, a sanctum…So around that sanctum or temple the forest is maintained…The people never cut the trees, they never take the leaves and not even a single branch will be wasted, it will be retained in the forest itself. If a tree has died because of the old age it will be made to fall there alone and this man will not touch it, he will not cut it…In India this tradition is strong, particularly the god adoration mentality is strong here. So therefore wherever the trees that grow around the temple, or the sanctum, he doesn't cut, he leaves. The sacred forests are maintained.[8]

This is echoed by the director of an environmental NGO in Virajpet, Coorg:

> So these *devarakadus*, no one used to really take anything from them. They were pristine undisturbed forests, not even fire-wood would be collected. This is why you still have these virgin forests, literally 'hotspots of biodiversity', because it hasn't been disturbed.[9]

The following section of this paper will assess the discourses surrounding the relationship between the ancient institution of the sacred grove and environmental conservation. To what extent are they the product of an elite environmentalist ideology or do they have a broader relevance?

*Sacred Groves: Repositories of Biodivinity or Hotspots of Biodiversity?*

While examples of these 'pristine forests' still exist across India, they are dwindling in number due to a range of factors. For example, in Coorg from 1905 to 1985 the extent of sacred groves, or *devarakadus*, shrunk from 15,506 to 6,299.61 acres because of 'encroachments, denudation, acquisition for coffee cultivation

---

[8]   Interview 1/5/97, Bangalore. Pradip Saha, Managing Editor of the Indian ecology magazine 'Down To Earth', suggested to me that sacred groves which are located on a steep gradient, tend to house more malevolent and ferocious deities than other groves. This is because such a forested hillside serves a particularly important ecological function to the land below and the more malevolent the deity the greater the deterrent against interfering in the grove (personal conversation 20/08/03).

[9]   Interview 11/2/98, Virajpet, Coorg.

and other commercial purposes' (Kalam, 1996, pp. 25–6). However, many of the people I interviewed also considered that sacred groves are decreasing because of the dilution of traditional values, westernisation and migration. As a postgraduate student from the University of Agricultural Sciences in Bangalore put it:

> Basically underlying this one is the greed you see. It is due to materialism and the influence of western culture. Because of that we have lost our values and culture…These things wouldn't have happened ten years back, twenty years back – it was unthinkable. Today they are encroaching, tomorrow the sacred groves will be denuded.[10]

While agreeing with this depiction, his tutor, Professor M.G. Chandrakanth, also stressed that for migrants who come to work on the plantations 'there is no sacredness of the forest. It is only for the Coorg people, because of their culture… Those who migrate from outside, even from Kerala, they just don't have any feeling…'.[11]

Thus, with respect to Coorg, the commercialisation of the land has lead to a transformation in 'traditional' farming practices and has brought changes to the institution of the sacred grove. Before the introduction of coffee into the region by the British in 1854, Coorg was almost completely covered with forest and in its eastern region with thick jungle (Pouchepadass 1990, p. 6). Thus, the land upon which the sacred groves stand acquired a new economic value and, while state level instruments theoretically exist to prevent enchroachment, many feel that politics and economics often get in the way of serious attempts to protect sacred groves across the country. Crucially, in Coorg, for instance, as one local environmentalist points out, 'there is a dispute about whom the land belongs to, whether it is to the revenue department or the forest department'[12] and this has slowed down measures to protect the remaining sacred groves in the region.

In order to understand the significance of this dispute, we need to look back to the British designation of forests into different types under the Forest Act of 1865 (Pouchepadass, 1990, p. 10). It is reported that the British considered sacred groves to be a 'contrivance' on the part of villagers to deny the state from claiming their rights over all forest lands (Chandran and Hughes, 1997, p. 423). Mr Thamiah, of the Deputy Commissioner's office, Madikeri, Coorg, explained to me that some sacred groves were classified as 'reserve forest' (a class of forest that was closed to all uses except those licensed by the state) while others were designated as 'protected forests' (a class of forest that could be used for small-scale activities such as timber and fuel collection, or grazing).[13] Where sacred groves became 'protected forests' communities found that they could no longer restrict access to

---

[10]   Interview 30/1/97, University of Agricultural Sciences, Bangalore.
[11]   Interview 30/1/97, University of Agricultural Sciences, Bangalore.
[12]   Interview 11/2/98, Virajpet, Coorg.
[13]   Interview 9/2/98, Madikeri, Coorg.

what had once been communally regulated lands (Chandran and Hughes, 1997, p. 422). In Coorg sacred groves became classified as 'protected forests' in 1905, placed under the control of the Revenue Department (which collects taxes on land belonging to the government), and have been heavily encroached (Kalam, 1996, p. 51). Although since 1985 there have been moves to reassign land that has not been heavily encroached (including *devarakadus*) to the category of 'reserve forest', which would place it under the control of the Forest Department, these transferences are slow in coming, with many blaming the Karnataka Government for bowing to pressure from powerful plantation owners (Sharma 2003). According to Mr Thamiah:

> There is a move to convert it into reserve forest. Reserve forest means that everything is prohibited even hunting, felling of trees: everything is prohibited. It is not reserve forest now, it is village forest[14]...At the moment it belongs neither to the Forest Department or to the Revenue Department. It is like that now. But the forest authorities are conducting a survey and they may take it shortly...[However,] they can't declare the *devarakadu* as reserve forest if it is under encroachment...what is the good of declaring it *devarakadu* if it is fully under cultivation, fully encroached by some people...The government can take action but the encroachers in some cases are very poor, if they are thrown out of the land it would be very difficult for them.[15]

While there is evidence to suggest that the absorption of sacred groves into secular management programmes has in many cases contributed to their decline, other scholars have pointed out that the use of sacred groves can change over time for religious reasons. For instance, the deities that live in sacred groves tend to be uniconic and not housed within any structure (Gadgil and Vartak, 1974b, p. 156). However, as Gadgil explained to me:

> We have done a study relating to sacred groves to show how when the Brahmin priests take control of deities located in sacred groves they deliberately tend to replace the worship of trees, of natural objects, by idols. They want to cut down the forest and use the money to construct a temple... As you come from the more remote villages to those which have better communication...the low caste indigenous priesthood is taken over by the Brahmin priests and when the Brahmin priests take over, and more sort of institutionalised religion comes into play, the worship of nature gives way to worship of idols in the temple and the sacred groves tend to be cut down.[16]

---

[14]   A category of protected forest (Pouchepadass 1990, p. 18). Chandrakanth and Nagaraja write that most *devarakadus* in Coorg are *paisari devara kadu*: 'owned by the government, and are jointly managed by the village and the government' (1997, p. 220).

[15]   Interview 9/2/98, Madikeri, Coorg.

[16]   Interview 4/2/97, Indian Institute for Science, Bangalore.

Although many commentators view the shift to Brahmanical religion as undermining more localised indigenous religiocultural practices, which preserved sacred groves intact, other scholars argue that this depiction may actually be misleading. While this process of *sanskritisation* has meant that some encroachments may be carried out 'on behalf of the divine' (Kalam, 1996, p. 51), in order to build temples to keep up with the changing times (Gadgil and Chandran, 1992, p. 187; Chandran and Hughes, 1997, p. 420), it cannot be assumed that the authentic form of the sacred grove is as 'pristine forest' (Jeffery, 1998).

Freeman's research on sacred groves (*kavus*) in Kerala, suggests that sacred groves have always taken a variety of forms that do not necessarily coincide with the modern environmentalist's idea of 'pristine relics from a primeval past' (1994, p. 11). He writes that a

> *kavu* may indeed result from the dedication of a patch of virgin forest to a deity, but I also know of those developed from what was once a stand of cultivated toddy-palms, from small stands of shrubbery on laterite hillocks, and in one case, from an old tank in the middle of paddy fields (1994, p. 11).

Moreover, a '*kavu* may refer to a temple that no longer has any associated grove, [thus] the semantic weight of the term rests with the dedication of the site to a deity, rather that with the flora of the site, *per se*' (1994, p. 12, fn. 14). The purpose of sacred groves is to provide a pleasure garden for the use of the deity and, whilst encroachment according to human needs is forbidden, it is often the case that 'what we might regard as human disturbance, resource exploitation, and encroachment are happily accommodated within the cultural framework of the grove as the deities' preserve' (1994, p. 11).

Freeman, in particular, has argued against the tendency of much discourse around the subject of sacred groves to assume, or at least to give the impression of, the existence of an ideal type of sacred grove as 'pristine forest' (1994, p. 9, fn. 11). He challenges the writing of Gadgil and Vartak (1981) as particularly vulnerable to this type of oversimplification. While their work generally concentrates upon the Western Ghats there is a tendency for it to read as though they are making more general points about sacred groves throughout India. Gadgil and Vartak are, however, by no means the only scholars whose work seems to generalise about certain features of sacred groves. Writing on sacred groves easily lends support to religious environmentalist discourse, where practices such as preserving sacred groves are seen as evidence of a 'primitive ecological wisdom' that predates colonial interference in natural resource management on the sub-continent.

By contrast, Freeman's research suggests that any protection of biodiversity was coincidental rather than intentional and that sacred groves were protected out of respect for the deity rather than because of an innate belief in the intrinsic value of nature. As Kalam points out: 'where was the need to preserve/conserve the forests as there was no danger at all of depletion of forest resources?' (1996, p. 52). Moreover, the protection of sacred groves does not match modern ecological thinking as it only affords protection to particular areas of nature rather than the entire natural environment. This *Romantic* belief that religious practices have preserved sacred groves intact has lead people to believe that they are rather more extensive than they actually are, with the effect of failing to realise the extent of their decline. According to Kalam, writing in 'Coffeeland News', a local Coorg publication:

> Till my 1996 publication *Sacred Groves in Kodagu District of Karnataka (South India): A Socio-Historical Study*, many people sincerely believed that the *Devarakadus* were indeed preserved and were in a good shape. Some even thought that being gods'/deities' abodes these were in fact conserved in almost virgin climax form. Such beliefs were subscribed to not only by the lay people but also by social and natural scientists (Kalam, 2000).

Nevertheless, there are many commentators who employ modern concepts to describe and explain the purpose and use of sacred groves in the past, or they embark upon a *Romantic* eulogy about a lost 'ecogolden age'. For instance, Chandran and Hughes make the unlikely claim that, 'sacred groves belong to a variety of cultural practices which helped Indian society maintain *an ecologically steady state* with wild living resources' (1997, p. 418, my emphasis). Similarly anachronistic is the assertion by Chandrakanth and Nagaraja that 'wherever a *devara kadu* has been preserved well by the village communities, there has been the altruistic motive and the recognition that birds and animals *also have rights*' (1997, p. 223, my emphasis). Other scholars and activists take a less romantic perspective. For instance, Professor P.S. Ramakrishnan[17] accepts that there are two viewpoints: those who consider that people were aware of the ecological value of conserving sacred groves and those who consider that environmental preservation was a biproduct of conserving sacred groves for religious reasons. However, rather than attempting to resolve this difference of opinion he concludes: 'without getting into this controversy of what is the reason behind it, I am interested in looking at it from a contemporary perspective in what way can we make use of it'.[18]

In line with this thinking, a number of the ecologists that I interviewed explained how they had become interested in sacred groves through a scientific and pragmatic interest in conservation. For instance, Madhav Gadgil told me how he had been studying sacred groves since 1973: 'I'm an ecologist and I was interested in finding examples of undisturbed, well preserved natural vegetation... the best examples, strikingly, were some of the sacred groves.'[19] Similarly, Dr K.G. Saxena[20] claimed to be interested in:

[17]   School of Environmental Sciences, Jawaharlal Nehru University, New Delhi.
[18]   Interview 24/4/98, Jawaharlal Nehru University, New Delhi.
[19]   Interview 4/2/97, Indian Institute for Science, Bangalore.
[20]   School of Environmental Sciences, Jawaharlal Nehru University, New Delhi.

the function of sacred groves in the environmental perspective, how sacred groves are related to the social mechanisms of resource users, restraints placed by society upon resource use...*The fundamental objective or challenge these days is in what way you promote sustainable resource management*...Instead of commanding and controlling the people you build on religion, culture. So that is one way of mobilising people's participation.[21]

Ramakrishnan echoed this concern to make use of traditional beliefs and practices. He explained that when he first went to work in the North East of India, 25 years previously, he was interested in why the government's development and conservation projects had largely failed: they were 'rejected by the local people'. He soon noticed, however, that there were small patches of forest that had been preserved: 'a few hectares to a few square kilometres which are protected by local communities...'[22] He became interested to:

> try to see what are the possibilities in terms of building upon this traditional knowledge base...in order to be able to define a strategy which adheres with the value system of the local communities [so that] they have a sense of participation in the process of development rather that something being imposed from outside...When I went there, and I started working on my mundane biological, ecological problems, every time I started working on it I hit against the human dimension...In whatever bits and pieces I could pick up, and among a whole variety of things that I did, the cultural dimensions of ecology became an important concern.[23]

Thus, the scientific community and conservation bodies are beginning to take this system of 'indigenous nature preservation' seriously (e.g. Jamir and Pandey, 2003; Upadhaya et al., 2003; Ramanujam and Cyril, 2003; Ramanujam and Kadamban, 2001). Ramanujam and Kadamban note, for example, with respect to their study of plant biodiversity in two forests near Pondicherry, South India, that the forest that had been maintained as a sacred grove was 'more species rich' (2001, p. 1203) than the other forest that had 'lost the status of a sacred grove because of its conversion to Eucalyptus plantations' (2001, p. 1203). They conclude that, 'the concept of sacred groves appears to be an efficacious tool in biodiversity conservation worth continuing into the next millennium' (2001, p. 1215).

However, it is important to note that from a scientific or conservationist perspective, the study of sacred groves forms one of the components of a broader concern with sustainable development and the preservation of biodiversity. Religious values in themselves are not generally seen as having any necessary role to play. As the director of an environmental NGO in Virajpet Coorg argued:

21 Interview 24/4/98, Jawaharlal Nehru University, New Delhi.
22 Interview 24/4/98, Jawaharlal Nehru University, New Delhi.
23 Interview 24/4/98, Jawaharlal Nehru University, New Delhi.

> Protecting and preserving *devarakadus* merely for superstitious beliefs does not
> bear relevance in this modern age...training at the grass roots level would help
> spread the message of the necessity to protect these *devarakadus* for scientific
> reasons (Belliappa, 1996).

While members of the scientific/conservation community are not immune to
holding romanticised views about the role that religion played in conservation in
the past (or about the authentic form of sacred groves as 'pristine forests'), they
are more likely to consider that religious institutions are in decline and that it is the
job of the ecologist to find other ways of preserving the biodiversity of the sacred
groves. Although some of the scientists I have spoken to genuinely lament the
decline in traditional values about the forest, others are not so concerned and are
happy to promote the introduction of secular management programmes to preserve
the remaining groves.

By contrast, the examples of religious environmentalism discussed in Chapter
5 and the first case study in Chapter 6, not only hold romanticised views about
the role that religion played in conservation in the past, but that religion has a
special and unique role to play in averting environmental problems more widely.
However, individuals that adhere to this 'strong' or 'romantic' version of religious
environmentalism are also more likely to be religious themselves and to have a
personal view of the Earth as sacred. Thus, a 'strong' or 'romantic' version of
the discourse can be contrasted with a 'weak' or 'pragmatic' expression. While
the former is committed to pursuing a religiously inspired environmentalism, the
latter considers that religion played a role in protecting biodiversity in the past
but that this is less relevant in the modern age (except where it is still strong or
as a means of encouraging participation in environmental projects). Moreover,
whereas the strong version of the discourse believes that sacred groves ought to be
protected because they are divine and, therefore, intrinsically valuable, the weaker,
scientific/pragmatic expression is more interested in preserving biodiversity for its
long-term practical benefits and for scientific interest.

Whilst this is a goal that should be encouraged in a country such as India,
where huge swathes of indigenous forest continue to be denuded year by year, it
cannot be assumed that the goals of scientific conservation will necessarily match
the cultural and economic needs of local communities, particularly where these
deny any human interference whatsoever. We need to ask why sacred groves
ought to be preserved intact: whose interests does such a goal serve? While one
might assume that the practical work of ecologists is more likely to benefit people
than the romantic vision that religion can liberate people from ecological disaster
(because religious traditions teach that the Earth has intrinsic value), it must be
remembered that scientific ecology is not a neutral enterprise. It makes use of elite
discourses that employ sophisticated language and concepts that often have little
relevance to the environmentally illiterate. In fact, where conservationists of both
the *Romantic* and the *pragmatic* types are keen to prevent any kind of interference
in sacred groves, traditional religious practice has allowed people to use the

forest in line with the wishes of the deity, even to the extent of clearing the grove and erecting a temple. Thus, it is not only environmentalists who are explicitly ecocentric and believe that nature has intrinsic value, who express the ethic of wilderness conservation, discussed at length by Guha (1989). It is also reflected in the thinking of more scientific and instrumental attitudes towards conservation, where sacred groves are of interest because of the protection of rare species that have medicinal properties or for their wider ecological function.

In the next section, I move on to look at another example of 'nature religion' in India that is often understood to imply environmental protection: the practice of recognising rivers as sacred. This example, in particular, enables us to discuss the critique that the 'Hindu civilizational' response to ecological problems in India is potentially dangerous because of its similarities with discourses employed by the Hindu Right.

## Sacred Rivers

The integration of religious life with rivers is common throughout India. Rivers are considered as sacred and are typically identified as a goddess. Those living along the riverbanks draw water for domestic needs, agricultural and industrial purposes. Rivers are a means of transport and a focus for recreation. However, they are worshipped daily by locals who consider that bathing in their sacred waters will purify them, both physically and spiritually. For instance, a temple at Talacauvery, in Coorg, South India, is located at the source of the river Cauvery and is considered to be the birthplace of the goddess Cauvery who manifests herself as the river. A booklet produced by the temple authorities indicates an attitude of reverence and gratitude towards the river:

> Sri Cauvery had showered Her blessings to the people of the states of Karnataka and Tamil Nadu. Lakhs of hectares of land in Karnataka and Tamil Nadu have been fertilised by the river waters of Sri Cauvery. Numerous industrial factories and business concerns are functioning in the states of Karnataka and Tamil Nadu on account of the perennial water resources of Sri Cauvery. Above all these facts, it is very significant that millions of people from ancient days to the modern times have derived spiritual consolation and benefit by bathing in the sacred waters of Sri Cauvery and worshipping her as the Divine Mother (Shankaranarayanabhat, 1997, pp. 9–10).

Devotees bathe in a large tank filled with water from the river, which is adjoined by a much smaller pool, the *brahmakundika*. This smaller pool is the source of the River Cauvery and it is in this form that the Goddess is present rather than as an icon. Attendant priests recite mantras, offer flowers into the pool and present *arati*, the sacred flame, to visiting pilgrims. Each October on *Tulasankramana*, or *Tulasankranti* day, after the monsoon, thousands of devotees come here to witness the emergence of a spring into the *brahmakundika*. They assemble to witness the level of the pool rise for a few seconds, 'like milk rising when it has been boiled' (1997, p. 24). This festival is called *Shri Cauvery Theertodbhava* and is considered to be the birthday of the goddess Cauvery. The *Tulasankramana* occurs on the first day of a month-long festival, the *Cauvery Jatra*, and pilgrims traditionally carry a pot of sacred water back to their homes. Many who cannot visit the temple on the first day come on pilgrimage in the course of the next month. It is believed that during this auspicious month the goddess Ganga and other river goddesses will be with Shri Cauvery. Behind the *brahmakundika*, higher up, is a very small *peepal* or *aswattha* tree smeared with vermilion and strung with a few flower garlands. Underneath is a statue of the Cauvery goddess. There is a story about how this tree was a special gift to the sage Agastya, the husband of Shri Cauvery, from Brahma, Vishnu and Shiva. The gods made a promise to Agastya that the tree would always remain in stunted form and that their presence would remain in it.

However, it is the Ganges, which is the most significant river in India: both materially and spiritually. It is around 2,500 km long, flowing through the western Indian states of Uttar Pradesh, Bihar and West Bengal, and also into Bangladesh. Its flood-prone basin is one of the most densely populated in the world, home to approximately five hundred million people, almost 10 per cent of the global population, including at least 30 per cent of the world's poorest billion people (Chapman, 1995, p. 3). At many places along the river, water quality is extremely poor, affected by both domestic and industrial effluent and since 1985 has been subject to the much-maligned Ganga Action Plan. The 'Ganga Action Plan' was initiated by the Ministry of Environment and Forests, New Delhi, (MOEFF) in 1985 with the specific aim of tackling such pollution and bringing it within acceptable limits. However, the River Ganges is also deeply ingrained in the religiocultural practices of the region. Hindus consider the river to be an embodiment of the goddess Ganga and places along the river attract pilgrims who come to bathe in her purifying waters: from its origins at Gangotri in Himachal Pradesh to where it flows through Shiva's city of Varanasi, to eventually enter the sea at Calcutta (Eck, 1985). To be cremated on the banks of the Ganges in Varanasi is to be assured entry into heaven and the attraction of the 2000 Ardh Kumbh Mela in Allahabad, which drew up to one hundred million pilgrims, was the opportunity to bathe in the confluence of the rivers Ganga and Yamuna (also a goddess).

*To What Extent is the Worship of Rivers Evidence of Environmental Values and Practices?*

Kelly Alley's fieldwork at Dasasvamedha Ghat in Varanasi, amongst the *pandas* (pilgrim priests) working there, is a good place to begin to think about this question.[24] She argues that whereas environmentalists in Varanasi are concerned

---

[24]   David Haberman's recent book (2006) takes up similar themes with respect to the River Yamuna, also worshipped as a goddess.

to clean the Ganga because it is polluted with wastes, which are a threat to human health as well as biodiversity, the *pandas* are more concerned about ritual purity and do not consider physical pollution to threaten the spiritual purity of Ganga: it is not a contradiction for something to be ritually pure but physically dirty. It is not that the *pandas* are unconcerned about the material pollution of Ganga but that they see this in terms of wider social degeneracy (that is given religious explanations) rather than in terms of population growth, urbanisation, and industrial and technological development which have brought a decline in ecological balance (1998, p. 299). Their aim is to keep Ganga happy through the performance of *arati* and *puja* so that she will continue to purify the cosmos, soul, body, and heart thereby avoiding complete collapse of the current moral order (1998, p. 311). Alley suggests that the separation of ideas of ritual purity (*shuddha* or *pavitra*) from physical pollution (*gandagi*) means that people tend not to be as bothered about projects to clean the Ganges as one would hope.

Alley has argued that the separation of ritual purity of the Ganges from her physical cleanliness means that many local people are not that concerned about the material pollution of the river: the Ganges is ritually pure and can look after herself! The weight of responsibility for the devotee lies in performing *arati* and *puja* rather than campaigning for adequate sewage treatment facilities. The problem lies not so much in lack of adequate facilities for treatment of sewage but in the broader social degeneracy of the present age, the *kali yuga*: complete moral decay is kept at bay by religious observances rather than removing rubbish from the River Ganges (the rubbish in the Ganges is a further symptom of degeneracy in general). People worship the River Ganges as the goddess *Ganga Ma* and consider that she is sacred, but this high religious value that is placed upon the river is not translated into environmental values. While people bathe in the Ganges to remove 'impurities' it seems as though little distinction is made between ritual and material impurity. Although *Ganga Ma* herself has an infinite capacity to remove ritual impurities, and remains ritually pure, the ecological health of the river is suffering from the failure to seriously consider that there is a limit to the volume of material wastes the river can effectively carry away. Thus, the high regard with which people hold *Ganga Ma* tends to lead them to the conclusion that there is nothing they can do to harm or pollute her (Alley, 1998; 2000).

Ritual bathing throughout India has become a hazardous practice owing to the pollution of India's rivers. As the Deccan Herald reports:

> In Patna, a few days after celebrating the Chhath festival on the banks of the river Ganga, several devotees had eruptions, red spots and skin irritation all over their bodies. Apparently it was the 'holy dip' which had led to this impious problem...For far too long have rivers in India been treated as glorified sewers. On the one hand, they are considered as sacred and, on the other, they are abused day in day out by the very populace that reveres them (Banerjee, 1998).

Similarly, *India Today* reports on the Ganga at Varanasi which along its 2,525 km supports over 33 million people living on its basin and absorbs over 1,340 million litres of sewage daily:

> [A] rotting corpse floats by. At the Dashashwamedh Ghat, the water has a blackish tinge from soot, ash, cinders, half-burnt wood of funeral pyres, and other pollutants. It is not just bodies, but domestic and industrial sewage that are polluting the Ganga. Tests...showed that the coliform count – an index of the bacteria – mainly from human waste – upstream was more than 13 times higher than the safe limit; downstream it was 300 times. Samples were only taken from where people bathe (Halarnkar 1997, pp. 119 ff).

A well-known NGO in Varanasi that is committed to cleaning up the river is the Sankat Mochan Foundation (SMF hereafter), located at the far end of the city, on the banks of the Ganges near Tulsi Ghat. The SMF was formed in 1982 by Veer Bhadre Mishra, a now-retired Professor of Civil Engineering at the famous 'Banaras Hindu University' (BHU), as well as a hereditary priest of the Hanuman Temple in the city. He is affectionately and respectfully also known as 'Mahantji'. By the early 1980s there were over eighty drains along the Ganges allowing untreated domestic waste to enter the river at Varanasi. Mahantji explains that whilst these have now been intercepted and diverted to sewage treatment plants, the measures introduced under the Ganga Action Plan have either failed or created further problems. For instance, when there are power cuts, often more than once a day, the pumps that take the water to the treatment plants do not work and raw sewage enters directly into the Ganges. Moreover, further downstream in Kanpur, the treated effluent is now used for irrigation but remains dangerously polluted, causing stomach problems, skin rashes and a decline in agricultural productivity. As Mr Sundd (one of the SMF volunteers) reported, it is becoming difficult to find young men to marry the girls at nearby Kamanti village, one of the areas affected by the water pollution. He lamented that concerned parents are now saying: 'why should we send our daughters to hell?'[25]

As part of their *Swatcha Ganga* (Clean Ganga) Campaign, SMF take daily measurements of water quality at several locations at ten metres from the bank. However, this representation or construction of the Ganges, as polluted with lesser or greater amounts of material wastes, does not resonate with the way in which many people living along the banks view the *Ganga*. One of the volunteers at the SMF, Vinay Pandey, described the following scenario:

> One day he had been working with a British documentary maker, interviewing people on the banks of the Ganges. He saw a devotee bathing near a sewage outlet and asked him whether he was aware he was bathing in polluted water.

---

[25]    Interviews, Sankat Mochan Foundation, 9/10/00.

The devotee turned to him in utter disbelief and furiously reprimanded him for even suggesting such a thing.[26]

Whereas our above discussion has looked at how pollution is dealt with in Varanasi when it is conceived of as 'material wastes', for the devotee in this story the primary and most important sense in which the idea of 'pollution' is understood is religious. The idea that Ganga can be polluted or impure is not only blasphemous but also illogical. It is important to make a careful distinction between the pollution of *Ganga Ma* and the pollution of *Ganga Ma's waters*.

Haberman notes a similar point with respect to his fieldwork along the banks of the Yamuna:

> How do Yamuna's devotees in Braj view modern pollution, and how does the presence of polluting substances in the river affect devotees' religious perspective and practice...I received roughly three types of response to my inquiries. Some denied that the pollution had any real effect on the river goddess or on living beings dependent on her; some acknowledged that the pollution harms living beings who come in contact with the water but does not affect the river goddess herself; and some contended that the pollution is having a harmful effect on beings who come in contact with the water as well as on the river goddess herself. I have observed that the latter group – and to some extent the second group – is much more inclined than the first group to engage in activities that the West would label as 'environmental activism' (206: 132–3).

Whilst NGOs, such as the Sankat Mochan Foundation, may argue that the Ganga Action Plan has been a failure, because it has wasted millions of rupees on inappropriate measures, we can point to a more subtle reason why it may not fulfil its desired outcomes or why the scientific jargon employed by NGOs such as Sankat Mochan Foundation falls on deaf ears. As Alley writes:

> Since environmental activists find that the belief in sacred purity ultimately allows residents to reject or opt out of projects to tackle the problems of *gandagi*, they should try to interact with local religious leaders to sort out how occupational interests linked to ritual purity can become more connected with the need for physical cleanliness (1998, p. 324).

So she is suggesting that if the priests can be persuaded to incorporate environmental cleanliness into their ritual activities then they could act as a conduit to transmit these environmentalist ideas to local people. In fact it is a traditional injunction that physical uncleanliness be kept away from ritually pure objects or spaces. However, being difficult to enforce this ideal has increasingly been ignored. This use of religion echoes that of two teachers in Varanasi, Dr Anuradha Banerjee

[26] Interview, Tulsi Ghat, Varanasi, 10/12/00.

and Dr Kamala Pandey, who have written a book called *Rakshata Gangam* (Save Ganga) (Tomalin and Crandall Hollick, 2004). They have reinterpreted Ganges mythology in terms of the contemporary need to protect the river from physical pollution.

While discussions about the preservation of sacred groves and sacred rivers are making an impact at the level of scientific conservation, religious institutions in India are much less concerned with environmental degradation than the more romantic religious environmentalists would lead us to believe (groups like the Vrindavan Forest Revival Project, discussed in the last chapter, are the exception rather than the rule). However, one area within mainstream religion in India where ecological issues are beginning to make an impact is amongst some affiliates of the Hindu Right. It is not only the case that a number of such high profile affiliates have recently shown an interest in environmental issues but that religious environmentalist discourse in India closely resembles the historicist strategies employed by the Hindu Right. To what extent is it possible to distinguish between those who employ such 'Orientalist' or 'neo-traditionalist' (Sinha et al., 1997) readings of Hinduism out of a genuine concern for the natural environment and those who eulogise about a grand Hindu past as a means of bolstering a divisive and aggressive nationalist agenda?

## Environmentalism and the Hindu Right

The writing of environmental history in India has largely occurred within the context of postcolonial critique (e.g. Gadgil and Guha, 1993; Shiva, 1988). While the writing of Grove (1998a), in particular, has attempted to debunk the idea that the British colonialists were completely unconcerned about ecological issues, such as deforestation, blame for the destruction of India's forests, for instance, has been consistently and uncritically traced to the British greed for timber. Sivaramakrishnan describes Indian scholarship on the environment as 'caught up in the critique of colonialism, the nation state, development and the transitions to capitalism that engrossed a wider nationalist and postcolonial historiography' (2003). However, in the search for an authentically Indian environmental history, many scholars of the environment in India have engaged in a process of romanticising and essentialising the past that has similarities with the narrow construction of history that bolsters the Hindu nationalist movement (Chakrabarty, 2000). Again, according to Sivaramakrishnan, environmental historians have been 'instrumental in propagating a strategically essentialist, celebratory, indigenism (inspired equally by Gandhian ideas and romantic primitivism). This perspective has on occasion stimulated ethnonationalism, regionalism, and forms of religious nationalism drawing upon the romanticized precolonial/premodern subject and society that they evoke in their writings' (2003). There is a rejection of modern science and the enlightenment as a western colonial project and 'new traditionalist' valorising of past cultural and religious traditions as authentically environmentalist (Sinha et al., 1997).

For instance, the writings of Vandana Shiva, fit this pattern. And as Nanda writes she 'has become a leading light of Hindu ecology, and makes regular appearances in neo-Hindu [i.e. fundamentalist] ashrams in North America. Her work is most respectfully cited in *The Organiser*, the official journal of the RSS, the cultural arm of Hindu nationalist parties' (2002, p. 30). Another example of the potentially dangerous romanticisation of a Hindu past is found in the 'ecological niche' theory of caste (Gadgil and Guha, 1993; Gadgil and Malhotra, 1998) which argues that the caste system served to prevent the exploitation of natural resources where the 'monopoly of lineages over particular resources in a given locality favoured the cultural evolution of social restraints on resource utilization, leading to their sustainable use' (Gadgil and Malhotra, 1998, p. 27). Similarly, Dwivedi writes that, 'in a sense, the Hindu caste system can be seen as a progenitor of the concept of sustainable development' (1996, p. 159). While the extent to which such a perspective is premised upon the belief that the caste system ought to be retained is unclear, many are critical for its implicit support for a system of social organisation principled on injustice (Baviskar, 1999, pp. 27–8). As Sharma warns, 'at certain times, environmental discourses, however well-intentioned, fall into the trap of valorisation and romanticisation of some dangerous forms of indigenism that aid obscurantist forces, albeit unintentionally' (2002). One of the major problems of this sort of uncritical promotion of a Hindu past is that it obscures the ways in which it has underpinned gender and caste discrimination, and more recently the outright oppression of religious minorities through the ascendancy of the Hindu Right.

Thus, while religious environmentalist discourse may have a very noble aim, it does run the risk of being taken up to support unintended causes, or of becoming implicitly aligned with unwelcome political forces. Religious environmentalism shares with Hindu nationalism the desire to search ever further back in history for evidence that supports its contemporary agenda. Where the religious environmentalist is concerned to prove that environmental awareness is an authentic feature of the Hindu tradition throughout its history, from pre-Vedic times to the present, the Hindu nationalist looks for evidence to support a view of Hinduism as the genuine and original Indian religiosity. Some scholars do not, however, make a clear distinction between those who employ a 'Hindu civilizational' response to argue for conservationist ethics and those who support the Hindu Right. Baviskar, for instance, seems to implicitly align those who look to the Hindu tradition for ecological ethics with the Hindu Right, because they employ a similar discourse. Thus, commentators such as Vandana Shiva (who famously argues that the Hindu tradition supports contemporary ecofeminist thinking) and Madhav Gadgil (with his ecological niche theory of caste) are not clearly differentiated from those who are associated with groups such as the *Rashtriya Swayamsevak Sangh* (RSS) and the *Vishva Hindu Parishad* (VHP). The recourse to a unified Hindu tradition that is superior to other Indian traditions, as well as western civilisation, is a potentially worrying force that has become dangerously politicised in recent decades. Is it possible to distinguish between those who look to the Hindu tradition as a means of encouraging ecological consciousness, or social justice, and those Hindu chauvinists who have 'hijacked' the environmental movement as a means of promoting a broader political agenda that otherwise has little to do with conservation? Is it a case of 'guilt by association'? (Mawdsley, 2006, p. 382).

*Guilty by Association?*

Sharma describes how the 'Vrindavana Forest Revival Project' in Uttar Pradesh, initiated by some prominent environmental and religious organisations in 1991, shares the same language as the Hindu Right (2002). He writes that:

> Vrindavana is seen as the birthplace of Krishna and after the Ram Janmabhumi liberation campaign and the destruction of the Babri Mosque, the 'liberation of Krishna Janmabhumi' has become central to the agenda of Hindu conservatives. The language of this environmental project underlines, as causes of environmental problems of Vrindavana, the 'abandonment of traditional Hindu values and technology', 'centuries of Muslim and British rule as detrimental to traditional Hindu culture and practices', 'forgetting the injunctions such as those found in *Manusmriti*', thereby offering solutions on entirely new socio-political grounds, going beyond trees, shrub planting and sewage systems (2002).

While the Vrindavan Forest Revival Project is first and foremost a conservation movement, its language and values would seem to echo broader Hindu nationalist sentiments within modern India. For instance, it invokes the mythology of Krishna and a yearning for the time when Krishna was visibly and perpetually present in Vrindavan, as the basis of an 'ecogolden age'. The fact that this type of language and imagery intersects with that of 'Hindu conservatives' is certainly problematic, but should not necessarily imply an identification of this reforestation project with political and religious nationalism. The problem facing those that resort to a 'Hindu civilizational' response, such as in the above passage, is that they are likely to be taken as showing support for the nationalist movement by critics of the Hindu Right. Mawdsley argues that 'fashionable neo-traditionalist discourses are problematically amenable to the promotion of chauvinist ideologies and agendas' (2006, p. 382).

Another example of the blurring of the boundaries between ecological and nationalist movements concerns the River Ganges. While attempts to encourage religious support for projects to clean up the Ganges have not been particularly successful, religious figures have been rather more prominent in voicing objections to the Tehri dam, which is being constructed on the River Bhagirathi, a tributary of the Ganges in the Himalayas (see Alley (2000) for a discussion of similar religious objections to the Ganges Canal in Haridwar in the early twentieth century). The veteran Gandhian activist Sundarlal Bahuguna has largely championed this protest. Sharma writes that the movement which was set up to originally oppose the dam, back in 1978, has routinely resorted to using Hindu myths to speak about the consequences of the dam and also actively seeks to gain the support of religious *sadhus* (2001; 2002). However, more recently an organised Hindu presence has become involved in the campaign through the VHP, and various rallies and marches have taken place to voice objection and garner support. Sharma quotes a *sadhvi* (female mendicant) attending a rally organised by the VHP in 2000: 'the Tehri dam is being constructed to imprison the Ganga forever. This is an organised conspiracy to demolish our religion and culture. The way we had to demolish the Babri mosque at our own risk, we have to get ready now for the demolition of the Tehri dam' (2001). This echoes Kipling's story 'The Bridge-Builders', set during the British colonial period, which relates 'Mother Gunga's' rage at being locked in by a newly constructed bridge and her appeal to the other Gods for help. They, on the other hand, have decided that it is time she backs down and takes 'her appointed place in the new imperial geography' (Prakash, 1999, p. 168).

For the original anti-dam movement, the recourse to religious ideas about the Ganges is one strategy for encouraging people to take to issue the seriously and has certainly raised the profile of the controversy surrounding the Tehri dam. By contrast, many of those who are stimulated by the religious rhetoric surrounding the dam seem more concerned with the Ganges as a symbol of Hindu culture and nation than with its ecological implications. In fact, Alley suggests that the Hindu Right hijacked the anti-Tehri dam campaign as a political tool during the 1998 election, but quickly lost interest once they secured victory (2002, pp. 223–6). She writes that interest in the dam issue arose 'because of the perspective and concerns of a particular sadhu-saint, a religious political leader who plays a prominent role in state and national politics' (2002, p. 223). Once that sadhu-saint, Swami Chinmayananda, however, was elected to office, 'the campaign against river pollution and the opposition to the Tehri dam fell away almost immediately' (2002, p. 226). Alley concludes that although opposition to the dam does periodically enter his political ideology, on the whole, he has not translated his earlier concern into a sustained critique of government policy.

Thus, religious environmentalist discourse has different roles in the anti-Tehri dam campaign where diverse movements and ideologies have coalesced over the issue: from the Gandhian idealism of Sunderlal Bahuguna to the divisive nationalism of the VHP. Nevertheless, Baviskar suggests that the distance between these two may not be so great. Bahuguna, for instance, has been reported as one of the VHP delegates to recently meet the Indian Prime Minister in a bid for the construction of a temple at the Babri mosque site (2004). Similarly, Sharma points out that Bahuguna has been observed 'invoking popular stereotypes about the Muslim community' (2002, p. 5). Thus, they query the extent to which this veteran of ecological activism is using instrumental devices to court the support of conservative Hinduism, or whether this more broadly reflects the spirit of the Hindu Right.

*'Hindu Ecology in the Age of Hindutva'*

One of the most outspoken critics of religious environmentalism in India is Meera Nanda (2005). Her article 'Hindu ecology in the age of Hindutva: the dangers of religious environmentalism' addresses the above critique head-on. She writes: 'what is wrong with making the ecological religious? Why should religion not have a role in environmental protection? Why shouldn't new social movements tap the popular religiosity of ordinary people for environmental protection?' (2005, p. 68). In spite of the apparent appeal of bringing religion and environmentalism together, she 'raises some fundamental questions regarding the use of Hindu symbols, rituals and cosmology in environmental activism in India' (2005, p. 70). She employs many of the same critiques that have been discussed in this book, but ultimately uses them to attempt to undermine religious environmentalism as a viable option in both India and abroad. My aim has not been to undermine religious environmentalism *per se* but to assess the extent to which it is a viable ecopolitical option. She makes reference to one of the key points raised throughout this book, that 'the underlying assumption of religious environmentalism – that a religious attitude of sacredness and reverence toward nature encourages wise use of nature – is not supported by sound evidence from field studies' (2005, p. 88). Moreover, she draws attention to the fact that

> Most poor people participate in environmental movements for secular reasons. In study after study it has come to light that the primary motivation of poor people to take action on behalf of the trees, rivers and land is their interest in a better life materially for themselves and for their children (2005, p. 88).

While I agree with both of these statements, what they fail to capture is the way in which a 'religious attitude of sacredness and reverence toward nature' might be re-directed towards 'wise use of nature' in the context of modern environmentalist initiatives. Thus, the poor might participate in environmental movements because it will benefit them materially, but these movements might be more successful if they are make recourse to local religiocultural values and narratives (e.g. the project in Vrindavan or ecologists' use of sacred grove discourses).

However, Nanda argues that a 'secular motivation for environmental action is an untapped resource for secular environmentalism. Rather than drape the cloak of sacredness on nature, environmentalism in India can become a source of secularism and a class-based collective action' (2005, p. 89). Nanda is writing from a position of concern about the rise of Hindu nationalism in India: her promotion of secularism is a response to this concern. Firstly, she argues that the dangers of co-option by Hindu nationalism are very real and that this undermines the religious environmentalist endeavour in India from the outset. Secondly, even if the above were not true then it would still be problematic 'because of the in-egalitarian, illiberal and irrational elements of the tradition' (2005, p. 73), particularly gender and caste hierarchies. To complete this chapter and our investigation of the extent to which its links with some features of Hindu Right challenge the validity, integrity and efficacy of religious environmentalism in India, it is worth looking at Nanda's argument more closely.

Nanda claims that the Hindu Right is actively seeking alliances with a host of neo-pagan movements in Europe and North America (2005, p. 71). According to her definition, this would include members of various radical EDA groups, such as those discussed in Chapter 5, since 'many in the deep-ecology/pagan environmentalism camp are either practicing Hindus, or at least profess a great affinity for Eastern spiritualities' (2005, p. 75). It is not entirely clear in what ways the Hindu Right is seeking this alliance, but later in the chapter she tells us that 'the Hindu-neo-pagan dialogue is still in its initial stages, and may not amount to anything more than one more Western fringe religion looking for inspiration from Hinduism and India' (2005, p. 82). She points out the Hindu influences of Gandhi and Sri Aurobindo upon the writings of the Deep Ecologist Arne Naess and the ways in which New Age and neo-pagan philosophies draw upon the non-dualistic monism of Vendanta (2005, p. 75). However, although Hindu thought is amenable to the liberal and egalitarian vision of various western new spiritualities, Nanda wishes to emphasise that it also has a 'dark side' and 'if protecting the environment means adopting a worldview which has a long history of supporting deeply egalitarian and anti-humanistic ideas, I recommend that we think twice' (2005, p. 78). She argues that 'the horrendous inequalities and superstitions that follow from this worldview somehow fail to register on the neo-pagan/New-Age mindset of pagan environmentalists, for they tend to see inequities as natural 'differences' in the chain of being which must be preserved against the onslaught of capitalist mass society' (2005, p. 77). In my experience, however, while 'pagan environmentalists' do adopt features of eastern traditions they tend to mould them to fit egalitarian social systems and are sharply critical of hierarchy and oppression. What they are taking on board are not unadulterated eastern traditions but something quite different: however, this does not make them guilty of endorsing the 'horrendous inequalities' of traditional Hinduism. Hinduism is, of course, not homogenous and since ancient times there have been various reformist movements seeking to purge the culture of caste discrimination in particular. But Nanda rejects the efficacy of reformist movements (even those of the late colonial period) in the face of the strong grip that tradition maintains.

One problem with this article is the way in which various neo-pagan religious environmentalists or ecospiritual radical environmentalists are lumped together with right wing racist pagan movements that do actively seek alliances with the Hindu Right in India. She writes: 'what is of concern to me, as to many other students of this stew of new ideologies, is the possibility of cross-fertilization of ideas between genuine spiritual seekers, the politically progressive anti-racist environmentalism, and the radical religious nationalists' (2005, p. 84). While Nanda tells us that 'racist neo-pagans routinely infiltrate non-racist radical ecology groups by espousing ecological themes' (2005, p. 88) in my experience they are much more likely to be rejected and denounced than to be in a position to effect some kind of mass brainwashing of individual activists who are fundamentally egalitarian in their worldview. I think that the alliance that she discusses is worthy of study and should be a cause for concern, but it does not, in my opinion, necessarily undermine all forms of religious environmentalism that draw upon Hinduism – in both India and abroad.[27]


## Conclusion

To date, the response of the Hindu Right to environmental issues has remained sporadic and largely confined to the issue of the Tehri dam. Alley, for instance, suggests that it has been particularly difficult for the Hindu Right to maintain an interest in campaigns to clean up the Ganges because the Muslim community, in particular, does not emerge as an obvious culprit to take the blame for its pollution (2000, p. 370). However, while she argues that 'the Muslim 'other' staged in struggles over sacred space fades away in discussions about Ganga's sacrality' (2000, p. 381), objection to the Tehri dam *does* employ anti-Muslim rhetoric. Although the depiction of the 'Muslim other' as responsible for the damming of the Ganges at Tehri is not clearly or consistently articulated, we do find the linking of the Tehri issue to the Ram Janmabhumi movement (Alley 2002, p. 224). This locates the concern of the Hindu Right for the damming of the Ganges within a broader political campaign against the Muslim community, which is considered to be intent upon destroying Hindu culture.

Whether or not the response of groups such as the VHP to the Tehri dam is sustainable, or likely to be repeated with respect to other ecological concerns, it is arguable that environmentalists in India ought to distance themselves from exclusively Hindu interpretations of ecological issues. This way they can avoid being identified with the Hindu Right. The elevation of the Sanskrit tradition has been one of the criticisms widely levelled at commentators such as Vandana Shiva (1988) and Banwari (1992), who invariably draw upon Brahmanical Hinduism to express their ecological ethics (Baviskar, 1999). This ignores or downplays the diversity of religiocultural traditions that exist in India from *adivasi* ('tribal'/indigenous) traditions to Islam, Sikhism, Christianity and Buddhism. In fact, although not without its problems, the literature surrounding sacred grove preservation is a welcome contribution to the over-emphasis upon the elite Sanskrit tradition that many feel has become synonymous with religious environmentalism in India (Baviskar, 1999). Unless the practice of preserving sacred groves can be linked to events or personalities of classical Hinduism (as with the example of Krishna's forests in Vrindavana), or to the 'Muslim enemy', the sacred grove is unlikely to appeal to the Hindu Right. While the literature on sacred groves does tend to classify sacred grove protection as part of the 'Hindu' tradition, it is

---

[27]    See Taylor (1998; 2002) for further discussion of radical environmental subcultures and links to racist movements.

more correctly to be seen as part of a religiocultural landscape that predates and exists alongside the pan-Indian elite Brahmanical tradition. In fact, the process of 'Sanskritisation' has had an impact upon the demise of the institution of the sacred grove, as regional deities become identified with the pan-Indian Gods and the groves are cleared to make way for temples. Nevertheless, much of the literature on sacred groves is limited by its failure to distinguish between the idea that aspects of Hinduism can be interpreted to support contemporary environmentalist thinking and the far stronger assertion that Hinduism *is* 'environmentally friendly': the recognition of 'biodivinity' does not make one an environmentalist.

In this chapter I have shown that religion often enters the environmental debate in India for pragmatic rather than romantic reasons. Whilst we still find the same religious environmentalist assumptions being made, the reasons for using religion are different. Religion is used to help maintain or encourage environmentally friendly behaviour but is not seen as necessary in itself. By contrast, in the environmental direct action movement, for example, I have shown that a spiritual approach to environmentalism is believed to be both necessary and of more than practical or ecological significance. I am suggesting that in the above examples religious environmentalist narratives are being used consciously and reflexively in order to contribute towards the preservation of sacred groves. Whilst the idealised image of Indian rural life that they invoke does not necessarily match up to the reality of lived experiences, as a form of rhetoric it may be useful. It is of course difficult to separate out a belief in the authenticity of this position from its use as a rhetorical device. However, the evidence suggests that some environmentalists are, at least some of the time, consciously using religion in order to achieve practical effects rather than to actually argue for a return to such a rural idyll.

# Chapter 8
# Conclusion

## Does Religious Environmentalism have Cross-cultural Significance?

The main aim of this book has been to investigate the extent to which 'religious environmentalism' has cross-cultural significance. Does the reliance of religious environmentalism upon a particular model of religion *and* understanding of nature limit its relevance for non-western contexts? Does religion have a role to play in ecological thinking and action in a country such as India, or is religious environmentalism a narrowly focused, colonial, postmaterialist and romantic ideology that has limited relevance in a developing context? It has been my argument that the sociocultural context of religious environmentalism has been under theorised. The two religious environmentalist narratives or assumptions are representations, *theory* typically presented *fact*, and we need to move beyond this in order to be able to examine the efficacy of the theory and to draw up its boundaries and limits. Whilst there is a vast literature that discusses the environmentalist interpretation of different religious traditions, there has been much less analysis of how these ideas translate into practical initiatives or how they affect people's lives. Neither has there been much critical reflection upon the religious environmentalist enterprise itself.

Larson, for instance, has suggested that the debate about whether or not religious traditions provide a basis for environmental ethics needs to be approached from a somewhat different angle. A more crucial question to ask is: 'why is it that we tend to think of the environmental crisis as a 'philosophical' or 'ethical' problem when it is obviously so much more than that?' (Larson, 1991, p. 276). An extension of this is to ask why we tend to think of it as a 'religious' or 'spiritual' problem. The very fact that such a debate exists in the first place needs to be carefully scrutinised as it tells us something about (western) society's self understanding or its 'anatomy' rather than whether or not religious traditions are environmentally friendly (Larson, 1991, p. 276). While in India, environmental problems are more likely to reflect the *local pragmatic* approach, much environmentalist rhetoric in the West is mediated by a *Romantic* belief that nature has rights or intrinsic value. Therefore, humanity's relationship with the natural world becomes an ethical issue and has attracted commentary upon the way in which this intersects with religious and spiritual traditions. If we turn to India, however, although such ethics can be derived from the Hindu tradition, for instance, their relevance and appeal is not so evident. As Van Horn's review of literature on Hinduism and ecology reveals (2004), a consequence of reading any of these religious environmentalist interpretations of Hinduism is likely to leave one with an inflated image of the significance of religious and cultural values to conservation of the environment in both past and present India.

## Globalisation and the Ethics of Representation

This book has also told a story about the consequences of globalisation. It has been concerned with the effects of globalisation on the nature of and understandings about environmental problems, as well as the use of religiocultural resources from across the globe to approach and solve the 'environmental crisis'. Globalisation has meant that for many, particularly in the West, the certainties of religious traditions have become less convincing and, moreover, that it is possible to choose from a global range of cultural and religious resources. Globalisation has created a situation where religious and cultural systems are increasingly treated as global resources, which can be shaped and crafted to support contemporary ideologies about the environment. They are frequently uprooted from their original contexts, both in terms of their geographical origin and their indigenous significance. Such ideas are being treated almost as if they were commodities that, as Larson writes, can be

> detached and 'dug out' as it were and then imported into our own frameworks…
> if they are to be utilized profitably, these 'resources' will have to be processed,
> manufactured, mass-produced, and finally, distributed…the market for the
> eventual product is worldwide or global, and in that sense we can congratulate
> ourselves that what we are doing will subsequently benefit not only Asia but all
> people everywhere. This, of course, is exactly the rationale that the British used
> in Indian during the Raj (1991, p. 270).

Lash and Urry, by contrast, argue that a commodification metaphor is not really appropriate since 'what (all) the culture industries produce becomes increasingly, not like commodities but advertisements. As with advertising firms, the culture industries sell not themselves but something else and they achieve this through "packaging". Also like advertising firms they sell 'brands' of something else' (1994, p. 138). Thus, the religious environmentalist assumptions may be seen as 'brands' of traditions of nature religion 'packaged' as religious environmentalism.

Many scholars have questioned the implications of the representation of religious traditions as environmentally friendly when the assumed beliefs and practices of non-industrial cultures as ecologically benign are idealised. One danger of this type of Orientalism is that more pressing and practical measures may become obscured (Baviskar, 1997). As Dentan writes, regarding the dangers of such 'fakelore' (Dorson 1976),

> It is important for reasons of ethnographic accuracy and proper respect, not
> to transform the lives of real people into utopias for the use of others. When
> members of a powerful society use a self-serving fakeloric version of another
> people's history or life as a myth for their own, they may deprive that people the
> chance to assert their own, differing version (Dentan, 1994, p. 95).

However, this sensitivity towards people's cultural integrity can also lead to a virtual sacralisation of cultures and traditions where it is argued that these must be preserved intact. Although the issue about 'cultural theft' is not just a concern about preserving tradition, but also about who has the right to interpret and transform tradition, this consideration too can become over-stated and over-inflated, when it fails to account for the instances when the poor appropriate environmental stereotypes about themselves to serve strategic ends (Brosius, 1999). Thus, the situation is not so straightforward, since alongside different elite discourses we also find indigenous/local/grassroots versions or responses. While globalisation does imply a certain level of uniformity and homogeneity, it can also foster diversity where local culture interacts with global discourses to produce strategic localised versions. Globalised discourses that represent other cultural systems, may stamp out diversity and silence voices, but they can also encourage the agency of different cultures to shape these discourses to their own ends (Brosius, 1999).

## *The Use and Relevance of Religious Environmentalist Assumptions*

Religious environmentalism represents a creative and innovative tendency, which aims to find support for contemporary environmentalist thinking within religious and cultural traditions. It is a new tradition that makes use of traditional ideas within a contemporary context. Whilst there are issues concerning the way in which such ideas are used, particularly if they result in oppression, marginalisation or the silencing of voices, these critiques can become over-extended and hyperbolic. There is a danger that the overuse of charges of 'cultural theft' or the 'myth of primitive ecological wisdom' can lessen the efficacy of these important critical tools: to 'essentialise the essentialisers' potentially undermines the more cautious, balanced and reflective use of such critiques. While I am sympathetic to the arguments of scholars such as Baviskar and Guha, that the discourses presented by the global environmental movement do often idealise and romanticise poor people, I am also interested in how these discourses are actually used within different groups and movements.

Within the examples of *Romantic* religious environmentalism described in Chapters 5 and 6 (EDA in Britain and the Rainbow Family in India) the myth of primitive ecological wisdom is a narrative that can be motivational; it provides meaning for the individuals who adopt it. This is interesting and relevant from a sociological perspective. Thus, in terms of description, explanation and analysis, there is a need to balance an appreciation the affective and motivational side of such 'myth making' (and not to dismiss it completely for its anachronistic viewpoint), with the impact and power relations involved in propagating such 'myths'. Religious environmentalism aims to reclaim a space for people's cultural and religious beliefs and how these shape attitudes towards the natural world, in reaction to the universalising tendencies of the scientific *managerial* approach to the conservation of natural resources. It aims to ethicalise the agenda of the dominant institutions within global society, which are often blind to the environmental consequences of their activities. While there is a sense in which religious environmentalism is itself often blind to its own deeper agenda and potential impact (it perpetuates an idealised image of the 'happy peasant' living in harmony with the natural world), it is important to contextualise this as part of a broader set of frustrations that many feel towards modern society. An idealisation of the countryside, of rural living or an unspoiled wilderness, are, in part, contemporary strategies to accommodate wider discontents with the totalising machinery of modern urban living and industrial culture.

In Chapters 6 and 7, I look at the ways in which these discourses are actually played out in an Indian context. What potential is there for Hinduism to be transformed into an ecological religion? What would such an ecological religion look like in India, where *Romantic* and postmaterial environmentalism is less convincing, and in what ways could it have an impact upon people's behaviour? And what challenges face such an ecologising of religion in the light of concerns about the 'Hinduisation of civil society'? In Chapter 6 I discuss two case studies: the first (a Rainbow gathering in the Himalayas) is an example of *Romantic* environmentalism, it closely resembles Charles Taylor's expressive ethical style (1989) and employs Hannigan's 'rhetoric of rectitude' (1995), whereas the second (the Vrindavan Conservation Project) employs the theistic ethical style (Taylor, 1989) and is an example of *local pragmatic* environmentalism. The latter employs *Romantic* discourses about nature, but this is blended with a focus upon immediate and practical ends (e.g. the planting of trees, the cleaning of the *parikrama* path etc.), rather than having as its proximate goal the total transformation of human-nature relations. The example of sacred grove protection, discussed in Chapter 7, where ecologists make use of *Romantic* discourses about nature as a strategic device (part of their repertoire of conservationist tactics), is described as an example of 'weak' religious environmentalism. This lies in contrast to the 'strong' version, where individuals strongly buy into or affiliate with the underlying values of the discourse.

Finally, I consider the critique that the 'Hindu civilizational' response (Baviskar, 2004) to environmental problems in India, is indistinguishable from a broader Hinduisation agenda, tied up with the aggressive and chauvinistic Hindu nationalist movement. I suggest that environmentalists in India ought to distance themselves from exclusively Hindu interpretations of ecological issues to avoid being identified with the Hindu Right. The elevation of the Sanskrit tradition has been one of the criticisms widely levelled at commentators such as Shiva and Banwari, who invariably draw upon Brahmanical Hinduism to express their ecological ethics (Baviskar, 1999). This ignores or downplays the diversity of other religiocultural traditions that exist in India, from *adivasi* ('tribal'/indigenous) traditions to Islam, Sikhism, Christianity or Buddhism. In particular, religious environmentalism has not engaged in any serious depth with the impact of cultural and religious traditions upon the 'subaltern masses' in India, as regards how they relate to their environment. As a specialist field of scholarly research, 'subaltern studies' aims to 'get beyond the broad, mainstream and biased overview of the "official" or "elitist" history of India in order to find the concrete and particular historical struggles of the "subaltern" masses in India' (Larson, 1995, p. 41). Larson points out that although subaltern scholars have recognised the importance of the 'religious consciousness' to the subaltern peoples, they have not yet pursued it to any great extent. Whilst this lacuna is yet to be filled, it is likely to reveal that there is no simple, linear relationship between religious and cultural values and how people relate to their natural environment. However, a more sensitive appreciation of such an interaction is essential on two counts; firstly, to challenge the romantic image of the Indian peasant and, secondly, to work towards a more effective understanding of what the environment represents to people.

*Biodivinity and Biodiversity: The Limits to Religious Environmentalism?*

So, does religion have a role to play in ecological thinking and action in a country such as India, or is religious environmentalism a narrowly focused, colonial, postmaterialist and romantic ideology that has limited relevance in a developing context? The answer to this question is not straightforward. Whether endorsing or critiquing religious environmentalism as a viable global ecopolitics one should be attuned to issues of context, interpretation and the politics of representation. This book has shown that whilst there is a place for religion within environmentalism, without critical reflection, applying more and more ethics and religion is perhaps no more useful than applying more and more science and technology. Moreover, as Larson warns, 'if we seriously think that we can find 'conceptual resources' in Asia, *and* that such an effort would have a serious impact upon the environmental crisis, then we really have not understood the environmental problem at all!' (1991, p. 271). Thus, on the one hand, the environmental crisis is unlikely to be a problem that is solvable through ethics or religion: just because religious and ethical solutions can be suggested it does not entail their efficacy. On the other hand, in an era that is likely to become increasingly pre-occupied with the realities and injustices of ecological disasters, religious solutions are perhaps no more limited or partial than others when taken alone. In both India and Britain, many people make clear links between thinking about and responding to ecological concerns (in ways that are both expressive and pragmatic) and the potential of religious teachings and ethics to challenge and transform individual behaviour. Religious environmentalism takes many guises and is by now a prominent and well-established feature of the contemporary environmental movement. Despite critics and those who doubt its efficacy, we do find both *Romantics* and *pragmatists* who are attracted to the notion that biodivinity has a role to play in preserving biodiversity, perhaps for different reasons and with different underlying motivations, but arguably in response to similar concerns and questions about the future of the planet.

# Appendix
# Religious Studies as a Discipline[1]

Religious studies emerged as a discipline in the 1960s to create space for the 'secular study of religion'. It sought to distinguish itself from theology, 'traditionally regarded as an insider discourse' (Flood 1999, p. 18), through adopting a '"non-confessional approach" which tried to treat religions as key dimensions of human culture which can be understood in ways akin to other discipline's understandings of their objects' (Flood 1999, p. 18). Whereas theology was confined to the Christian tradition,[2] was carried out by 'insiders' and rested upon an acceptance of the truth claims of the tradition, religious studies had as its object all religious traditions, and was proclaimed to be founded upon the 'value-free exploration of religious meaning and institutions' (Flood 1999, p. 19). As Flood writes 'the language of theology is a language which *expresses* religion whereas the language of religious studies is a language *about* religion' (1999, p. 20).

The intellectual basis for this 'scientific' study of religion (as opposed to theology) is a legacy of earlier scholarly developments since the eighteenth century, particularly within anthropology, sociology, psychology and philosophy. Scholars provided both functional (what religion *does*) and substantive/essentialist (what religion *is*) definitions of religion; they sought to explain the nature of religious phenomena (often reducing them to social or psychological causes rather than 'supernatural'); and they contributed towards a body of literature which generated new knowledge about religious belief and practice across the globe. The German scholar Max Muller had a particular influence upon the emergence of what we now call 'religious studies'. He called for a new comparative and non-confessional scientific study of religion – *Religionswissenschaft*. However, what was distinct about this new approach to the study of religion, was the assertion that the subject matter of religious studies ('religion') was itself unique and was not reducible to the categories of the social sciences (it was *sui generis*). Moreover, this band of scholars also objected to the 'Eurocentric' tendencies of anthropological and 'Orientalist' accounts of religion when they implied that

---

[1]  The material in this Appendix is based on work first published in Tomalin 2007, pp. 3–9. That work is copyright of the University of Birmingham (2007) and is an output of a project funded by the UK Department for International Development (DfID) for the benefit of developing countries. The views expressed here are not necessarily those of DfID.

[2]  The study of Christian theology developed within western institutions but is now studied and taught across the globe. Today the term theology is sometimes also applied to the study of religious traditions (other than Christianity alone) when it is undertaken by 'insiders' and may reflect a 'confessional' perspective.

such traditions were inferior to, or to be contrasted with, the Christian tradition. The challenge facing 'religious studies' was to develop a methodology that was capable of two things. First, it needed a methodology that enabled the production of scholarly reflection upon *all* religious traditions on their own terms, but by researchers who stood 'outside' the religious traditions they were studying (unlike theology, where theologians were 'insiders'). Second, it was deemed important that this method should remain 'agnostic' about the truth of religious beliefs, since to reduce them to naturalistic explanations was to take something away from the religious subject's account and to affirm them would imply a theological position.

To meet this challenge, a *phenomenological* methodology had become popular by the 1960s, which demanded that the researcher 'bracket' his/her own interpretation of religious phenomena and instead endeavour to enter into 'empathy' with the believer in order to 'bring out what religious acts mean to the actors' (Smart 1996, p. 2). As Erricker writes,

> The notion of a phenomenological study of religion was really an attempt to justify the study of religion on its own terms rather than on the terms of the theologian or the social scientist. The sentiment behind this was and still is liberal in character, arguing for the importance of equal consideration being given to different 'religious cultures', whether past or present, empathizing with and seeking to understand the viewpoints of different traditions across the spectrum of religious practices and constructing a case for the importance of the study of religious within the academic world (1999, p. 83).

While this was undoubtedly seen as a welcome contrast to the Eurocentric 'Orientalist' construction of religious traditions, which emerged from within colonial encounters, the extent to which this method successfully bridges the gap between theology and social sciences, in the 'value-free' way that it wants to, has been challenged (see Dubuisson, 2003; Fitzgerald, 2000; McCutcheon, 1997; Tomoko, 2005). As Shaw writes 'by making it [*sui generis* religion] central to their discourse, scholars in the history of religions are effectively insulated from uncomfortable questions about standpoint and privilege' (1995, p. 70).[3]

---

[3]   A second critique, which is not so relevant to this study, rests upon the extent to which this method distinguishes the discipline from theology. It is argued that the 'methodological agnosticism' (agnosticism about the truth claims or origins of religions), which dominates religious studies, is, after all, a theological standpoint. The phenomenological method treats religion as *sui generis* (a thing of its own type, which cannot be explained in terms of other phenomena), which implies an acceptance of the claims made by believers (Fitzgerald, 2000; McCutcheon, 1997; 1999). Fitzgerald argues that this reliance upon a notion of religion as *sui generis* is a thinly disguised 'ecumenical liberal theology' (2000, p. 7). He argues that the phenomenological approach to religion actually belies a 'theological' commitment after all, since it implicitly supports a non-naturalistic explanation for religious

McCutcheon is similarly concerned that this privileging of the category rel.̣
as effectively 'sociopolitically autonomous' has made it difficult for religious
studies to engage with the ways in which religious traditions are implicated in
maintaining difference and exploitation (1997, p. 4). He writes that religious
studies scholars are 'like their Christian Theological predecessors who claimed
that the Christian message to be equally autonomous and unique, they are
effectively insulated from political and historical analysis' (1997, p. 4). He
continues:

> The implications of exclusively constructing religion in this one manner...
> effectively segments people from their complex sociopolitical and historical
> relationships and contributes to manufacturing a cultural context conducive
> to such segmentation. Although it is possible, even probable, that a significant
> number of the global population find the poverty suffered by large segments of
> the global population and the tremendous wealth of others to be reprehensible,
> the consequence of one of their primary suppositions (that certain aspects of
> human life are free from the taint of sociopolitical interactions) shares in a
> strategic marginalization of historical humans (1997, p. 23).

Thus, in treating the accounts of religious subjects as beyond scrutiny
(*sui generis*) the phenomenology of religion avoids comment upon the social,
economic or political contextuality of religious phenomena. In trying to
understand what religious acts mean to the believer, the focus shifts away from
religions as products of particular contexts, both in terms of how they have been
shaped by external factors as well as the influence that they have upon the those
factors in turn (McCutcheon, 1997, p. 62). So, for instance, a gender analysis of
religion would be discouraged by an 'extreme' phenomenological method (King
1995).

So how does my study draw upon the above discussion? I am sympathetic
to retaining, as one methodological tool, 'the attentive and detailed *description*
of the phenomena packaged as "religion"...[and] paying close attention to the
"believer's own account" as part of the explanatory process' (Sutcliffe 2004,
p. xxiii). However, I also argue that the subjective accounts of believers 'require
social, cultural and historical contextualization if adequate analysis is to be

---

phenomena. Thus, religious studies is considered to be 'crypto-theology' and critics argue
that it then becomes unclear why is should remain a separate discipline with its own
unique methodology. Fitzgerald, for instance, argues that 'religious studies be rethought
and represented as cultural studies' (2000, p. 10) and McCutcheon suggests that religious
studies scholars should abandon their claim to have a unique methodology (which is based
upon the notion of *sui generis* religion) and should instead invest themselves in 'developing
interdisciplinary connections with their colleagues in the social sciences' (1997, p. 201).
Thus, religious studies scholars are considered to be apologists for the truth behind religious
belief even when they claim to be 'value-free'.

achieved' (2004, p. xxvi) and that in drawing on various methodologies (historical, textual, ethnographic etc...) 'qualitative approaches construct religion not as an ahistorical essence...but as a "social formation"...embedded in and generated by particular cultural and political contexts and essences' (2004, p. xxvii). This extra 'hermeneutical step' is now common within religious studies, which routinely draws upon critical methodologies which have developed outside the discipline of religious studies, including gender analysis, post-colonial critique and, increasingly, postmodern thought.

# Bibliography

Adams, William M., *Future Nature: A Vision for Conservation* (London: Earthscan, 1996).

Aitken, Robert, 'Gandhi, Dogen and Deep Ecology', in Bill Devall and George Sessions (eds), *Deep Ecology: Living as if Nature Mattered* (Salt Lake City, UT: Gibbs Smith, 1985), pp. 232–5.

Ajit, Shine Kiran, *Quest for Good Governance: Contribution and Potential of Religious Institutions as Stakeholders* (Presented at 'The Quest for Good Governance' organized by the Monash Governance Research Unit and Monash Institute for the Study of Global Movements, 27 August, 20, 2004, www. buseco.monash.edu.au/mgt/research/governance/pdf-downloads/k-shinde-wshop.pdf (last accessed 18/07/08).

Alley, Kelly, 'Idioms of Degeneracy: Assessing Ganga's Purity and Pollution', in Lance Nelson (ed.), *Purifying the Earthly Body of God* (New York: State University of New York Press, 1998), pp. 297–330.

Alley, Kelly, 'Separate Domains: Hinduism, Politics and Environmental Pollution', in Christopher Chapple and Mary E. Tucker (eds), *Hinduism and Ecology* (Cambridge: Harvard University Press, 2000), pp. 355–87.

Alley, Kelly, *On the Banks of the Ganga: When Wastewater Meets a Sacred River* (Ann Arbor: University of Michigan Press, 2002).

Almond, Philip C., *The British Discovery of Buddhism* (Cambridge: Cambridge University Press, 1988).

Anderson, Benedict, *Imagined Communities: Reflections on the Origin and Spread of Nationalism* (Cambridge: Harvard University Press, 1981).

Anderson, Jon, 'Researching Environmental Resistance: Working Through Secondspace and Thirdspace Approaches', *Qualitative Research*, 2/3 (2002): 301–22.

Anderson, Jon, 'The Ties that Bind? Self- and Place-identity in Environmental Direct Action', *Ethics, Place and Environment*, 7/1–2 (2004a): 45–57.

Anderson, Jon, 'Spatial Politics in Practice: The Style and Substance of Environmental Direct Action', *Antipode*, 36/1 (2004b): 106–25.

Anon and Anon, 'And the single issue said to the totality', *Do or Die*. No. 5 (1996): 93.

Apffel-Marglin, Frederique and P.C. Mishra, 'Sacred Groves Regenerating the Body, the Land, the Community', in Wolfgang Sachs (ed.), *Global Ecology A New Arena of Conflict* (Halifax, Nova Scotia: Fernwood Publishing, 1993) pp. 197–207.

Apffel-Marglin, Frederique and Pramod Parjuli, 'Sacred Grove and Ecology: Ritual and Science', in Christopher Key Chapple and Mary Evelyn Tucker (eds), *Hinduism and Ecology: The Intersection of Earth, Sky, and Water* (Cambridge: Harvard University Press, 2000) pp. 291–316.

Arnold, David and Ramachandra Guha (eds), *Nature, Culture, Imperialism: Essays on the Environmental History of South Asia* (New Delhi: Oxford University Press, 1995).

Babb, Lawrence A., *The Divine Hierarchy: Popular Hinduism in Central India* (New York and London: Columbia University Press, 1975).

Banarjee, Rajat, *A Gloomy, Grubby Gutter Called Ganga* (Deccan Herald, Sunday Herald. February 8th, 1998).

Banuri, Tariq and Frederique Apffel Marglin (eds), *Who Will Save the Forests: knowledge, power and Environmental Destruction* (London and New Jersey: Zed Books, 1993).

Banwari, *Pancavati: Indian Approach to the Environment* (New Delhi: Shri Vinayaka Publications, 1992).

Barry, Andrew, 'Demonstrations: Sites and Sights of Direct Action', *Economy and. Society*, 28/1 (1999): 75–94.

Barthes, Roland (trans. Annette Lavers), *Mythologies* (London: Cape, 1972).

Baviskar, Amita, *In the Belly of the River: Tribal Conflicts over Development in the Narmada Valley* (New Delhi: Oxford University Press, 1995).

Baviskar, Amita, 'Tribal Politics and Discourses of Environmentalism', *Contributions to Indian Sociology*, 31/2 (1997): 195–224.

Baviskar, Amita, 'Vanishing Forests, Sacred Trees: A Hindu Perspective on Eco–Consciousness', *Asian Geographer*, 18/1–2 (1999): 21–31.

Baviskar, Amita, 'Between Violence and Desire: Space, Power, and Identity in the Making of Metropolitan Delhi', *International Social Science Journal*, 55/1 (2003): 89–98.

Baviskar, Amita, 'Red in Tooth and Claw? Looking for Class in Struggles over Nature', Raka Ray and Mary Fainsod Katzenstein (eds), *Social Movements in India: Poverty, Power, Politics* (Lanham, MD.: Rowman and Littlefield, 2004) pp. 161–78.

Beck, Ulrich, 'Risk Society and the Provident State', in Scott Lash, Bronislaw Szerszynski and Bryan Wynne (eds), *Risk, Environment and Modernity: Towards a New Ecology* (London: Sage, 1996) pp. 27–43.

Beckford, James A., *Religion and Advanced Industrial Society* (London: Unwin Hyman, 1989).

Beckford, James A., 'The Sociology of Religion and Social Problems', *Sociological Analysis*, 51/1 (1990): 1–14.

Belfrage, Sally, *Flowers of Emptiness* (London: Women's Press, 1981).

Bellah, Robert, 'Religious Evolution', *American Sociological Review*, 29 (1964): 358–74.

Belliappa, Jyotsna, *Devarakadus – Hotspots of Biodiversity in Coorg District, Karnataka* (Conference report, the Centre for Environmental Education (CEE), Virajpet, Coorg, 1998).

Berger, Peter L., Brigitte Berger and Hansfried Kellner, *The Homeless Mind: Modernization and Consciousness* (New York: Random House, 1973).

Beyer, Peter, 'Privatization and the Public Influence of Religion in Global Society', *Theory, Culture, Society*, 7/2–3 (1990:): 373–95.

Beyer, Peter, 'The Global Environment as a Religious Issue: A Sociological Analysis, *Religion*, 22/1 (1992): 1–19.

Beyer, Peter, *Religion and Globalization* (London: Sage, 1994).

Beyer, Peter, 'The Religious System of Global Society: A Sociological Look at Contemporary Religion and Religions', *Numen*, 45/1 (1998): 1–29.

Bhatt, Chetan, *Hindu Nationalism: Origins, Ideologies, and Modern Myths* (Oxford, United Kingdom: Berg Publishers Limited, 2001).

Bircham, Emma and John Charlton, *Anti–Capitalism: A Guide to the Movement* (Bookmarks Publications: London, 2001).

Bird, Elizabeth A.R., 'The Social Construction of Nature: Theoretical Approaches to the History of Environmental Problems', *Environmental Review*, 11/4 (1987): 255–64.

Bloch, Jon P., 'Alternative Spirituality and Environmentalism', *Review of Religious Research*, 40/1 (1998a): 55–73.

Bloch, Jon P., 'Individualism and Community in Alternative Spiritual Magic', *Journal for the Scientific Study of Religion*, 37/2 (1998b): 286–302.

Bookchin, Murray, *The Ecology Of Freedom: The Emergence And Dissolution Of Hierarchy* (Palo Alto, Calif.: Cheshire Books, 1982).

Bookchin, Murray, *Post-scarcity Anarchism* (Montréal: Black Rose Books, 1986).

Bookchin, Murray, *The Ecology of Freedom: The Emergence and Dissolution of Hierarchy* (Oakland, California: AK Press, 2005).

Bopp, Judie, *The Sacred Tree: Reflections on Native American spirituality* (Twin Lakes: Lotus Light Publications, 1985).

Bradford, George, *How Deep is Deep Ecology?* (Evansyon, Illinois: Times Change Press, 1989).

Brechin, Steven R. and Willett Kempton, 'Global Environmentalism: A Challenge to the Postmaterialism Thesis', *Social Science Quarterly*, 75/2 (1994): 245–69.

Brosius, Peter, 'Analyses and Interventions: Anthropological Engagements with Environmentalism', *Current Anthropology*, 40/3 (1999): 277–309.

Bruce, Steve, *Religion in the Modern World: From Catholics to Cults* (Oxford: Oxford University Press, 1996).

Bryant, Barbara, *Twyford Down* (London: E. and F.N. Spoon/Chapman and Hall, 1996).

Butler, Beverley, 'The Tree, the Tower and the Shaman: The Material Culture of Resistance of the No. M11 Link Roads Protest of Wanstead and Leytonstone, London'. *Journal of Material Culture*, Vol. 1, No. 3 (1996): 337–63.

Calhoun, Craig, 'New Social Movements of the Early Nineteenth Century', *Social Science History*, 17/3 (1993): 385–427.

Callicott, J. Baird, 'Traditional American Indian and Western European Attitudes Towards Nature: An Overview', *Environmental Ethics*, 4/4 (1982): 293–318.

Callicott, J. Baird and Roger T. Ames (eds), *Nature in Asian Traditions of Thought: Essays in Environmental Philosophy* (New Delhi: Sri Satguru Publications, 1991).

Campbell, Colin, 'The Cult, the Cultic Milieu and Secularization', in *The Cultic Milieu: Oppositional Subcultures in an Age of Globalization*, Jeffrey Kaplan and Heléne Lööw (eds), (Walnut Creek/Lanham/New York/Oxford: Altamira, 2002), pp. 12–25.

Cant, Sarah and Ursula Sharma (eds), *Complementary and Alternative Medicines: Knowledge in Practice* (London: Free Association Books, 1996).

Carson, Rachel, *Silent Spring* (Boston: Houghton Mifflin, 1962).

Carter, Lewis F., *Charisma and Control in Rajneeshpuram: The Role of Shared Values in the Creation of Community* (Cambridge: Cambridge University Press, 1990).

Chakrabarty, Dipesh, 'Postcoloniality and the Artifice of History: Who Speaks for "Indian" Pasts?', in *A Subaltern Studies Reader, 1986–1995*, Ranajit Guha (ed.) (New Delhi: Oxford University Press, 2000), pp. 263–93.

Chandrakanth, M.G. and M.G. Nagaraja, 'Existence Value of Kodagu Sacred Groves Implications for Policy', in Anil Agarwal (ed.), *The Challenge of the Balance: Environmental Economics in India. Proceedings of the National Environment and Economics Meeting, January 1994* (Centre for Science and Environment: New Delhi, 1997) pp. 217–24.

Chandrakanth, M.G. and Jeff Romm, 'Sacred Forests, Secular Forest Policies and People's Actions', *Natural Resources Journal*, 31/4 (1991): 741–56.

Chandran, M.D. Sugash and J. Donald Hughes, 'The Sacred Groves of South India: Ecology, Traditional Communities and Religious Change', *Social Compass*, 44, No. 3 (1997): 413–27.

Chapman, Graham, 'The Ganges and the Brahmaputra Basins', in Graham Chapman and Michael Thompson (eds), *Water and the Quest for Sustainable Development in the Ganges Valley* (London and New York: Mansell, 1995) pp. 3–24.

Chapman, Graham, Keval Kumar, Caroline Fraser and Ivor Gaber, *Environmentalism and the Mass Media: the North-South divide* (London: Routledge, 1997).

Chapple, Christopher Key, *Nonviolence to Animals, Earth, and Self in Asian Traditions* (New Delhi: Sri Satguru Publications, 1995).

Chapple, Christopher Key, 'Toward an Indigenous Indian Environmentalism, in Lance E. Nelson (ed.), *Purifying the Earthly Body of God: Religion and Ecology in Hindu India* (Albany: State University of New York Press, 1998) pp. 13–37.

Clark, J. and Rose, T., 'British Anarchists Plan Seattle Riot', *The Sunday Times*, 28 November (1999): 11.

Cohn, Norman, *The Pursuit of the Millennium: Revolutionary Millenarians and Mystical Anarchists of the Middle Ages* (London: Pimlico, 1970).

Commoner, Barry, *The Closing Circle: Nature, Man and Technology* (New York: Knopf. 1971).

Cotgrove, Stephen, *Catastrophe or Cornucopia: The Environment, Politics and the Future* (Chichester: John Wiley and Sons, 1982).

Cotgrove, Stephen and Andrew Duff, 'Environmentalism, Values and Social Change', *British Journal of Sociology*, 32/1 (1981): 92–110.

Coward, Harold G., 'Purity in Hinduism, with Particular Reference to Patanjali's Yoga Sutras', in Harold G. Coward, Julius J. Lipner, and Katharine K. Young (eds), *Hindu Ethics: Purity, Abortion and Euthanasia* (Delhi: Sri Satguru Publications, 1991), pp. 9–40.

Cronon, William, 'Nature, History and Narrative: A Place for Stories, *Journal of American History*, 78/4 (1992): pp. 1347–76.

D'Anieri, Paul, Claire Ernst, Elizabeth Kier, 'New Social Movements in Historical Perspective' *Comparative Politics*, 22/4 (1990): 445–58.

Dalton, Russell, Manfred Kuechler and Wilhelm Burklin, 'The Challenge of New Movements', in Russell Dalton and Manfred Kuechler (eds), *Challenging the Political Order* (Oxford: Oxford University Press, 1990) pp. 3–20.

Dankelman and Davidson, *Women and Environment in the Third World: Alliance for the Future* (London: Earthscan in association with IUCN, London, 1988).

DasGupta Sherma, Rita, 'Sacred Immanence: Reflections of Ecofeminism in Hindu Tantra', in Lance Nelson (ed.), *Purifying the Earthly Body of God: Religion and Ecology in India* (New York: State University of New York Press, 1998) pp. 89–132.

Dekker, Paul, Peter Ester and Masja Nas, 'Religion, Culture and Environmental Concern: An Empirical Cross-national Analysis, *Social Compass*, 44/3 (1997): 443–58.

Dentan, Robert Knox, 'Surrendered Men: Peaceable Enclaves in the Post Enlightenment West', in Leslie E. Sponsel and Thomas A. Gregor (eds), *The Anthropology of Peace and Nonviolence* (Boulder, Colorado and London: Lynne Reinner, 1994) pp. 69–108.

Deudney, Daniel, 'In Search of Gaian Politics: Earth Religion's Challenge to Modern Western Civilisation', in Bron Taylor (ed.), *Ecological Resistance Movements: The Global Emergence of Radical and Popular Environmentalism* (Albany: State University of New York Press, 1995) pp. 282–99.

Devall, Bill and George Sessions, *Deep Ecology* (Salt Lake City, Utah: Gibbs M. Smith, 1985).

Dodson, Sean, 'History of Anti–Capitalism Protests', *The Guardian*, 30 April (2003): www.guardian.co.uk/mayday/story/0,7369,481489,00.html (last accessed 18/07/08).

Doherty, Brian, 'Paving the Way: the Rise of Direct Action against Road-building and the Changing Character of British Environmentalism', *Political Studies*, 47/2 (1999): 275–91.

Doherty, Brian, Matthew Patterson and Benjamin Seel, 'Direct Action in British Environmentalism', in Benjamin Seel, Matthew Patterson and Brian Doherty (eds), *Direct Action in British Environmentalism* (London and New York: Routledge, 2000) pp. 1–24.

Doherty, Brian, Alexandra Plows and Derek Wall, '"The Preferred Way of Doing Things": The British Direct Action Movement', *Parliamentary Affairs*, 56/4 (2003): 669–86.

Donga, Alex, 'The Rise (And Fall) Of The Ego Warrior?' *Do or Die*, 5 (1996): 89.

Dorson, Richard M., *Folklore and Fakelore: Essays Toward a Discipline of Folk Studies* (Cambridge, Massachusetts: Harvard University Press, 1976).

Douglas, Mary, 'Environments at Risk', in Jonathan Benthall (ed.), *Ecology: The Shaping Enquiry* (London: Longman, 1972) pp. 129–45.

Driver, Thackwray S. and Graham Chapman (eds), *Time-scales and Environmental Change* (London: Routledge, 1996).

Dubuisson, Daniel, *The Western Construction of Religion* (Washington, D.C.: Johns Hopkins University Press, 2003).

Dubois, Abbe J.A., *Hindu Manners, Customs and Ceremonies* (Calcutta: Rupa and Co., 1993 [1905]).

Dwivedi O.P., 'Global Dharma to the Environment', *Indian Journal of Public Administration*, 39/2 (1993a): 566–76.

Dwivedi O.P., 'Human Responsibility and the Environment: A Hindu Perspective', *Hindu-Christian Studies Bulletin*, 6 (1993b): 19–26.

Dwivedi, O.P., 'Satyagraha for Conservation: Awakening the Spirit of Hinduism', in *This Sacred Earth Religion, Nature, Environment*, Roger S. Gottlieb (ed.), (London and New York: Routledge, 1996) pp. 151–63.

Dwivedi O.P., 'Environmental Protection in the Indian Tradition', in George A. James (ed.), *Ethical Perspectives on Environmental Issues in India* (New Delhi: APH Publishing Corporation, 1999), pp. 161–88.

Dwivedi, O.P. and B.N. Tiwari, *Environmental Crisis and Hindu Religion* (New Delhi: Gitanjali Publishing House, 1987).

Earle, Fiona, Alan Dearling, Helen Whittle, Roddy Glasse and Gubby, *A Time to Travel? An introduction to Britain's newer Travellers* (Lyme Regis, Enabler Publications, 1994).

Easthope, Gary, *Healers and Alternative Medicine: A Sociological Examination* (Aldershot, Hants: Gower, 1986).

Eck, Diana L., *Darshan: seeing the divine image in India* (Chambersburg, Pennsylvania: Anima Books, 1985).

Eck, Diana L. 'The Goddess Ganges in Hindu Sacred Geography', in John Stratton Hawley and Donna Marie Wulff (eds), *Devi: Goddesses of India* (Berkeley: University of California Press, 1996) pp. 137–53.

Eckersley, Robyn, 'Green Politics and the New Class: Selfishness or Virtue?', *Political Studies,* 37/2(1989): 205–23.

Eder, Klaus, *The Social Construction of Nature* (London: Sage, 1996).

Ehrlich, Paul, *The Population Bomb* (New York: Ballantine Books, 1968).

Ellen, Roy F., 'What Black Elk Left Unsaid: On the Illusory Images of Green Primitivism', *Anthropology Today*, 2/6 (1986): 8–12.

Entwistle, Alan W., *Braj: Centre of Krishna Pilgrimage* (Groningen: E. Forsten, 1987).

Erricker, Clive, 'Phenomenological Approaches', in Peter Connolly (ed.), *Approaches to the Study of Religion* (London: Cassell, 1999) pp. 73–104.

Evans, David, *A History of Nature Conservation in Britain* (London and New York: Routledge, 1997).

Evernden, Neil, *The Social Creation of Nature* (Baltimore and London: Johns Hopkins University Press, 1992).

Eyerman, Ron and Andrew Jamison, *Social Movements: A Cognitive Approach* (Cambridge: Polity Press, 1991).

Fairservis, Walter M., *The Roots of Ancient India: The Archaeology of Early Indian Civilisation* (London: Allen and Unwin, 1971).

Feldhaus, Anne, *Water and Womanhood: Religious Meanings of Rivers in Maharashtra* (New York: Oxford University Press, 1995).

Fernandes, Ruben Cesar, 'A Night for the Earth', *The New Road: The Magazine of WWF's Conservation and Religion Network*, June–September (1992): 7.

Fischer, Louis, *The Life of Mahatma Gandhi* (London: Granada, 1982 [1951]).

Fitzgerald, Timothy, 'Hinduism and the "World Religion" Fallacy', *Religion* 20 (1990): 101–18.

Fitzgerald, Timothy, *The Ideology of Religious Studies* (New York: Oxford University Press, 2000).

Flood, Gavin D., *Beyond Phenomenology: Rethinking the Study of Religion* (London: Cassell, 1999).

Freeman, John Richardson, *Forests and the Folk: Perceptions of Nature in the Swidden Regimes of Highland Malabar* (Pondicherry: Pondy Papers in Social Sciences, 15, 1994).

Freeman, John Richardson, 'Gods, Groves and the Culture of Nature in Kerala', *Modern Asian Studies*, 33/2 (1999): 257–302.

Friedmann, John and Rangan, Haripriya (eds), *In Defense of Livelihood: Comparative Studies in Environmental Action* (Hartford, CT: Kumarian Press, 1993).

Gadgil, Madhav, 'Husbanding India's Natural Resources: The Tradition and the Prospects', in Carla M. Bonden (ed.), *Contemporary Indian Tradition* (Washington and London: Smithsonian Institution Press, 1989) pp. 323–31.

Gadgil, Madhav and Subash M.D. Chandran, 'Sacred Groves', *India International Centre Quarterly*, 19/1–2 (1992): pp. 183–7.

Gadgil, Madhav and Ramachandra Guha, *This Fissured Land: An Ecological History of India* (New Delhi: Oxford University Press, 1993).

Gadgil, Madhav and Ramachandra Guha, *Ecology and Equity: The Use and Abuse of Nature in Contemporary India* (London: Routledge, 1995).

Gadgil, Madhav and K.C. Malhotra, 'The Ecological Significance of Caste', in *Social Ecology*, Ramachandra Guha (ed.) (Delhi: Oxford University Press, 1998) pp. 82–8.

Gadgil, Madhav and V.D. Vartak, 'Sacred Groves of India: A Plea for Continued Conservation', *Journal, Bombay Natural History Society*, 72/2 (1974a): 198–205.

Gadgil, Madhav and V.D. Vartak, 'The Sacred Groves of Western Ghats in India', *Economic Botany*, 30 (1974b): 152–60.

Gadgil, Madhav and V.D. Vartak, 'Studies on Sacred Groves along the Western Ghats in Maharashtra and Goa: Role of Beliefs and Folklores', in S.K. Jain (ed.), *Glimpses of Indian Ethnobotany* (New Delhi: Oxford and IBH Publishing Company, 1981) pp. 272–8.

Gandhi, Maneka, *Brahma's Hair: On the Mythology of Indian Plants* (New Delhi: Rupa and Co., 1994).

Giddens, Anthony, *Consequences of Modernity* (Cambridge: Polity Press, 1990).

Gombrich, Richard and Gananath, Obeyesekere, *Buddhism Transformed: Religious Change in Sri Lanka* (Princeton, New Jersey: Princeton University Press, 1988).

Gosling, David L., *Religion and Ecology in India and Southeast Asia* (New York: Routledge, 2001).

Gottlieb, Roger S., *This Sacred Earth: Religion, Nature, Environment* (London: Routledge, 1996).

Gnanadason, Aruna, 'Toward a Feminist Eco-Theology for India', in Rosemary Radford Ruether (ed.), *Women Healing Earth: Third World Women on Ecology, Feminism, and Religion* (Maryknoll, NY: Orbis Books, 1996) pp. 74–81.

Graham, Helen, *Complementary Therapies in Context: The Psychology of Healing* (London: Jessica Kingsley, 1999).

Green, Cathy, Susan Joekes and Melissa Leach, 'Questionable Links: Approaches to Gender in Environmental Research and Policy', in Cecile Jackson and Ruth Pearson (eds), *Feminist Visions of Development* (London and New York: Routledge, 1998) pp. 259–83.

Grove, Richard H., *Ecology, Climate Change and Empire: The Indian Legacy in Global Environmental History 1400–1940* (New Delhi: Oxford University Press, 1998a).

Grove, Richard, H., Vinita Damodaran and Satpal Sangwan (eds), *Nature and the Orient: The Environmental History of South and Southeast Asia* (New Delhi and Oxford: Oxford University Press, 1998b).

Guha, Ramachandra, 'Ideological Trends in Indian Environmentalism', *Economic and Political Weekly*, December 3rd (1988): 2578–81.

Guha, Ramachandra, 'Radical American Environmentalism and Wilderness Preservation: A Third World Critique', *Environmental Ethics*, 11 (1989): 71–83.

Guha, Ramachandra, 'Toward a Cross Cultural Environmental Ethic', *Alternatives*, 15 (1990): 431–45.

Guha, Ramachandra, *The Unquiet Woods: Ecological Change and Peasant Resistance in the Himalaya* (New Delhi: Oxford University Press, 1994).

Guha, Ramachandra, 'Mahatma Gandhi and the Environmental Movement', in Ramachandra Guha and Juan Martinez-Alier, *Varieties of Environmentalism: Essays North and South* (London: Earthscan, 1997) pp. 153–68.

Guha, Ramachandra and Juan Martinez-Alier, *Varieties of Environmentalism: Essays North and South* (London: Earthscan, 1997).

Gupta, Shakti M., *Plant Myths and Traditions in India* (London: E.J. Brill, 1971).

Gruzalski, Bart, 'The Chipko Movement: A Gandhian Approach to Ecological Sustainability and Liberation from Economic Colonisation', in Ninian Smart and Shivesh Thakur (eds), *Ethical and Political Dilemmas of Modern India* (New York: St. Martin's Press, 1993) pp. 100–125.

Haberman, David L., 'River of Love in an Age of Pollution', in Christopher Key Chapple and Mary Evelyn Tucker (eds), *Hinduism and Ecology: The Intersection of Earth, Sky, and Water* (Cambridge: Harvard University Press, 2000) pp. 339–54.

Habermas, Jurgen, *The Theory of Communicative Action*, Vol 2 (Cambridge: Polity, 1987).

Halarnkar, Samar, 'The Rivers of Death', *India Today*, January 15th (1997): 115–23.

Hannigan, John A., 'Social Movement Theory and the Sociology of Religion: Towards a New Synthesis', *Sociological Analysis*, 52/4 (1991): 311–32.

Hannigan, John A., *Environmental Sociology: A Social Constructionist Perspective* (London and New York: Routledge, 1995).

Hansen, Thomas Blom, *The Saffron Wave: Democracy and Hindu Nationalism in Modern India* (Princeton, NJ: Princeton University Press, 1999).

Hardman, Charlotte and Graham Harvey (eds), *Paganism Today* (London: Thorsons, 1996).

Harre, Rom, (Author), Jens Brockmeier, Peter Mulhausler, *Greenspeak: A Study of Environmental Discourse* (Thousand Oaks, California: Sage, 1999).

Harris, Adrian, 'Sacred Ecology', in Charlotte Hardman and Graham Harvey (eds), *Paganism Today* (London: Thorsons, 1996) pp. 149–55.

Harris, Ian, 'How Environmentalist is Buddhism?', *Religion*, 21/2 (1991): 101–14.

Heelas, Paul, *The New Age Movement: The Celebration of the Self and the Sacralization of Modernity* (Oxford: Blackwell, 1996).

Hemment, Drew, 'Dangerous Dancing and Disco Riots: The Northern Warehouse Parties', in George McKay (ed.), *DiY Culture: Party and Protest in Nineties Britain* (London: Verso, 1998) pp. 208–27.

Hetherington, Kevin, *Expressions of Identity Space, Performance, Politics* (Thousand. Oaks, CA: Sage Publications Ltd, 1998).

Hetherington, Kevin, *New Age Travellers: Vanloads of Uproarious Humanity* (Cassell: London, 2000).

Hobbes, Thomas, *Leviathan or the Matter, Forme and Power of a Commonwealth Ecclesiastical and Civil* (Oxford: Blackwell, 1960 [1651]).

Holland, Dorothy, Debra Skinner, William. Lachicotte Jr. and Carol Cain, *Identity and Agency in Cultural Worlds* (Cambridge, MA: Harvard University Press, 1998).

Hutchinson, Thomas and Ernest De Selincourt (eds), *Wordsworth: Poetical Works* (London: Oxford University Press, 1969).

Inden, Ronald, 'Orientalist Constructions of India', *Modern Asian Studies*, 20/3 (1986): 401–46.

Inglehart, Ronald, *The Silent Revolution: Changing Values and Political Styles Among Western Publics* (Princeton, New Jersey and Guildford: Princeton University Press, 1977).

Inglehart, Ronald, 'Public Support for Environmental Protection: Objective Problems and Subjective Values in 43 Countries', *Political Science and Politics*. 28/1 (1995): 57–72.

Jackson, Cecile, 'Doing What Comes Naturally? Women and Environment in Development', *World Development*, 21/12 (1993a): 1947–63.

Jackson, Cecile, 'Women/Nature or Gender/History? A Critique of Ecofeminist "Development"', *The Journal of Peasant Studies*, 20/3 (1993b): 389–419.

Jackson, Cecile, 'Gender Analysis and Environmentalisms', in Michael Redclift and Ted Benton (eds) *Social Theory and the Global Environment* (London: Routledge, 1994) pp. 113–49.

Jackson, Cecile, 'Radical Environmental Myths: A Gender Perspective, *New Left Review*, 210 (1995): 124–40.

Jacobsen, Knut A., 'Bhagavadgita, Ecosophy T, and Deep Ecology', in Eric Katz, Andrew Light and David Rothenberg (eds), *Beneath the Surface: Critical Essays in the Philosophy of Deep Ecology* (Cambridge, MA: MIT Press, 2000) pp. 231–52.

Jaffrelot, Christophe, 'Hindu Nationalism: Strategic Syncretism in Ideology Building', *Economic and Political Weekly*, March 20–27 (1993): 517–24.

Jain, S.K. (ed.), *Glimpses of Indian Ethnobotany* (New Delhi: Oxford and IBH, 1981).

James, George A., 'Ethical and Religious Dimensions of Chipko Resistance', in Christopher Key Chapple and Mary Evelyn Tucker (eds), *Hinduism and Ecology: The Intersection of Earth, Sky, and Water* (Cambridge: Harvard University Press, 2000) pp. 499–530.

Jamir, S.A. and H.N. Pandey, 'Vascular Plant Diversity in the Sacred Groves of Jaintia Hills in Northeast India', *Biodiversity Conservation*, 12/7 (2003): 1497–510.

Jeffery, Roger (ed.) *The Social Construction of Indian Forests* (Edinburgh and New Delhi: Centre for South Asian Studies and Manohar Publishers, 1998).

Jeffery, Roger and Nandini Sundar (eds), *A New Moral Economy for Indian Forests? Discourses of Community and Participation* (New Delhi, London: Sage, 1999).

Jordan, G. and Maloney, W.A., *The Protest Business: Mobilizing Campaign Groups* (Manchester: Manchester University Press, 1997).

Joshi, Vasant, *Education, Environment and Meditation* (paper submitted for presentation at the World Philosophers Meet, Pune, November 24–30, 1996).

Jury, Lousie, 'Buried 50ft Down in Sodden Red Clay, Swampy Plots Britain's Biggest Fight Yet with the Car!', *Independent*, 9th October (1996): 1.

Kalam, M.A., *Sacred Groves in Kodagu District of Karnataka (South India): A Socio-historical Study* (Pondicherry: Pondy Papers in Social Sciences, 21, 1996).

Kalam, M.A., 'Devarakadus: Conservation for Posterity or Confiscation as Property?', *Coffeeland News*, Nov. 6th (2000) http://www.kodava.org/CoffeeLand/Nov2000/coffee110600.htm (last accessed 29/03/04).

Kamath, Suryanath U. (ed.), *Ancient Indians' Attitudes Towards Nature and Environment* (Bangalore: The Mythic Society, 1994).

Kauffman, L.A. 'The Anti-Politics of Identity', *Socialist Review* 20/1 (1990): 67–80.

Khoshoo, T.N., *Mahatma Gandhi: An Apostle of Applied Human Ecology* (Bombay: Tata Energy Research Institute, 1995).

Khurana, Indira, 'Best Kept Sacred', *Down To Earth*, April 30 (1998): 34–9.

Killingley, Dermot, *Rammohun Roy in Hindu and Christian Tradition* (Newcastle upon Tyne: Grevatt and Grevatt, 1993).

Kindred, Glennie, *The Earth's Cycle of Celebration* (Self Published, 1995).

King, Anna S., 'Spirituality: Transformation and Metamorphosis', *Religion*, 26/4 (1996): 343–51.

King, Richard, 'Orientalism and the Modern Myth of Hinduism', *Numen*, 46/2 (1999): 146–85.

King, Ursula (ed.), *Religion and Gender* (Oxford: Blackwell, 1995).

Kinsley, David, *Ecology and Religion: Ecological Spirituality in Cross-Cultural Perspective* (New Jersey: Prentice Hall, 1995) pp. 54–67.

Klostermaier, Klaus, *A Survey of Hinduism* (New York: State University of New York Press, 1994).

Knott, Kim, *Hinduism: A Very Short Introduction* (Oxford: Oxford University Press, 2000).

Kothari, Ashish, Saloni Sur and Neena Singh, 'People and Protected Areas: Rethinking Conservation in India', *The Ecologist*, 25/5 (1995): 188–94.

Larson, Gerald James, 'Conceptual Resources in South Asia for "Environmental Ethics", in J. Baird Calicott and Roger T. Ames (eds), *Nature in Asian Traditions of Thought: Essays in Environmental Philosophy* (New Delhi: Sri Satguru Publications, 1991) pp. 207–78.

Larson, Gerald James, *India's Agony Over Religion* (New York: State University of New York Press, 1995).

Lash, Scott and John Urry, *Economies of Signs and Space (Theory, Culture & Society)* (London: Sage Publications, 1994).

Leach, Melissa, 'Earth mother myths and other ecofeminist fables: How a strategic notion rose and fell', *Development and Change* 38/1 (2007): 67–85.

Lee, David, 'The Natural History of the Ramayana', in Christopher Key Chapple and Mary Evelyn Tucker (eds) *Hinduism and Ecology: The Intersection of Earth, Sky, and Water* (Cambridge: Harvard University Press, 2000) pp. 245–68.

Lee, Martha, *Earth First!: Environmental Apocalypse* (New York: Syracuse University Press, 1995).

Leopold, Aldo, *A Sand County Almanac: And Sketches Here and There* (London: Oxford University Press, 1968 [1949]).

Letcher, Andy, 'The Scouring of the Shires: Fairies, Trolls and Pixies in Eco-Protest Culture' *Folklore*, Vol. 112, No. 2 (2001): 147–61.

Levi-Strauss, Claude, *The Savage Mind* (London: Weidenfeld, 1962).

Lewis, C.S., *The Discarded Image: An Introduction to Medieval and Renaissance Literature* (Cambridge: Cambridge University Press, 1964).

Locke, John, *Two Treatises of Government*, ed. P. Laslett (Cambridge: Cambridge University Press, 1963[1689]).

Lorenzen, David, 'Who Invented Hinduism?' *Comparative Studies in Society and History*, 41/4 (1999): 630–59.

Lovelock, James, *Gaia: A New Look at Life on Earth* (Oxford: Oxford University Press, 1979).

Lovelock, James, *The Ages of Gaia: A Biography of our Living Earth* (Oxford: Oxford University Press, 1995).

Lowe, P.D., 'Values and Institutions in the History of British Nature Conservation', in A. Warren and F.B. Goldsmith (eds), *Conservation in Perspective* (Chichester: John Wiley, 1983) pp. 329–52.

Lowe, Philip and Jane Goyder, *Environmental Groups in Politics* (London: George Allen and Unwin, 1983).

Luckmann, Thomas, *The Invisible Religion: The Problem of Religion in Modern Society* (New York: Macmillan, 1967).

MacKenzie, John M., *The Empire of Nature: Hunting, Conservation and British Imperialism* (Manchester: Manchester University Press, 1988).

Macnaghten, Phil and John Urry, *Contested Natures* (London: Sage, 1998).

Madan, T.N., *Religion in India* (New Delhi: Oxford University Press, 1992).

Maffesoli, Michel, *The Time of the Tribes: The Decline of Individualism in Mass Society* (London: Sage, 1996).

Mandelbaum, David G., 'Transcendental and Pragmatic Aspects of Religion', *American Anthropologist*, 68 (1966): 1174–91.

Martin, Bernice, *A Sociology of Contemporary Cultural Change* (Oxford: Basil Blackwell, 1981).

Martin, David, *Tongues of Fire: The Explosion of Protestantism in Latin America* (Oxford: Basil Blackwell, 1990).

Martinez-Alier, Juan and Eric Hershberg, 'Environmentalism and the Poor: The Ecology of Survival', *Items (Social Science Research Council)*, 46/1 (1992): 1–5.

Masuzawa, Tomoko, *The Invention of World Religions* (Chicago: University of Chicago Press, 2005).

Mawdsley, Emma, 'After Chipko: From Environmental to Region in Uttaranchal', *Journal of Peasant Studies*, 25/4 (1998): 36–54.

Mawdsley, Emma, 'India's Middle Classes and the Environment', *Development and Change*, 35/1 (2004): 79–103

Mawdsley, Emma, 'The Abuse of Religion and Ecology: The Vishva Hindu Parishad and Tehri Dam', *Worldviews: Environment, Culture, Religion*, 8/2 (2005): 1–24.

Mawdsley, Emma, 'Hindu Nationalism, Postcolonialism and Environmental Discourses in India', *Geoforum*, 37/3 (2006): 380–90.

McCutcheon, Russell T., *Manufacturing Religion: The Discourse on Sui Generis Religion and the Politics of Nostalgia* (New York, Oxford: Oxford University Press, 1997).

McCutcheon, Russell T., *The Insider/Outsider Problem in the Study of Religion: A Reader* (London; New York: Cassell, 1999).

McKay, George, *Senseless Acts of Beauty: Cultures of Resistance Since the Sixties* (London: Verso, 1996).

McKay, George (ed.), *DiY Culture: Party and Protest in Nineties Britain* (London: Verso, 1998).

McNeish, Wallace, 'The Vitality of Local Protest: Alarm UK and the British Anti-Roads Movement', in Benjamin Seel, Matthew Patterson and Brian Doherty (eds), *Direct Action in British Environmentalism* (London and New York: Routledge, 2000) pp. 183–98.

Mellor, Philip, 'Protestant Buddhism? The Cultural Translation of Buddhism in England', *Religion*, 21/2 (1991): 73–92.

Melucci, Alberto, *Nomads of the Present: Social Movements and Individual Needs in Contemporary Society* (London, Hutchinson, 1989).

Melucci, Alberto, 'A Strange Kind of Newness: What's "New" in New Social Movements?', in Hank Johnston, Enrique Larana, Joseph R. Gusfield (eds), *New Social Movements: From Ideology to Identity* (Philadelphia: Temple University Press, 1994) pp. 101–30.

Melucci, Alberto, *Challenging Codes: Collective Action in the Information Age* (Cambridge: Cambridge University Press, 1996).

Merchant, Carolyn, *Radical Ecology: The Search for a Livable World* (London and New York: Routledge, 1992).

Milton, Kay (ed.) *Environmentalism: The View from Anthropology* (London and New York: Routledge, 1993).

Milton, Kay, *Environmentalism and Cultural Theory: The Role of Anthropology in Environmental Discourse* (London and New York: Routledge, 1996).

Mosse, D., *The Rule of Water: Statecraft, Ecology and Collective Action in South India* (New Delhi, Oxford, New York: Oxford University Press, 2003).

Mullen, Bob, *Life as Laughter: Following Bhagwan Shree Rajneesh* (London: Routledge and Kegan Paul, 1983).

MVDA, *Vrindavan – Future Work Plan* (report for development in Vrindavan, prepared by the Secretariat, Mathura Vrindavan Development Authority (MVDA), Mathura, India, 2001).

Naess, Arne, 'The Shallow and the Deep, Long Range Ecology Movement', *Inquiry*, 16 (1973): 95–100.

Nanda, Meera, *Breaking the Spell of Dharma and other Essays* (Three Essays Press: New Delhi, 2002).

Nanda, Meera, 'Hindu Ecology in the Age of Hindutva: The Dangers of Religious Environmentalism', in Meera Nanda, *The Wrongs of the Religious Right: Reflections on Science, Secularism and Hindutva* (Three Essays Collective: New Delhi, 2005) pp. 67–91.

Nandy, Ashis, 'The Twilight of Certitudes: Secularism, Hindu Nationalism, and Other Masks of Deculturation', *Alternatives*, 22/2 (1997): 157–76.

Nash, Roderick, *Wilderness and the American Mind* (New Haven and London: Yale University Press, 1973).

Nelson, Lance (ed.), *Purifying the Earthly Body of God: Religion and Ecology in India* (New York: State University of New York Press, 1998a).

Nelson, Lance, 'The Dualism of Nondualism: Advaita Vedanta and the Irrelevance of Nature,' in Lance Nelson (ed.), *Purifying the Earthly Body of God: Religion and Ecology in India* (New York: State University of New York Press, 1998b) pp. 61–88.

Niman, Michael I., *People of the Rainbow: A Nomadic Utopia* (Knoxville: The University of Tennessee Press, 1997).

Nirpunge, D.S., M.S. Kunbhojkar and V.D. Vartak, 'Studies on Sacred Groves of Maharashtra Part I: Observations on Sagdara Grove in Pune District', *Indian Journal of Forestry,* 2/4 (1988): 282–6.

Nye, Malory, *A Place For Our Gods: the Construction of a Hindu Temple Community in Edinburgh* (Centre for South Asian Studies Series, London: Curzon Press, 1995).

Oelschlaeger, Max, *The Idea of Wilderness: From Pre-history to the Age of Ecology* (New Haven and London: Yale University Press, 1991).

Oelschlaeger, Max, *Caring for Creation: An Ecumenical Approach to the Environmental Crisis* (New Haven and London: Yale University Press, 1994).

Offe, Claus, 'New Social Movements: Changing Boundaries of the Political', *Social Research*, 52 (1985): 817–68.

O'Flaherty, Wendy D. and Derrett, J. Duncan M. (eds), *The Concept of Duty in South Asia (*New Delhi: Vikas; London: University of London, School of Oriental and African Studies, 1978).

O'Riordan, Tim, 'Environmentalism and Education', *Journal of Geography in Higher Education*, 5/1 (1981): 3–18.

Palmer, Martin and Anne Nash, *Advent and Ecology: Resources for Worship, Reflection and Action* (Surrey: WWF, 1988).

Palmer, Martin and Victoria Finlay, *Faith in Conservation: New Approaches to Religion and the Environment* (World Bank: Washington DC, 2003).

Palmer, Susan J. and Arvind Sharma, *The Rajneesh Papers: Studies in a New Religious Movement* (New Delhi: Motilal Barnasidas, 1993).

Patz, Jonathan A., Diarmid Campbell-Lendrum, Tracey Holloway and Jonathan A. Foley, Impact of Regional Climate Change on Human Health, *Nature*, 438, 17 November (2005): 310–17.

Pederson, Poul, 'Nature, Religion and Cultural Identity: The Religious Environmentalist Paradigm', in Ole Bruun and Arne Kalland (eds), *Asian Perceptions of Nature: A Critical Approach* (Richmond, Surrey: Curzon Press, 1995) pp. 258–76.

Pepper, Stephen, *The Roots of Modern Environmentalism* (London and New York: Routledge, 1986).

Pereira, Winin and Jeremy Seabrook, *Asking the Earth: Farms, Forestry and Survival in India* (London: Earthscan, 1990).

Pichardo Nelson A., 'New Social Movements: A Critical Review', *Annual Review of Sociology*, 23/1 (1997): 411–30.

Pintchman, Tracy, 'The Ambiguous Female: The Conception of Female Gender in the Brahmanical Tradition and the Roles of Women in India', in Ninian Smart and Shivesh Thakur (eds), *Ethical and Political Dimensions of Modern India* (London: St. Martin's Press, 1993) pp. 144–59.

Pintchman, Tracy, *The Rise of the Goddess in the Hindu Tradition* (New York: State University of New York Press, 1994).

Plows, Alex, 'Earth First! Defending Mother Earth, Direct Style', in George McKay (ed.), *DiY Culture: Party and Protest in Nineties Britain* (London: Verso, 1998) pp. 152–73.

Pouchepadass, Jacques, *The Ecological History of the Central Western Ghats in the Modern Period: A Preliminary Study* (Pondicherry: Pondy Papers in Social Sciences, 6, 1990).

Prakash, Gyan, *Another Reason: Science and the Imagination of Modern India* (Princeton, New Jersey: Princeton University Press, 1999).

Prime, Ranchor, *Hinduism and Ecology: Seeds of Truth* (London: Cassell, 1992).

Purkis, Jonathan, 'Modern Millenarians?: Anticonsumerism, Anarchism and the New Urban Environmentalism', in Benjamin Seel, Matthew Patterson and Brian Doherty (eds), *Direct Action in British Environmentalism* (London and New York: Routledge, 2000) pp. 93–111.

Radice, William (ed.), *Swami Vivekananda and the Modernization of Hinduism* (New Delhi, Oxford: Oxford University Press, 1998).

Rajneesh, Bhagwan Shree, *The True Sage* (Pune, Inda: The Rajneesh Foundation, 1976).

Rajneesh, Bhagwan Shree, *From Sex to Super-Consciousness* (New Delhi: Harper Collins India, 1997).

Ram Manohar, P. (Trans.), 'Fragile and Fantastic Kerala's Amazing "Kavus"', *Amruth*, February (1997): 3–7.

Ramakrishnan, P.S. 'Conserving the Sacred: From Species to Landscape', *Nature and Resources*, 32/1 (1996): 11–19.

Ramakrishnan, P.S., K.G. Saxena and U.M. Chandrashekara (eds), *Conserving the Sacred for Biodiversity Management* (Enfield, New Hampshire: Science Publishers, Inc., 1998).

Ramanujam, M.P. and D. Kadamban, 'Plant Biodiversity of Two Tropical Dry Evergreen Forests in the Pondicherry Region of South India and the Role of Belief Systems in their Conservation', *Biodiversity Conservation*, 10/7 (2001): 301–11.

Ramanujam, M.P. and K.P.K. Cyril, 'Woody Species Diversity of Four Sacred Groves in the Pondicherry Region of South India', *Biodiversity Conservation*, 12/2 (2003): 289–99.

Rangarajan, Mahesh, *India's Wildlife History: An Introduction* (Delhi, India: Permanent Black in association with the Ranthambhore Foundation, 2001).

Rodda, A. (ed.), *Women and the Environment* (London and New Jersey: Zed Books Ltd, 1991).

Roof, Wade Clarke, *Spiritual Marketplace: Baby Boomers and the Remaking of American Religion* (Princeton, NJ: Princeton University Press, 1999).

Rootes, Christopher, 'The Transformation of Environmental Activism: Activists, Organizations and Policy Making', *Innovation*, 12/2 (1999): 155–73.

Rootes, Christopher, *Environmental Protest in Western Europe* (Oxford: Oxford University Press, 2007).

Routledge, Paul, 'The Imagineering of Resistance: Pollok Free State and the Practice of Postmodern Politics', *Transactions of the Institute of British Geographers*, New Series, 22/3 (1997): 359–76.

Roy, Arudhati, 'Democracy: Who's She When She's at Home?', *Outlook India*, 6th May (2002), http://www.sedos.org/english/roy.htm (last accessed 18/07/08).

Rubin, Charles T., *The Green Crusade: Rethinking the Roots of Environmentalism* (The Free Press: New York, 1994).

Rucht, Dieter, 'The Strategies and Action Repertoires of New Movements', in R.J. Dalton and M. Keuchler (eds), *Challenging the Political Order,* (Cambridge: Polity Press, 1990) pp. 156–75.

Rudig, Wolfgang, 'Peace and Ecology Movements in Western Europe', *West European Politics*, 11 (1988): 26–39.

Saberwal, Vasant K. and Mahesh Rangarajan (eds), *Battles over Nature: Science and the Politics of Conversation* (Madras: Sangam Books, 2003).

Saberwal, Vasant K, Mahesh Rangarajan and Ashish Kothari, *People, Parks and Wildlife: Towards Coexistence* (Hyderabad: Orient Longman, 2000).

Sarkar, Tanika, *A Will to Violence* (http://indiatogether.org/women/violence/will2viol.htm, 2002, last accessed 29/06/07).

Sassoon, Joseph, 'Ideology, Symbolic Action and Rituality in Social Movements', *Social Science Information*, 23/4–5 (1984): 861–73.

Scott, Alan, *Ideology and the New Social Movements* (London: Unwin Hyman, 1990).

Seed, John, Joanna Macy, Pat Flemming and Arne Ness, *Thinking Like a Mountain: Towards a Council of all Beings* (Philadelphia: New Society Publishers, 1988).

Seel, Benjamin, Matthew Patterson and Brian Doherty (eds), *Direct Action in British Environmentalism* (London and New York: Routledge, 2000).

Seel, Benjamin and Alexandra Plows, 'Coming Live and Direct: Strategies of Earth First!', in Benjamin Seel, Matthew Patterson and Brian Doherty (eds), *Direct Action in British Environmentalism* (London and New York: Routledge, 2000) pp. 112–32.

Sen, Geeti (ed.), *Indigenous Vision: People's of India Attitudes to the Environment* (New Delhi: Sage and New Delhi: India International Centre, 1992).

Shankaranarayanabhat, Aedurkala K., *Sri Cauvery – the Ganga of the South* (Kodagu, Karnataka: Sri Ramakrishna Prakashana, 1997).

Sharma, Mukul, 'Nature and Nationalism', *Frontline*, 18/3 (2001): http://www.frontlineonnet.com/fl1803/18030940.htm (last accessed 18/07/08).

Sharma, Mukul, 'Saffronising Green', *Seminar* 516 (2002): http://www.india-seminar.com/2002/516/516%20mukul%20sharma.htm (last accessed 18/07/08).

Sharma, Ravi, 'Questionable Transfers', *Frontline*, 20/6 (2003): http://www.frontlineonnet.com/fl2006/stories/20030328001305200.htm (last accessed 18/07/08).

Shaw, Rosalind, 'Feminist Anthropology and the Gendering of Religious Studies', in Ursular King (ed.), *Religion and Gender* (Oxford: Blackwell, 1995) pp. 65–76.

Shinn, Larry D., 'The Inner Logic of Gandhian Ecology', in Christopher Key Chapple and Mary Evelyn Tucker (eds), *Hinduism and Ecology: The Intersection of Earth, Sky, and Water* (Cambridge: Harvard University Press, 2000) pp. 213–41.

Shiva, Vandana, *Staying Alive: Women, Ecology and Survival in India* (New Delhi: Kali for Women, 1988).

Shivaram, Choodie, 'Sacred Plants Resort', *Hinduism Today*, 4/18 (1996): http://www.hinduismtoday.com/archives/1996/4/1996-4-16.shtml (last accessed 18/07/08).

Sinha, Subir, Shubhra Gururani and Brian Greenberg, 'The "New Traditionalist" Discourse of Indian Environmentalism', *The Journal of Peasant Studies*, 24/3 (1997): 65–99.

Sivananda, Swami, *Mother Ganga* (Tehri Garwal: The Divine Life Society, 1994).

Sivaramakrishnan, K. 2003 *Nationalisms and the Writing of Environmental Histories*, *Seminar* 522, www.india-seminar.com/2003/522/522%20k.%20sivaramakrishnan.htm (last accessed 18/07/08).

Smart, Ninian, *Dimensions of the Sacred: An Anatomy of the World's Beliefs* (London: Harper Collins, 1996).

Smith, Mick, 'The State of Nature: The Political Philosophy of Primitivism and the Culture of Contamination', *Environmental Values*, 11/4 (2002): 407–25.

Smith, W. Cantwell, *The Meaning and End of Religion: A New Approach to the Religious Traditions of Mankind* (New York: New American Academy, 1964).

Sundar, Nandini, Roger Jeffery and Neil Thin, *Branching Out Joint Forest Management in India* (New Delhi: Oxford University Press, 2001).

Sutcliffe, Steven (ed.), *Religion: Empirical Studies: A collection to mark the 50th Anniversary of the British Association for the Study of Religion* (Aldershot: Ashgate, 2004).

Sutcliffe, Steven and Marion Bowman (eds), *Beyond New Age: Exploring Alternative Spirituality* (Edinburgh: Edinburgh University Press, 2000).

Szerszynski, Bronislaw, 'Performing Politics: The Dramatics of Environmental Protest', in Larry Ray and Andrew Sayer (eds), *Culture and Economy after the Cultural Turn* (London: Sage, 1999) pp. 211–28.

Szerszynski, Bronislaw, 'Ecological Rites: Ritual Action in Environmental Protest Events', *Theory, Culture and Society*, 19/3 (2002): 305–23.

Szerszynski, Bronislaw, *Nature, Technology and the Sacred* (Oxford: Blackwell Publishing, 2005).

Szerszynski, Bronislaw and Tomalin, Emma, 'Enchantment and its Uses: Explicit and Implicit Religion in Direct Action Politics', in Jonathan Purkis and James Bowen (eds), *Changing Anarchism: Anarchist Theory and Practice in a Global Age* (Manchester: Manchester University Press, 2004) pp. 199–212.

Tarrow, Sidney, *Power in Movement* (Cambridge: Cambridge University, 1994).

Taylor, Bron (ed.) *Ecological Resistance Movements: The Global Emergence of Radical and Popular Environmentalism* (Albany, New York: State University of New York Press, 1995).

Taylor, Bron, 'Earth First: From Primal Spirituality to Ecological Resistance', in Roger S. Gottlieb (ed.), *This Sacred Earth: Religion, Nature, Environment* (London and New York: Routledge, 1996) pp. 545–57.

Taylor, Bron, 'Earthen Spirituality or Cultural Genocide?: Radical Environmentalism's Appropriation of Native American spirituality', *Religion*, 27/2 (1997): 183–215.

Taylor, Bron, 'Religion, Violence and Radical Environmentalism: From Earth First! to the Unabomber to the Earth Liberation Front', *Terrorism and Political Violence*, 10/4 (1998): 1–42.

Taylor, Bron, 'Earth and Nature-Based Spirituality (Part 1): From Deep Ecology to Radical Environmentalism,' *Religion* 31/2(2001a): 175–93.

Taylor, Bron, 'Earth and Nature-Based Spirituality (Part II): From Earth First! and Bioregionalism to Scientific Paganism and the New Age,' *Religion*, 31/3 (2001b): 225–45.

Taylor, Bron, 'Diggers, Wolves, Ents, Elves and Expanding Universes: Bricolage, Religion, and Violence from Earth First! And the Earth Liberation Front to the

Antiglobalization Resistance', in Jeffrey Kaplan and Heléne Lööw (eds), *The Cultic Milieu: Oppositional Subcultures in an Age of Globalization* (Walnut Creek/Lanham/New York/Oxford: Altamira, 2002) pp. 26–74.

Taylor, Bron, 'A Green Future for Religion?', *Futures*, 36 (2004): 991–1008.

Taylor, Bron, 'The Tributaries of Radical Environmentalism', *Journal of Radicalism* 2/1 (2008): 27–61.

Taylor, Bron, *Dark Green Religion* (University of California Press, 2009, forthcoming).

Taylor, Charles, *Sources of the Self: The Making of the Modern Identity* (Cambridge, MA: Harvard University Press, 1989).

Taylor, Guy, We Haven't Gone Away, *The Observer*, 21 July (2002): http://www.observer.co.uk/worldview/story/0,11581,759092,00.html (last accessed 18/07/08).

Thapar, Romila, 'Imagined Religious Communities? Ancient History and the Modern Search for a Hindu Identity', *Modern Asian Studies* 23/2 (1989): 209–31.

Thomas, Keith. *Religion and the Decline of Magic: Studies in Popular Beliefs in Sixteenth and Seventeenth-Century England* (Harmondsworth: Penguin Books, 1973).

Thomas, Keith, *Man and the Natural World: Changing Attitudes in England 1500–1800* (London: Allen Lane, 1984).

Thompson, Edward Palmer, *The Making of the English Working Class* (London: Victor Gollanz Ltd., 1963).

Thompson, Judith and Paul Heelas, *The Way of the Heart: The Rajneesh Movement* (Wellingborough, Northamptonshire: The Aquarian Press, 1986).

Tillich, Paul, *Dynamics of Faith* (London: Harper and Row, 1957).

Tipton, Stephen M., *Getting Saved from the Sixties: Moral Meaning in Conversion and Cultural Change* (Berkeley, California and London: University of California Press, 1982).

Tobias, Michael (ed.), *Deep Ecology*, (San Diego, California: Avant Books, 1985).

Tomalin, Emma, 'Bio-divinity and Biodiversity: Perspectives on Religion and Environmental Conservation in India', *Numen* 51/3 (2004): 265–95.

Tomalin, Emma, '*Religious Studies and Development: a literature review*' (working paper 6, Religions and Development Research Programme, 2007) www.rad.bham.ac.uk/files/resourcesmodule/@random454f80f60b3f4/1202734412_WP6.pdf (last accessed 18/07/08).

Tomalin, Emma and Julian Crandal-Hollick, 'Making a radio documentary series about the river Ganges', *Contemporary South Asia*, 11/2, (2002): 211–26.

Touraine, Alain, *The Voice and the Eye: An Analysis of Social Movements* (Cambridge: Cambridge University Press, 1981).

Upadhaya, K., H.N. Pandey, P.S. Law and R.S. Tripathi, 'Tree Diversity in Sacred Groves of the Jaintia Hills on Meghalaya, Northeast India', *Biodiversity Conservation*, 12/3 (2003): 583–97.

Van Horn, Gavin, 'Hindu Traditions and Nature: Survey Article', *Worldviews: Environment, Culture, Religion*, 10/1 (2006): 5–39.

Varshney, Ashutosh, 'Contested Meanings: India's national identity, Hindu nationalism, and the Politics of Anxiety', *Daedalus*, 122/3 (1993): 227–61.

Vartak, V.D. and Madhav Gadgil, 'Studies on Sacred Groves along the Western Ghats from Maharashtra and Goa: Role of Beliefs and Folklores, in S.K. Jain (ed.), *Glimpses of Indian Ethnobotany* (New Delhi: Oxford and IBH Publishing Company, 1981).

Vidal, John and Helena Nowicka, 'Chaos as 5,000 Join Motorway Party', *Observer*, 14th July (1996): 2.

Wadley, Susan S., *Shakti: Power in the Conceptual Structure of Karimpur Religion* (Chicago: University of Chicago, Department of Anthropology, 1975).

Wall, Derek, *Earth First! and the Anti-roads Movement* (London: Routledge, 1999).

Wall, Derek, 'Snowballs, Elves and Skimmingtons? Genealogies of Environmental Direct Action', in Benjamin Seel, Matthew Patterson and Brian Doherty (eds), *Direct Action in British Environmentalism* (London and New York: Routledge, 2000) pp. 79–92.

Wallis, Roy *The Elementary Forms of the New Religious Life* (London: Routledge, 1984).

Warren, A. and F.B. Goldsmith (eds), *Conservation in Perspective* (Chichester: John Wiley, 1983).

Warren, Karen, *Ecological Feminist Philosophies*, Bloomington: Indiana University Press, 1996).

Webb, James, *The Occult Establishment* (La Salle, Illinois: Open Court, 1976).

Weber, Max, *The Protestant Ethic and the Spirit of Capitalism* (London: Unwin Paperbacks, 1985 [1920]).

Weber, Thomas, *Hugging the Trees: The History of the Chipko Movement* (New Delhi: Viking, 1989).

Weightman, Simon, *Hinduism in the Village Setting* (Milton Keynes: The Open University Press, 1978).

White Jnr., Lynn, 'The Historical Roots of our Environmental Crisis', *Science*, 155/3767 (1967): 1203–7.

Wilson, Bryan, *Religion in Sociological Perspective* (Oxford University Press, Oxford, 1982).

Winternitz, Maurice, *A History of Indian Literature. Vol 1* (New Delhi: Motilal Barnasidas, 1980).

Woodhead, Linda and Paul Heelas (eds), *Religion in Modern Times: An Interpretive Anthology* (Malden, Mass.: Blackwell Publishers, 2000).

Wordsworth, William, *Lyrical ballads, with other poems. In two volumes. Second edition* (London: T.N. Longman and O. Rees, 1800).

Worster Donald, *Nature's Economy: A History of Ecological Ideas* (Cambridge: Cambridge University Press, 1994 [1977]).

Wright, Mary Anna, 'The Great British Ecstasy Revolution', in George McKay (ed.), *DiY Culture: Party and Protest in Nineties Britain* (London: Verso, 1998) pp. 228–42.

WWF, *The Assisi Declarations: Messages on Man and Nature from Buddhism, Christianity, Hinduism, Islam and Judaism* (WWF: London, 1986).

WWF India, *Sacred and Protected Groves of Andhra Pradesh* (Hyderabad: WWF, 1996).

Yearley, Stephen, *Sociology, Environmentalism, Globalization: Reinventing the Globe* (London: Sage, 1996).

Yellapa Reddi, *Sacred Plants* (Karnataka State Forest Department, 1988).

Zinnbauer, Brian J., Kenneth I. Pargament, Brenda Cole, Mark S. Rye, Eric M. Butter, Timothy G. Belavich, Kathleen M. Hipp, Allie B. Scott and Jill L. Kadar, 'Religion and Spirituality: Unfuzzying the Fuzzy', *Journal for the Scientific Study of Religion*, 36/4 (1997): 549–64.

# Index